Soaring in Life Endorsements

Many books and speakers have told me where they were and where they are now — but I've always wanted a roadmap of how they got from there to here. That's what this remarkable book does — it clearly shows the potholes and speed traps to avoid on the path to enlightenment — to connection with our souls! I'm seventy-four years old and have read thousands of self-help/awareness/growth books and never before have I found a book which so vividly and concretely describes the path from there to here. It shows us how to get form discomfort and regret to joyful awakened living!

Open this book anywhere and read a few pages. You'll find freedom as you recognize yourself in these pages. Whether you're a highly-paid executive or a struggling housewife, a student or a professor, you'll find yourself here.

— Rose Wolfenbarger
   Former Personal Assistant to *Neale Donald Walsch*
   Coordinator of Communication for the Conversations with
   God Foundation

If you have read the first chapter of *Soaring in Life* and find it painfully close to home...don't give up....keep reading! Life can be challenging: Those kids! Your spouse! That boss! Whittle offers a step by step guide to transforming those relationships and creating deeper connections with others. *Soaring in Life* is a guide to finding the extraordinary in the ordinary and turning life into a growing, learning, Sacred experience.
   — Cathy Muller
      Director of Lifespan Religious Education
      Unitarian Universalist Congregation of Columbia

Author Mary Whittle's passion for meaningful living is evident in her book *Soaring in Life*. With an insightful perspective on the rat race that is the average American's lifestyle ("The Way of the Flock"), she offers heartfelt guidance on accepting the choices we are afforded, and then choosing well among them. By nurturing our innate ability to be more aware, more deliberate, and more engaged, Whittle promises deeper and more meaningful living. I suspect the average American is not ready to stray from her flock. But for one who is ready, Whittle's book may be just the right guide toward transformation and restoration.

—Paige Getty,
   Minister
   Unitarian Universalist Congregation of Columbia

SOARING IN LIFE

A Way of Living
That Nourishes and Restores Your Soul

By
Mary Whittle, M.S.

PublishAmerica
Baltimore

First printing

Special thanks to the following authors and publishers for allowing the use of quotes from their works:

"Jonathan Livingston Seagull's Proclamation," from *Jonathan Livingston Seagull* by Richard Bach, copyright (C) 1970 by Avon Books. Used by permission of Simon & Schuster.

"Skin Stealer," from *A Light in the Attic* by Shel Silverstein, copyright (C) 1981 by Evil Eye Music, Inc. Used by permission of HarperCollins Publishers and Edite Kroll.

"Things as They Are," from *The Te of Piglet* by Benjamin Hoff, copyright (c) 1992 by Benjamin Hoff. Used by permission of Dutton, a division of Penguin Group *USA) Inc.

"Ikkyu's Story of Attention," from *The Five Stages of the Soul* by Harry Moody, published by Anchor Books 1997, used by permission of Doubleday, a division of Random House, Inc.

ISBN: 1-4137-3459-6
PUBLISHED BY PUBLISHAMERICA, LLLP
www.publishamerica.com
Baltimore

Printed in the United States of America

For Nathan and Shaun

May you practice flying joyously
May you realize you're Soaring
May your restoration be complete

Je vous aime

Acknowledgments

Sitting down to write these acknowledgments, I wondered how I could possibly thank all the people who have contributed in some way or another to the birth of this book. After all, the contents of this book come from a culmination of every influence I have had in my life—everyone that has ever contributed to my own evolution. Wouldn't that take *another book* to write? Though it is an impossible task, I am undertaking it, because there are times when the gratitude fills me so completely that it becomes difficult to even speak. Tears suffice at that point. I write now in the swelling of this gratitude.

For Miranda Prather, Executive Director at PublishAmerica, I thank you for your warmth and your patience as we corresponded, me—mostly posing questions, you—mostly answering them. To Meg Phillips, whose humor and lightness helped me so much while I was gathering all the material requested during that initial submission, I thank you for the warmth. And to Carrie Dennison, the editor, otherwise known as the midwife for the birth of this book, I genuinely thank you for your tedious work, for your candidness, openness and patience throughout the birthing process. I don't think the labor pains were that bad, do you? At the time of this writing, I have not yet formed relationships with the rest of the people at PublishAmerica who will be involved in the production of this book. To those I cannot name at this time, I am thanking you in advance. Even though you are not named here, you will be receiving "Thank yous" all along the way.

I am truly blessed to have in my life many people who I consider both friends and teachers. Each of these people has contributed in some way or another to the birth of this book. Heidi Arimes, we have cried and laughed together, watched each other struggle, explored and reinforced many different spiritual ideas with each other. I want to thank you for your constant synchronous presence in my life. And also for being so bold a few years ago to tell me that you had no idea what I was talking about after reading the first chapter of this book. Your comments caused a necessary rewrite. I think that it's clear now, don't you? Thank you for always speaking your truth.

Jeffrey Chappell—you started out as my piano teacher and without you even being aware of it, became my spiritual teacher. Your presence was powerful enough to launch me into a forgotten meditation. And your lessons on the piano extended into the realm of the spiritual. You taught by example. I am privileged to call you my friend.

There is a click that happens when you meet some people. You feel as if you have known this person all of your life and the conversation between you plunges to deep levels very quickly. I have a few friends in my life who I must have known before. Deanna Boggart is one of them. The intensity of our conversations means that we can only see each other occasionally, but time doesn't seem to be an issue. The connection with you, Deanna, is Soul food for me and I feel deeply grateful.

All of my teaching and the workshops blossomed from humble beginnings at the Unitarian Universalist Congregation of Columbia. My learning to teach started with Cathy Muller, the Director of Religious Education, who prodded me for a couple of years to teach one of the children's classes. (She had no idea at the time that she was combating a resistance born of terror—terror of speaking in front of groups…) Finally, I relented and began teaching. Cathy, in this way, you are directly responsible for the sheer joy that I get when I teach now. In my gratitude, I wish that I could more directly share some of it with you. And you gave me an enthusiastic "Yeah!" when I suggested teaching that first *Soaring 101* class. But more than in all these ways that you have contributed in your professional capacity, you have been my friend. I have shared with you tidbits of the joys and pieces of the dark nights, and you were there to listen. Thank you.

And to Sue Greer, who provided perfect insight in a timely way. You were both gentle and straight with me. And by the way, I'm "out there" now, hun.

Rose Wolfenbarger provided rays of light and hope and love in the dark times of rejection slips. Working with Neale Donald Walsch, she is no doubt inundated with letters from people that she doesn't know.

I was one of those people. Rose, you took the time to read an early version of this book and you lovingly responded with such positive feedback that you literally kept me going through all of those rejections. If it weren't for your enthusiasm and energy during those dark times, this book might never have been published. And you continue to sprinkle light and love into my life with your emails. I'm looking forward to sitting with you one day, talking, being silent, and laughing.

For all of the teachers who will go unnamed, those events of life, those authors who books affected me profoundly, I am truly grateful. Your appearances in my life seemed to be perfectly timed. Why am I not surprised?

There are many other people too, who constantly support the classes and workshops that I teach. *You* are the reason that I do what I do and can continue to do it. My gratitude goes deep for not only your support, but for the lessons that *you* have taught *me* as well.

And to the Invisible Ones — you have played every role possible in my life. You poked and prodded through intuition to begin writing and then, you helped me in the writing itself. You have weathered my bitterness and anger, my joy and elation, my slowness to "get it." You have given me answers when I demanded them, sometimes in forms that I didn't agree with or didn't understand until later, but the answers were always there. Your patience and support is boundless. You are the Source. Thank you for the glimpses.

My mother, Julie Bailey, has been an endless source of support throughout the entire journey. You never stopped believing, never stopped supporting me in any effort that I undertook. From the tiny to the monumental, your effort in contributing both to my own evolution and to the production of this book was relentless. Though there were times when I pushed you out of my life, you waited patiently and probably painfully for me to return. And as my own Alignment progressed, I was able to recognize you for who you are and was finally able to embrace your love once again. Thank you for your patience, your understanding and your never ending faith in me.

And to John, who sacrificed quietly and enormously, sometimes reluctantly, giving up your own dream so that I could follow mine. I'm planning to give it back to you one day. Just keep looking into my eyes, okay?

Lastly, to Nathan and Shaun, the lovely children who have been temporarily placed in my care—you are the ones who forced me to look inward to begin with. You are the ones who started me on the deepest search of my life. For it was you who mirrored back both the grime that surrounded my Soul and the beauty that was inherently there. You have taught me well. I have listened. In my gratitude and love for you, I will give you all that I can, teach you all that I can, in the way of example and in the way of words, but mostly in the way of love. May you practice flying joyously. May you realize you're Soaring. May your restoration be complete.

Soaring in Life
The Beginning

Focusing on Flying
An Answer to the Search for Meaning and Purpose in Life

The Way of the Flock
Our Usual Way of Living and the Dissatisfaction,
Regrets, Exhaustion and Frustrations That Result

the Way of
Jonathan Livingston Seagull
A Meaningful Way of Living That Focuses on Our
Alignment to the Sacred

The Basic Positions of Flying
The Basic Perceptual Approaches to Life That Are Consistent with This Focus

Winds That Can Blow Us Off Course
An Exploration of the Interfering Effects of Thoughts and Emotions Run Wild

Practicing Staying On Course
The Methods and Techniques of This Way of Living

Clearing Flying Patterns That Keep You From Soaring
A Review of the Common Process of Transcending a Deeply Rooted Issue

"Are We Soaring Yet?"
The Effects of This Way of Living

The Beginning
The Practice Begins...

SOARING IN LIFE
The Beginning

Soaring in Life

What if I were to tell you that there is a way of living
Where you could feel the pulse of peace
No matter what was happening in your life?
What if I were to tell you that there is a way of living
Where you could sense the depth of beauty
in the people around you
No matter what they were doing?
What if I were to tell you that there is a way of living
Where you could know with a depth of certainty
that is beyond imagining,
That meaning lies in every second of your life?
Would you be willing to listen?
Would you be patient enough to hear me out?
Would you be willing to put effort into a practice
That could lead you to an ultimate peace
So that you could laugh along with your Soul?
Would you Soar with me?

I will show you what I have found,
But first we must look into the darkness.
For the darkness will show us; the darkness will teach us.
Peer into the darkness
You will see that it is empty of meaning.
Peer into the darkness…
You will see how we're missing the point of it all,
Missing the essence of life itself.
Peer into the darkness…
You will see yourself reacting from ego,
When you could be acting from Soul.
Peer into the darkness…
You will see the wasted repetition of lessons unlearned.
The darkness has much to teach us.
Are you willing to peer into it with me?

I will show you now a glimpse into meaning.
I will show you a new meaning of success
　　That has nothing to do with how much money you make,
　　How much you own,
　　How big your house is.
I will show you that it is O.K. to be who you are,
　　No matter what choices you make in your life.
I will show you what it means to breathe in the essence of the life,
　　Of the peace,
　　Of the Sacred that surrounds you.
I will show you the Sacred that is within you,
　　An honored place of infinity, peace and love.
I will show you what it means to live from that place,
　　The place of the Sacred,
　　The place of the Soul.
Will you allow me to show you what I've found?

You want to know peace,
　　I teach you acceptance and meaning.
You want to know peace,
　　I teach you just how precious and joyous
　　The moments of life can be.
You want to know peace,
　　I teach you the value of pain.
Will you listen?

Would you like to know why
　　Your path is so difficult?
Would you like to know why
　　Life seems so empty sometimes?
Would you like to know why
　　You react so easily to life's situations?
Would you like to know why
　　You miss the essence of life itself?
Would you let me show you some reasons?

If you will let me, I will show you
　　A practice,

A path of conscious living,
    A path of peace and love.
Walk with me now,
    Into awareness,
    Into the consciousness that attention can bring.
Walk with me
    Into peace as you become aware of the Sacred around you.
    We can both let go of the old ways that lead to meaninglessness.
    We can both learn to embrace the clarity of objectivity.
We can both learn to see from Soul.
Will you walk with me?

Let us continue the practice,
    Even when the path becomes hazy.
Let us continue the practice
    Even when we do the same stupid behaviors
    Over and over and over again.
I can show you a bit about how to transcend those patterns.
    I can show you a method,
    But that's all I can show you.
The repetitions are uniquely yours
    And so are the answers.
Are you willing to tackle some of the toughest challenges
    On your own?

You want to know what Soaring in Life means?
I can tell you.
It means lightness.
It means joy.
It means spontaneity, meaning and laughter.
It means freedom.
It means transformation.
It means compassion, peace, harmlessness and…love.
It means setting your Soul free.

Would you Soar with me?

FOCUSING ON FLYING

An Answer to the Search
for Meaning and Purpose in Life

What if I were to tell you that there is a way of living
  Where you could feel the pulse of peace
  No matter what was happening in your life?
What if I were to tell you that there is a way of living
  Where you could sense the depth of beauty
  in the people around you
  No matter what they were doing?
What if I were to tell you that there is a way of living
  Where you could know with a depth of certainty
  that is beyond imagining,
  That meaning lies in every second of your life?
Would you be willing to listen?
Would you be patient enough to hear me out?
Would you be willing to put effort into a practice
  That could lead you to an ultimate peace
  So that you could laugh along with your Soul?
Would you Soar with me?

The Voice That Calls Us to Search for Meaning and Purpose

The day begins. It starts with the harsh sound of an alarm, which is intended to rouse you from your sleepy state of consciousness into a wakeful alertness. More often, though, that alarm rouses irritation. It's a rather bracing reminder that we need to be up and doing…well, something. Of course, hitting snooze means that you are already behind and you have to hear that grating buzz a second time. So you silence the drone of that alarm with a solid smack and conform to its calling. You're up. While you're dressing, you're wondering whether the kids have eaten and glance at the clock to see how much time is left. *Is there enough time for oatmeal or will it be cereal?* Your child wanders in the room. He is excited and wants to tell you about the visitation to his school today from the local zoo. You hear a word or two squished in between your thoughts.

"And snakes too…"

Does he already have his shoes on? You glance at his feet. *No. I think that I saw one of his shoes next to the refrigerator.*

"…might let a hawk sit on my shoulder…"

Where is that shirt I wanted to wear today? There it is hanging on the door. While putting your shirt on, you walk into the kitchen and check to see if your theory about the shoe location was correct. Yes! Meanwhile, your child has followed you and is still talking.

"I going to try to sit next to Zachary cause he always…"

You respond with, "Zachary, yes…" *Where is that other shoe? There it is under the dining room table.* You put the shoes on while he is still talking.

It is only the first few minutes of the morning and already, your mind and body are blurs of activity. You want to, but there doesn't seem to be enough time to have that conversation with your child.

Guilt doesn't have time to get beyond the pores of the skin because you have to get on with the next set of things to take care of. The work day, the evenings are all pretty much the same way, blurs that whiz by. The pace that started with that alarm just keeps going. Sometimes you're even better than the Energizer bunny. Toward the end of this whirling day, when you do finally have a moment to yourself, you're probably too tired to do anything else. Feeling mostly mind numbed from the incessant rapid fire of thoughts and activities that began with that raw alarm, you flop down in front of the tube to let your mind be distracted.

Whether you have children or not, this type of day probably sounds all too familiar, for here is a cross section of our usual way of living. We rush forward into the day and push through it until the end, when, too exhausted to even consider any other engaging activity, we numb ourselves in front of that TV. This is a rushing pace of living, a way of living in which we allow the details of the day to swell to an unwieldy importance and consume our energy so completely that there just doesn't seem to be any space for relishing the essence of life itself, for feeling the peace that comes from relaxing into the experience of life. In this usual way of living, we focus on the details and rush to get them done.

We don't often stop and reflect too much about it, but if we did make a tiny pause and look backward at the line of days, we might notice that this sort of withering pace, this tendency to become consumed in the details of our lives has been going on for quite some time. But it didn't start out that way, did it? No, life didn't start with a raw alarm and a jump-start into a swimming current of thoughts and activities. It was more like a sudden wail or curious, blurry look around that signaled the new consciousness. Yet somewhere between that early beginning and now, we learned and adapted a rapid fire pace of living, an unreflecting, active focus on details for their own sake.

In elementary school, we focused our attention and anxiety on those math and spelling tests. We worried over and practiced our reading so that we wouldn't be embarrassed in front of our reading group when we were asked to read out loud. We basked in our social and physical successes, as we were picked first for the basketball game because we were tall. And we relished the new school supplies that our parents bought for us every new school year. (Especially those color markers, since not everyone got those!) Even in these early years the details take on a heavy significance.

And, if that rapid fire pace of living didn't start in elementary school, then we were certainly familiar with it by the time we were in high school. Here, life seemed to become more complicated. We still had to deal with the schoolwork like before, (those quadratic equations *were* challenging, at least for some of us), and added to that was a consuming guilt over dumping our best friend for another friend who was more popular. *And* we had to figure out how to deal with our parents, even though we'd rather not deal with them at all, for they suddenly seemed to have gotten sort of geeky.

Then, after high school, there's college, (if we were lucky). Of course, the pace keeps going, and, as with every age, the focus shifts slightly. We've got to figure out exactly what we're going to do for a career and who we're going to live with. Marriage might be in the picture. And there's the question of where to live to work out.

At each stage in our living, we hone our energy and attention to whatever focus comes up naturally in our lives. With each age, there is a "to do" list and we try to figure out what is on that list and get to it. The pace increases and the details swell and consume us. And, while we can't point to a specific day, we could say that we learn this usual way of living early on. Just like the Energizer bunny, we keep going and going. Certainly, there is the occasional glance backward. This is when we grin at ourselves and marvel how we could have ever worried so furiously over why we couldn't spell the word "stupendous" correctly, or why we turned bright red when we stumbled over the word "luscious" while reading out loud to our group. Most often, though, the glance is brief and we continue in the usual way of living.

We may even think, *hey, I can do this life thing pretty well. And I am doing what I'm supposed to be doing.*

Then, with eyebrows raised and a quick glance around at the other folks who are our age for verification, we add a bit more quietly and less boldly, *at least...this is what everyone else is doing...*

We go along living in our usual way and time begins to slip by quite stealthily. Then one day, we hear it. The voice.

"This isn't it."

It's a small voice, barely a whisper, sometimes more like a breath. We hear it, though. Somewhere deep down, there is a resounding quiet that pulses a message upward. The message is that we are *missing something*. Somehow, though we figured out and followed that "to do" list, we missed a point, a *major* point. What this little voice is telling us is that we have somehow missed the purpose behind all of these details, that somehow our usual way of living doesn't exactly add up to a meaningful existence.

"*What?*" we say, (sometimes even out loud). "Hey, hold on a minute. I've been around long enough to know what I'm doing here and I've been doing life this way for awhile now. It's working pretty well so far."

Here, we mentally point out where we stand in life. We quickly scan through the stable career, the comfortable home, the steady family life.

"See," we tell ourselves, "we're doing alright." We wait for the response and then we get it.

"This isn't it."

Infuriating and relentless, the little voice comes back. At this point we might just decide that this little wispy nagging was indeed the wind. After all, it is difficult to begin to reevaluate a way of living that we have invested ourselves in so heavily. We've been living like this most of our lives! Questioning our method is certainly going to make us uncomfortable, leave us twitching slightly in our seats. For we know deep down that if we listen to this voice, it means that we'll be doing some reflecting and maybe even some changing. Reevaluation and change will naturally bring up the fear in most of us, so — without too much more thought, we might decide that the wind does indeed sound a bit like someone is talking. Then we'll laugh, shrug our shoulders and squiggle right back down into the old way.

But life won't let us continue to take that position forever, because the voice that we decided was the wind, gets louder. We hear it more and more often through the events of our lives. One thing or another will happen to trigger the voice again. You're peering in the mirror at some blemish on your face when you see it. The grey hair.

Whoa, you think, *how long has that been growing there?* The same quiet thought speaker answers, *long enough to be as long as the other hairs.*

Or the triggering event could be your child's graduation from kindergarten, or elementary school or college. Your child is changing and growing at an astonishing rate and you begin to wonder, *but am I?* Even at this point, though, even with a full acknowledgment of that voice, we can still manage to wriggle out of deep reflection. We trip over the voice, hear it and respond with no more than a blink reaction. We simply regain our balance and go on.

What am I getting so worked up about? It was only one grey hair. No big thing, really. Besides, I don't have time to think about that now. I'm going to be late getting the children from the bus stop. And we bolt out of the bathroom with our minds already consumed by the next few hours' activities, that voice a fading echo in our minds. Fading, that is, until the next prompting event occurs.

We all have our versions of reacting to the voice that prompts us to question and reflect. We might try to deny its existence and run like hell in another direction. Or we might simply put it off as something to think about later. Procrastination in the face of the potential discomfort that comes from reevaluation is common. Wait too long, though, and the voice changes from a quiet whisper to a loud roar. Now the prompting for reevaluation is more radical. You are jolted with adrenaline as you sit across the desk from your doctor and try to absorb the fact that she has just diagnosed you with a terminal disease.

Why is she so calm? you wonder. Then you wonder, *why am I?* It is the beginning of an existential slap that will take you on to tidal wave reflections over the next few weeks. You're going to be woozy and rocked, without a doubt. Whether the process is prompted in a breezy, gentle way and we actually listen or whether we wait for that rocky jolt, at some point, we begin to reflect on ourselves and our lives. We begin to search for the underlying meaning and purpose of living.

When we finally do get past the denial and procrastination, we may greet this voice with action.

"Okay," we say, as we take a hard look around at what makes up our lives, "if my life lacks meaning, then I will put some into it."

This statement goes with the serious, determined look that furrows the eyebrows. Action does it, so we make the massive changes that we think will insert that ever-elusive meaning. We change or quit our jobs. We change or quit our marriages. Radical hurricanes of change shock our significant others.

No more complacency! we silently scream in our minds. We take on the search with full wind and plunge into reading or religion or therapy. Or even more radical, we quit our lives and join a monastery in India.

There is an assumption that lurks under these massive shock waves of change. We assume that somehow the answers to our search lie in the dressings of our lives. Here's where we run into some "if onlys."

"If only I could find my Soul partner, someone to share my life…"

"If only I could find a job that is fulfilling…"

"If only I could find a religion that fits…"

"If only I could get away from all this stress, this spouse, this…"

If only we could make these changes in our external environment, then we would be content and our lives would be meaningful. If this is the assumption or the conclusion, or both, then we direct our energies to making the necessary changes in the external environment. We may decide to sweep our lives free of external debris in the name of these "if onlys" and at the price of twisting our hearts. This is when the old and now stale dissatisfaction with the marriage turns into a call for divorce and the two parties involved wrench their lives apart in search. What upheaval! Certainly we wouldn't expose ourselves to so much pain were we not motivated by our intentions of finding some meaning in our new lives without our partners or in the next relationship. Or we quit that job, heaving a fresh sigh of relief as we walk toward the elevators for the last time with our small box of personals. *Finally,* we think, *I am leaving this confining place, with its confining people!*

It's funny, though. After you change the externals, after you find that new job or that new partner, the respective honeymoon period begins to wear off. And you hear again that gentle whisper of longing. It's the voice again.

"This isn't it."

You whip your head around in a double take, certain that it *must* be the wind this time. After all, haven't you taken care of this longing? Haven't you expended massive amounts of physical and emotional energy making those changes? Haven't you just spent the last year of your life in emotional turmoil as you trudged through the transition, not to mention the bucks on therapy? Quickly, before you hear it again, you assure yourself with perhaps a bit too much vehemence that it *was* the wind. Then you set your shoulders and go around convincing you and everyone else just how glad you are to have made the changes you did and how you are in a much better place. We can pass through many years becoming masters of this spin.

But, perhaps, eventually, the voice becomes too loud to ignore. The itch of our search becomes unbearable and we must scratch. And so we do. We go through the whole cycle of change once again. We focus again on what is wrong with our partner, our job, our external environment. We run away from that situation and into a new one. Or maybe we just bow our heads in a sort of depressive acceptance, thinking that it could be better, but we don't know how to get it. We may run from dissatisfaction or we may accept it. Yet we are still dissatisfied. The voice is still there, a gentle relentless prodding.

Sometimes we may stumble upon a hint of truth, a slice of meaning in some activity or belief system. Intuitively, we recognize it. It's a feeling, something that we just know. Your friend introduced you to yoga and you decided to take a class. During practice one day, you found that your mind and your body were in the most relaxed, peaceful state. It is difficult for you to describe the sensation, but you are certain that there was some existential truth in that state of being. You felt so full, so complete. So you practice yoga as much as you can and begin to think of work as a means to make enough money to live so that you can finally get to the heart of the day, your yoga practice. Or perhaps you relish playing golf. You haven't mentioned it to your golfing buddies, but the reason you like golf so much has nothing to do with the score. You like it because of its quietness and because of the slow walking on the earth. You like to hit the ball, sure, but what you *really* look forward to is the walk *between* hits. The solitude and the peace that you feel during these in-between walks permeates deeply. You haven't told your buddies about this. They wouldn't understand, but you call them as often as possible to schedule a round. You can even manage to squeeze one in after work on some days.

When we find a piece of truth, our tendency is to grasp at it, to hold it so we can be certain that it doesn't get away. It is as if we put parentheses around whole chunks of our lives. We tenderly point to these chunks and call them special.

"There is the meaning, over there, when I play golf." So we wait with a drooling anticipation for the hour of that golf game to arrive and schedule as many tee-off times as possible. The parentheses remain in place clearly marking the specialness, the meaning in these moments.

As for the rest of it? As for the ordinary daily activities that make up such a major portion of our lives?

"Well...," we stammer, "well, at least *this* aspect, my yoga practice, has meaning."

This is how we console ourselves about the rest of it. The rest of it may be pointless. The rest is only good so that we can get to our yoga or that golf game. With those parentheses solidly in place, meaning congeals into a corner of our lives, to be retrieved when we can find the time. The other aspects of our lives, those mundane parts, are done so that we can finally get to the meaningful part. Sweeping the floor, doing the job, eating, talking with your spouse about the day and what bills haven't been paid, washing the dishes, deciding about whether or not to keep that stray cat that seems to have adopted you last week, getting the children ready for school; these are the mundane activities that cannot be avoided, but really aren't perceived as contributing much to meaning in life. These events and activities are dull and colorless compared to the rainbow radiance of yoga or golf. We recognize a difference. So we trudge through the black and white of the mundane so that we can wallow in the color of meaning.

Indeed, the black and white all too often seems to get in the way. It can be irritating. All that mundane activity and the stress of the job, relationships, responsibilities of children. It all seems to interfere with that inner peace or sense of connection that you've found, resulting in another set of "if onlys" that float up to consciousness.

"If only I could do yoga more often, I'm sure that I would treat others better."

"If only I could play golf more, then I could feel serene more often..."

"If only I could get away from the job and the stresses in my family, I could stay in that peaceful place."

And we may attempt to expand that meaningful corner into a room or a career. You might become a yoga teacher. Now your small piece of truth has stretched into a major portion of your day and you congratulate yourself on granting more meaning and purpose in your life. Those parentheses surround a larger chunk of your life. But you still have to prepare your meal for the evening. Or at the very least, you have to eat it. Then there are those troublesome relationships that disturb your inner tranquility. So you sigh and accept that you will always probably have a little black and white in your life. *Let's be realistic*, you think.

Then maybe the thought occurs to you that you don't have to be realistic. There really are monasteries that still exist. You *could* actually join one. You could simply drop out of all those externals that you have built up around you. No more job, no more stress from that demanding boss, no more relationships issues with the spouse. No responsibilities for house or children. Yep. Dropping out would eliminate most of the distractions from your life and enable you to devote yourself exclusively to that meaningful corner which, with such a decision, will now become the meaningful existence. Disillusion occurs somewhere along the way, though, and you realize that even in such a sterile, supportive environment, you will still have relationships. There will be others in the community, all with different personalities and opinions, opinions that you will be dealing with. And there will still be the mundane maintenance of daily living. You will still have to brush your teeth, wash dishes, and sweep. With this disillusion comes the idea again that a little black and white will always be there.

In a way, we have come back to where we started, keeping the rattled pace of activity set off by that cry or curious look that followed our births. Only now, the activity is linked to search for meaning. Yet despite our enormous efforts to change, despite our enormous efforts to expand any chunks of meaning that we may have stumbled upon, we still hear that same small wisp of a voice.

"This isn't it."

Very small, quietly loud and at this point, probably infuriating. For, no longer are we denying that our usual way of living lacks meaning or purpose. No longer are we avoiding or procrastinating in the reevaluation process. At this point, we have taken action,

31

sometimes undergone massive upheaval and changes in the name of this search, only to find ourselves still facing this nagging wisp. So we learn, perhaps the painful way, that swishing our jobs, our marriages, our life circumstances around doesn't necessarily contribute to finding the meaning. And we learn that the corner of meaning we so desperately clung to, doesn't quite fill us up like we thought it would — since, despite our efforts to expand its role in our lives, there is the lingering edge of black and white that comes with the mundane. We want full-blown radiant color, rainbows of brilliant meaning and purpose shining through every moment of our lives! Somewhere, down deep, we just *know* that it's possible. So what are we missing?

The Meaning and Purpose of Life

Do you remember the classic book, *Jonathan Livingston Seagull*, where Richard Bach introduced us to a metaphorical world of seagulls? Somewhere on your bookshelf, you've probably got a yellowing copy. But, in case you don't, I'll remind you about his story since it points so poetically to that missing element.

Jonathan lives in a flock of seagulls. Most of those seagulls follow a prescribed path, the way of the flock. They focus on getting the food and shelter that they need in order to survive and stay alive for as long as possible. Their complete energy and attention is consumed by this focus. They know no other. As young gulls, they are taught the skills that will serve them successfully. They learn how to find the fishing boats, how to fly and dive for the fish, how to swerve out of the way of boats and fishermen as necessary and how to find a good shelter. Later, they learn about finding mates and taking care of their own families. Again, their energy and attention are focused on all of this. They teach their little gulls the skills that they will need, the usual ways of the flock. And, generation after generation, the beat goes on. (If this is beginning to sound familiar, then you're getting the point.)

Then, of course, there is Jonathan. Jonathan is an *unusual* sort of seagull. He's not so interested in diving for food or finding the best fishing boats or the most comfortable napping beach. Jonathan is interested in flying for the sake of flying itself. At first, even he doesn't understand why he is so fascinated by flying. Perhaps he noticed the magic of flight one day. Perhaps he became absorbed by the entire experience of the wind swishing under his wings, the lilt, the changing points of view that the movement itself gave him. Changing direction, he could make the sun shimmer on the water like a reflective, hard surface or he could position himself to use the sun's rays to see into the depths of the water. Maybe it was an experience like this that caused the magnetic pull to fly for the sake of flying. Or maybe it was the speed of flight, which was always a strong lure for him. But, for whatever reason, Jonathan does something that no other gull in the flock ever did. He turns his focus away from the fishing boats, away from the diving and search for shelter; he starts to focus on flying itself.

His parents aren't happy that he spends so much of his time flying for no reason. (Well, at least that's how they thought of it.) So they pressure him to conform to the usual ways of the flock. Miserably he tries to conform and, for awhile, he flies like the other seagulls do. He dives for fish and keeps his flying in that "normal" range. And miserable is the word for the feelings that saturate him during this miserable time. Finally, though, as if pulled by a force beyond his control, he gives in and starts practicing flying again. When confronted by the rest of the flock about his misguided focus, (well, that *is* how they thought of it), he tries to explain.

"How much more there is now to living! Instead of our drab slogging forth and back to the fishing boats, there's a reason to life! We can lift ourselves out of ignorance, we can find ourselves as creatures of excellence and intelligence and skill. We can be free! We can learn to fly!"

The response he gets is piercing screeches.

"Outlandish!" they squeal, "We already know how to fly!"

They outcast him because of their insecurity. (That's how *I* think of it.) But even through the pain of this massive rejection and loneliness, Jonathan continues to focus on flying.

You see, at this point, he doesn't have that much of a choice. The certainty of his intuition is far too strong. Intuitively, he recognizes that this focus, this way of living is inherently more meaningful than any other focus that the flock could point to. Intuitively, he realizes that he has *discovered a higher purpose to flying: to Align himself to the*

33

Sacred that is both within him and outside of him. And he uses flying to do it. Focusing on the details of flight, he Aligns himself to the Sacred that surrounds him and his Soul is nourished by the peace that the Sacred contains. Focusing on becoming better at flying, he Aligns himself to the Sacred that is within him and he works on his spiritual evolution by allowing his Soul to guide his flight. Jonathan is using flying to Align himself with the Sacred, the Sacred that surrounds him, the Sacred of his Soul. *And this focus lets him Soar.*

Maybe this is what we've been missing. Perhaps we are here in this realm of existence *to Align ourselves with the Sacred, to recognize the Sacred that surrounds us, to recognize the Sacred that is within us, to use life itself as the means to do this. Letting life show us the Sacred that surrounds us, our Souls are nourished by the peace that the Sacred contains. Letting life show us the Sacred within us, we can work on our own spiritual evolution by allowing our Souls to guide our lives. And perhaps this focus will let us Soar.*

This is the assumption made here. Life is the potent, fertile arena that will show us the Sacred that is around us and within us. We will be nourished by the peace of it. We will evolve to the point that we allow Soul to direct our lives because of it. We can Soar.

This nourishment and evolution is happening already. Through the circumstances of our lives, we encounter exactly what we need both to nourish our Souls and to move us forward in our evolution, Aligning ourselves with the Sacred all along the way. The trouble is that many of us remain *unaware* of this process, which means that we move forward blindly. This is the usual way of living, when the focus remains embedded in the details and the rushing pace, when we fail to perceive the radiance of the beauty that surrounds us or the significance of the events and how they can contribute to our evolution. *But when we begin to assume that the purpose of our lives is our Alignment with the Sacred, to be nourished by the peace that it contains and to evolve to the point that we allow Soul to direct our lives, then our whole perception of life itself changes.*

From this point of view, you can look back at that elementary school experience when you stumbled over the word "luscious" in front of your reading group and do more than simply giggle at your youthful anxiety. Instead, you can clearly see an experience that could've led you to understand that mistakes are truly minor, that they don't say anything about your worth as an individual or about your intelligence. But without the help of an adult at the time, you were not aware of this. Your heated embarrassment at missing that word injected you with determination that you would *never* be embarrassed again, so you went home and redoubled your efforts to study *all* of the words.

"I will *never* miss another word," you told yourself with the gritted teeth of determination.

Of course, you did. The circumstance naturally came up again so that you could understand the *real* meaning of the experience, the one that had nothing to do with words at all. But without an adult to help you see it or without the training of learning to perceive life with the higher purpose in mind, you remained unaware of the meaning behind the experience.

Later on, in high school and beyond, our minds have advanced enough for us to perceive this higher purpose without the aid of another, yet we still tend to miss it. We get swallowed up in the smaller points of the situation and fail to see its significance in terms of our nourishment or evolution.

We might have to go through several intense relationships, maybe even a divorce or two, for example, to find out that the problem wasn't with our partner, but with us.

It might take several relationships to realize that the question was not, "Why are men so wimpy?" but "What is it about me that I need to dominate in my relationships?" instead.

What often happens is that this person needs to be able to understand and answer this question, to work through this need to dominate, so she attracts the exact type of man that, in turn, needs to be dominated. What a perfect match. Both are in the relationship that they need to be in, in order to learn about themselves, in order to realize that being dominant or submissive in a relationship is not in Alignment with the Sacred within them. Yet, without awareness, that learning is going to be stumbling and slow. Indeed, they may wrench themselves apart before they actually learn it. The recovery period is likely to be followed by another relationship start-up, which, if nothing was learned, is going to be a repeat of the previous one. Same relationship. Different person. Our Soul recognizes that we didn't learn enough that last time and thus naturally seeks out another situation or circumstance to provide us a new opportunity for learning and evolving. This cycle can go on indefinitely or at least until we learn. This might be one adult version of that same stumbling learning. The learning occurs. We *do* eventually evolve. We *do* eventually overcome the barriers that get in the way of Alignment. We just stumble around along the way.

But if we were to begin to assume that Aligning ourselves with the Sacred that is both outside us and within us, that our nourishment and evolution are indeed the reasons for our existence in these bodies, then we would know with certainty that *all* of our experiences are geared toward this higher purpose. What this would mean then, is that *every circumstance, every event, every thought and emotion, every moment is precious and potentially fertile for this Alignment, for experiencing the nourishing peace of the Sacred and for evolving to the point that we allow our Souls to direct our lives.* And we would approach the moments of our lives with a reverence, knowing that within each moment lies the potential for moving towards the Sacred. Then, with this perception firmly planted in place, we could actively pursue a way of living that would enhance the whole process. In other words, we learn to recognize the opportunities for nourishment and evolution that naturally surround us and attempt to enhance this process in every way that we can. We try to ensure that the nourishment is full and the evolution complete. This is the way of Jonathan Livingston Seagull. It is not the usual way. It is a way of living that attempts to continually hold in the foregrounds of our minds this higher purpose and then, through relentless practice and effort, to actively move toward our own nourishment and evolution. This is focusing on flying. And like Jonathan, once we start to perceive living with this higher purpose in mind, we may never see life in quite the same way again.

From this new perspective, some of the details of today fade in their importance, while others seem to glow with the color of…well, meaning. And when we can see the difference between what is important to this higher purpose and what doesn't contribute so much, then we can choose how we will be. We can actively engage in this process of Alignment to the Sacred that is within us and around us.

That raw alarm sounds, so you bolt out of bed, and the mind and body take off. When your child wanders in and starts to tell you about the zoo visit to the school today and you realize that you're not listening, that you're thinking about his shoes, you can stop yourself. You can sit down and listen. You can decide to fully engage in the conversation with your child, knowing that five minutes more is not going to have a gagging effect on the schedule, knowing that a full immersion into the simplicity and the Sacredness of this moment will nourish both you and your child. And you consider briefly that you might think later about changing how you do the mornings. But that's later.

"Now," you say, "tell me...did you say that they might let a hawk sit on your shoulder?" And you allow the image of the hawk sitting on that small shoulder to float up into consciousness and smile.

Being five minutes later suddenly seems to matter so much less. Having a connecting conversation with your child seems to matter so much more. With a focus on flying, you can recognize the Sacred that lies dormant in this tiny conversation and you can choose to honor it and be nourished. With a focus on flying, you can recognize that the Soul tends to sag under the weight of such a frenzied pace, then you can actively seek a change, a change that leads toward evolution. This tiny cross section of life is teeming with potential for nourishment and evolution, for that Alignment with the Sacred. *All of life is.* We only need change our way of living.

Once we assume that all of life, from that first blurry look around at birth to the last fading sound at death, is geared toward this higher purpose, then we can begin to understand some of the more weighty implications of this assumption. First, that meaning which seemed so mysterious, so endlessly in the future and just beyond our grasp, now stands boldly in front of us, in the here and now of our lives *as they already are, not as we think they ought to be.* Before, there was that long process of upheaval and change as we attempted to sculpture a life, incarnate an ideal of a life that would hold meaning. The voice would call and we would envision the "meaningful life," then set ourselves to the task of swirling around the externals circumstances so we could create that vision. So let it be envisioned; so let it be done. But it never quite worked. We always seem to find ourselves hearing that same irritating voice.

Yet, coming from this new perspective, the circumstances of our lives *as they are* provide exactly the necessary conditions to maximize our process. Whatever the externals are that make up our lives, they are exactly what we need to help us in our nourishment and evolution. What this means is that the relationship you are *already* in, is the ideal one for you at this moment, so that you can learn what you need to learn to progress and be fulfilled. (By no means does this imply, however, that you should stay in a relationship that is harmful. Indeed, what you may need to learn about this relationship is that the time has come to end it!) The point here is that the meaning, the potential for nourishment and evolution, for Alignment with the Sacred lies right under your nose in your life as it already is.

The person who has the need to dominate in relationships can discover this need without going through a long line of submissive partners. She can begin with a reflective questioning about the relationship she is currently in.

Questions like, "Why does power seem so important?" or "Why do I always feel so drained of energy after a conversation with my spouse?" or "Why does he tend to prick my anger so easily?" can be asked and answered, moving her forward in Aligning herself to the Sacred within her.

These questions come from the mirrored reflection that the current relationship provides. The current relationship holds the meaning that we seek because the potential for spiritual evolution is there. Another relationship is not going to change the questions or alter that potential. The reflection will remain the same. Without the questions, without focusing on what she can learn through the relationship, this person will simply carry her need to dominate into the next one. So there is grand futility in swirling the external circumstances of our lives around to get away from something internal. You carry you with you wherever you go, and the lessons that you need to learn, go with you too.

The meaning that we so arduously sought before comes up in another way as well. For no longer is that meaning restricted to the corners of our lives, where we so carefully placed that piece of truth we discovered. The yoga or the golf or whatever other piece of the truth that we have fitted to ourselves must move over now and share the spotlight with the *mundane*. That's right, the mundane, those ordinary activities that we couldn't seem to get away from, no matter what type of life we sculpted for ourselves, that old black and white, is actually full of potential for Aligning ourselves with the Sacred, for our nourishment and evolution. For now, from this new perspective, every moment is fertile. *Every single moment* holds the potential for nourishment and evolution; the yoga, golf and the rest of it. We must simply learn to see that potential, to embrace it and enhance it.

This potential lies in the smallest incidences of living. Simple, tiny cross sections of our lives carry it. You can walk away from a connecting conversation and feel completely refreshed, energized and intimate with the other person. You have been nourished and you might have received a message about your growth. Or the nourishment of the Sacred can be felt while you study the beauty of the delicate green of a plant against the creamy background of a candle. A small appreciation of gentle beauty is quite refreshing as the Alignment with the Sacred is felt in a quiet, peaceful way. Even sweeping the floor can have this effect, if we allow ourselves to appreciate the rhythmical motion and brushing sound.

We come to realize that all of those events, all of those tiny occurrences that we so casually tossed into the category of the mundane are really not black and white at all. Gradually, with some effort and practice, we understand that we are actually surrounded by color. We can slowly turn around a full 360 degrees and see the color of meaning everywhere.

"Wow," we say with the long exclamation of having been zapped with disillusionment, "it was there all along. I could just never see it."

Yep. We could just never see it. Illusions are like that. Elusive, masking, insidious little suckers.

Eventually, we understand that meaning is not some evasive ghost of the future. It lies in the circumstances of our lives as they already are. It lies in the big and small events of our lives. When we focus on the higher purpose on Aligning ourselves to the Sacred that is both within us and around us, of our nourishment and evolution, *meaning is wherever we are. Meaning is in the living itself.* A warm, cushy sort of life partner, meaning is.

Perhaps now, we know what we have been missing. It shows up in the usual way that we live our lives. There is a misguided focus, a focus that we intuitively know will never fill us. We sense it. We experience it through that nagging voice, that droning call that points out the hollowness, and fills us with a sad longing. We may ignore it, or radically change our lives in search, but it still seems to haunt us. The haunting, the hollowness and longing all point to the missing meaning, the lack of a higher purpose.

But if we view this life as the fertile arena for Aligning ourselves with the Sacred that is within us and around us, for experiencing the nourishing peace of the Sacred and for evolving to the point where we allow Soul to direct our lives, then the meaning and the higher purpose are automatically and naturally present. We are here, living and learning and evolving. This process happens whether we are aware of it or not. Our little seagull friend shows us how a shift to awareness of this higher purpose will change how we view our lives. We can begin to see how each experience, from the tiny moment of the mundane, to the grand, sweeping experiences that leave marks on our minds, affects our nourishment and evolution. Then, knowing this, we can actively pursue a way of living that enhances this higher purpose. We can energize our Alignment to the Sacred, our nourishment and spiritual evolution. From this perspective and with these efforts to enhance this process, we know that meaning bounds at us in every nuance of every second. We must simply focus on Aligning ourselves with the Sacred, on experiencing the nourishing peace of the Sacred and on evolving to the point where we allow Soul to direct our lives. We must simply focus on flying. And, with this focus, that voice is finally and peacefully silent.

We Are Evolving Towards ... Restoration

This book is about pursuing a way of living in which we actively pursue Aligning ourselves with the Sacred that is both within us and around us. It is about our own nourishment and evolution. This is the primary focus. It is about allowing the higher purpose to saturate our lives. It is about how to begin to live in this way. But this book is about something else as well. It is about transformation. For adopting such a way of living gradually leads to transformation.

We saw it with Jonathan. His relentless focus on flying, all of that constant practice and work led him toward a gradual transformation. Eventually, he entered another existence, where a focus on flying was all that was known. The skills that he could learn in this new existence were greater and farther reaching than he had ever imagined. Of course, he started working on these new goals right away. Yet, although he was intuitively drawn to this focus, although he was assured by the presence of these others with the same focus, he still wasn't entirely sure what they were working and evolving towards. Then, one of his teachers talks to him about love. Glimmers of understanding reached him. They were evolving toward a complete Alignment with their Souls, toward restoring themselves to their original state: a state of pure love. They were steadily learning to let their Souls Soar into their lives.

A state of pure love.

This is what we are evolving towards—a state of pure love. The Soul has an intimate relationship with love, for pure love *is* Soul. Thus, if we actively focus on Aligning ourselves with the Sacred that is within us and around us, toward our own nourishment and evolution, we will gradually witness the restoration of ourselves to our original state. Can we even begin to fathom the massive transformations that will occur if we are living from such a state? What will it be like to be so completely Aligned that we *become* pure love? Most certainly, how we perceive and approach our lives will be transformed. This almost goes without saying, since what we are talking about here is an approach to living. But this rippling transformation will infiltrate every other aspect as well: how we think, how we feel, what we value, what activities and choices we make and eventually, how we behave. A virtual blooming will occur. More and more often, the expressions of our energy—our thoughts, our emotions, and our behaviors—will reflect the Sacred, the Soul of love that lies within each of us. We will be Aligning ourselves with this pulsing center of our beings. *As we focus on our nourishment and evolution, this inner core, the Soul, will start to radiate outward and show up in our lives. Love will show up in our lives. We will be Soaring in Life. And what we begin to see, in ourselves, in our thoughts, emotions, and behavior are love, wisdom, serenity and compassion, (and probably peace, abundance and contentment as well, since these tend to be by-products of love.)*

It is a transformation that leaves us glowing with energy, pulsating with love. But these transformations, both the tiny and the monumental will not only affect the individual. Sure, you will feel it—profoundly. *But the others around you will feel it too.* And the ones that watch us most closely, the ones who will absorb it most deeply are our children. With the eyes of falcons, they watch how we live. They listen to the values that we exude through our behaviors as well as through our voices. So, when we openly acknowledge the higher purpose of living and shift to a focus on the Alignment of ourselves with the Sacred, on experiencing the nourishing peace of the Sacred and on evolving to the point where we allow Soul to direct our lives, they will absorb this way of being and automatically attempt to imitate it. What a lovely gift to pass on. Most certainly better than Legos.

* * * *

Now that you have been introduced to this central idea of focusing on flying, to the Alignment of self to the Sacred, to nourishment, evolution and to the eventual restoration and transformation that can result from such a focus, you might want to know what's coming next. Well, to start, we'll take a deeper look into how we ordinarily live and the results of the usual way. It's not pretty, but the darkness of the negative makes the positive look all that much brighter. You'll see how exasperation, dissatisfaction, frustration and regret are commonplace when we continue in our usual way of living in the next chapter, called *The Way of the Flock*.

The following chapter is *The Way of Jonathan Livingston Seagull*, which is, in turn, a deeper exploration of a *Focus on Flying*, a focus on Aligning ourselves with the Sacred that is within us and around us, on our nourishment and evolution. As you might expect, this is the brighter of the two choices of ways of living that are presented. Here it is revealed that the nourishment for the Soul comes from absorbing the essence of life itself, the Sacred, which is found in the present moment, and that evolution starts by paying attention to the meaningful significance of life's events. Also, here you will be introduced to some of the ways that the Soul gets blocked from shining right into our living.

The Basic Positions of Flying covers three perceptual approaches to living that are consistent with the way of Jonathan. How we perceive the events and circumstances of our lives greatly influences our ability to keep in line with our primary focus and these perceptual positions help us to keep the higher purpose in mind.

Winds That Can Blow Us Off Course is the next chapter. It consists of a deeper exploration of how thoughts and emotions, when given free rein, can interfere with our focus.

The next chapter, called *Practicing Staying On Course*, is the heart of this way of living. Here, you will learn some specific methods for Aligning yourself to the Sacred in your life. You will learn methods for Aligning to the Sacred outside of you as well as methods for Aligning to the Sacred within you. In other words, you will learn how to be nourished and how to evolve. You will see that the simple act of paying attention is central, since paying attention is how we can stay in the present moment and thus how we can Align ourselves with the Sacred outside of us, thereby nourishing our Souls. Paying attention is also the method for capturing the messages that life holds in front of us through events and experiences, which enhances your spiritual evolution. You'll read about specific techniques for maintaining attention in order to counter the interfering effects of thoughts and emotions. Also, you'll find out how you can observe life events from different points of view. This is so that you can learn the most about the messages for your evolution and eventual restoration. At the end of the chapter, you'll find methods of practicing.

Clearing Flying Patterns That Keep You From Soaring gives you an idea about the process of transcending some of the deeply rooted issues that can block your restoration. This is about the deeper aspect of learning and evolution.

Finally, *"Are We Soaring Yet?"* revisits the central idea of a focus on flying, specifically with regard to the idea of the transformation, Soaring and the lovely results of living in this way.

Recommended Readings:

Bach, Richard. *Jonathan Livingston Seagull: a story.* Avon 1970.
  Go on and dig this book out from under the dust. It's worth
  another read.

Oriah Mountain Dreamer. *The Invitation.* Harper San Francisco 1999.
  Don't let the author's name deter you or attract you to this book.
  Just allow the invitation to sink in. It is a call to live life in a real
  way. This book is a true gift, a must read.

Redfield, James. *The Celestine Prophecy.*
  Prophetic and entertaining at the same time, this book will be read
  for a long time to come. While easy to read, this work holds
  profound implications for our evolution. In addition to *The
  Celestine Prophecy*, James Redfield has written a few other follow
  up books and even an experiential guide. Let one book lead you to
  another. The vision doesn't get any better than this.

Walsch, Neale Donald. *Conversations with God.* G.P. Putnam's Sons,
1996.
  Mr. Walsch has written a series of books about Conversations with
  God. These books are absolutely golden in their capacity to ignite
  ways of thinking and ways of being that are move us beyond our
  ordinary way. The *Conversations with God* series are packed with
  wisdom. Read them all and be inspired.

Warren, Rick. *The Purpose-Driven Life: "What on Earth Am I Here For?"*
Zondervan, 2002.
  This is a lovely account of what it means to put God first in your
  life. From a traditional Christian perspective, Rick Warren literally
  defines life in terms of God. In non-traditional language, this *is*
  Aligning yourself with the Sacred that is within you and around
  you, for God permeates all. For Christians or non-Christians, this
  book holds much inspiration and wisdom.

Wilber, Ken. *The Atman Project.* Quest Books 1996.
I always find Ken Wilber's intelligence quite amazing. It comes through here as well as he explores human development from a transpersonal perspective. Psychology and spirituality are interwoven in what I found to be an extremely thought provoking work. It's thick in some places, a gentle challenge.

Williamson, Marianne. *A Return to Love: Reflections on the Principles of A Course in Miracles.* HarperCollins, 1992.
Marianne Williamson's energy is propelled throughout this book and the others that she has written, probably propelled by the love and the power of her Soul. I list this book here because it is a beginning to reading her words, but the other books are full of wisdom as well.

Zukav, Gary. *The Seat of the Soul.* Simon & Schuster 1989.

THE WAY OF THE FLOCK

*Our Usual Way of Living and the
Dissatisfaction, Regrets, Exhaustion and
Frusturations That Result*

I will show you what I have found,
But first we must look into the darkness.
For the darkness will show us; the darkness will teach us.
Peer into the darkness
  You will see that it is empty of meaning.
Peer into the darkness...
  You will see how we're missing the point of it all,
  Missing the essence of life itself.
Peer into the darkness...
  You will see yourself reacting from ego,
  When you could be acting from Soul.
Peer into the darkness...
  You will see the wasted repetition of lessons unlearned.
The darkness has much to teach us.
Are you willing to peer into it with me?

The "Prescribed Paths" and "Success"

Here we begin our exploration of the usual way of living, the way of the flock. The focus here has little to do with Alignment of ourselves to the Sacred within us and around us. The focus here is on survival and learning the skills to do it well. In a world of seagulls, this would mean learning to fish, learning where the best fishing areas are, finding a safe beach to sleep on, maybe finding a mate and having little gulls. In the human world, we start with an extensive training period called "school," (at least in most societies that's what it's called.) The school gives us the mental and social training that we need to move us toward the selection of a job or career. And somewhere along the way, we may seek out a partner and choose to have our own little gulls. Then there's retirement and the enjoyment of the fruits of a lifetime's labor. This series of tasks is the focus of the usual way of living, a prescribed path of survival that we ordinarily follow.

At first glance, this series of tasks of the prescribed path may appear simply as what life is. After all, isn't it natural and normal to get training until adulthood through school? Isn't it logical that we support ourselves and society through a job? And isn't falling in love a normal part of living? Yes, yes and yes. These series of tasks are a natural part of what life is. The problem does not lie within these normal tasks of living, but in *how* we go about them and in the *criteria* we use for "success."

We start by checking out the yardstick that the flock holds up to measure our "success" in life or our personal worth as an individual. Not only are we supposed to complete these series of survival tasks, but we are supposed to do them *well*. What this translates into is that we're supposed to do them better than anybody else, or at least better than most.

Now consider for a minute, just how difficult this set up truly is.

49

We've got these natural developmental hurdles to jump. They are hard enough to tackle. But luck, that seeming randomness of life, steps in to favor one person over the other. You come from a wealthier family, so you'll have more opportunities open to you than your buddy in school. Or you are born with a social disability while ninety percent of your classmates are free of this problem. We are born into certain circumstances with certain gifts. These circumstances and gifts are unique to who we are, and they may put us ahead of the rest of the flock or behind. No matter what the circumstances or gifts are, though, we are still attempting to jump those developmental hurdles and do it in a way that puts us at the top few percent of our generation. Unless you're born into a prime environment, with loads of innate gifts, the set up is not likely to lead to success.

And if we finally do "arrive," there is an implied promise that we will experience a general satisfaction, a full feeling of meaning. When we look into the future, we can envision a quiet afternoon in our retirement rocking chair where we mentally survey our lives, both current and past. We can anticipate a peaceful smile of satisfaction when we get there, not unlike the satisfaction we feel after a Thanksgiving meal.

We think that we'll be able to say to ourselves, "You did good."

Let's take a more concrete view at this whole idea. This is how a prescribed path looks for *one subgroup of one country in the West.* Please keep in mind that it is only one possible version in one country.

In some parts of America, in the early school years, you'll want to try to be good at something. Being smart counts, especially if you're generally smart in many subjects. You'll want to be good at sports too. Being good at sports particularly helps you if you're not as smart as you'd like to be. You don't want to be bad at sports. You'll know you're bad if you get picked last for a team, as if the eye rolls of the team members aren't enough to tell you just how bad you are. Being smart and athletic is the best combination and will ensure your popularity, which is extremely important. Try to be in the top clique of your elementary school and the top few popular cliques of middle and high school. Better to avoid being the teacher's pet, since this causes resentment and disdain among the other students. Extracurricular activities ensures being perceived as a "well-rounded" individual, so join the clubs and teams and do the lessons that interest you. Focusing on getting good grades will help you get into a college, but don't make too big a deal of studying or you'll lose popularity. Dating is good — it means that you are attractive. Careful not to go too far with sex, at least not before everyone else does. When you go to the university, it's a jump toward freedom, so you're expected to celebrate for the first two years. Then you get serious about your studies. You follow the behavioral laws of the fraternity or sorority you joined, keeping a close eye on any of the values that your parents taught you, in case they attempt to come out. When they do, just bury them for now. With a sense of independence and self-confidence, you embark into the world after college and find your first job. It was a lucky break to find the job in your field. The first few years show you climbing in the company. When another company offers you a higher paying job, you accept and when you begin work at the new place, you meet someone fabulous. You fuel the relationship and the love develops. Marriage is next on the agenda anyway. With the first child on the way, a new house out from the city in a quieter place is called for. The next section of life you spend juggling the demands of work and home, while the family grows larger and the promotions are regular. And as the family grows, the houses and expenses and responsibilities grow. Soon the children are moving on to college themselves and you stay in the same position at work. After all, you are one of the top executives now and the workload has decreased somewhat. Pension promises to be good. Just a few more years until that golf game can be full time. Maybe you'll get your own golf cart. Grandchildren might be coming soon.

This is only one version of a prescribed path for one subgroup of one country. Notice how in the above version, that the focus is on the details of the tasks of whatever age we find ourselves. We focus on sports and academics, then dating, then on whatever looms ahead in the next task. *The focus is on the details of the task itself and not on their significance in our evolution.* We can get so caught up that we are completely consumed and spellbound by them. We were picked last for the team, the eye rolls sunk deep fangs into our confidence, so we went home and started pumping iron and practicing. But we missed the point of significance. What we were supposed to learn is that being picked last for the team says nothing about our worth as a person. Or we were so concerned with being popular in high school, that the guilt for dumping our best friend for someone higher in the social ranks, barely even made it into the conscious mind before we were pushing it out again with rationalizations. Any more reflection in that situation would have caused too much pain, so we moved on. The significance behind the events gets overlooked. The potential for learning something that could move us toward Alignment with the Sacred goes unnoticed. We're too busy dealing with the events themselves to be aware of the meaning and purpose underlying them.

And there is an incessant hint of competition, an underlying push to get ahead of the rest, so that we can measure up to the yardstick of success. We look around and compare ourselves to the rest of the flock in our generation. *How am I doing?* To those ahead of us, we might sneer or be jealous of, or attempt to imitate. To those behind us, we might gloat, or feel disdain, or feel superior to. It can become quite nasty.

The problem is that most of us can't keep up with the competition or the demands of that yardstick. Certainly, we go along and give it our best shot. We might have been smart in school, but, even with the effort oozing out with the sweat, we just weren't genetically wired to be athletic. Strike one. We couldn't really fit in with the popular crowd in high school, so we clicked in with the outcasts. At least we belonged to a group. Strike two. College was okay, but we weren't really sure about direction, so we got a "temporary" position as an office assistant. After the divorce ten years later, we're still working at the same office in the same position. Strike three. With any reflection at all, we evaluate ourselves according the expected criteria and we don't measure up. We're out. At this point, despair may creep in. Or cynicism or disillusionment. Unhappiness and bitterness may pervade our way of being or we may come to a resolved acceptance of how we have come to perceive reality. And we know better than to expect to experience that quiet afternoon in our retirement rocking chair. No, we're not likely to have faces smeared with satisfaction.

Then, there are those who actually manage to keep up with the prescribed path, who, with some uncanny luck, seem to *actually* follow it. These are the folks who just seem to hit home run after home run; math whiz, high school basketball star, popular, student president, secure job at Microsoft, etc. They zoom along the prescribed path, gifted enough and smart enough to use those gifts so

52

that they stand out from the rest of the crowd. By the yardstick of the flock, they have succeeded.

We might assume, then, that they would be happy, content and loving life after all those successes. It's odd, though. The ones who actually managed to do it will experience the same dissatisfaction with life as the ones who couldn't quite keep up, only the successful followers don't know why they feel dissatisfied. Didn't they do everything they were supposed to do? Why is it, then, when they do that broad, sweeping survey of their lives from that rocking chair, that there is still so much black and white there? Where is the meaning that was promised them?

What's wrong? they think, as they glance about them at the lucky, well-manicured life they have made. *What's missing?*

Of course, what's missing is the meaning and the higher purpose. The flock broke its promise. When we get to this point, we begin to realize that the flock doesn't really have much insight about meaning or purpose. So in their ignorance, they hold up some superficial trophies and point to the tasks of the prescribed path in order to aim towards…something. The illusion can soothe us for awhile, at least until we get to a place of disappointment or we stumble on some event in our lives that makes us wonder and start to question. And by now, we are already quite familiar with the voice. The voice will fill us with a sense of emptiness, which is then followed by a pulsing desire to inject some meaning and purpose. This is when we stir our lives with massive upheavals of change or we run desperately to that corner of yoga or golf.

When we follow the way of the flock, we are taking a path that measures our personal worth against a yardstick that is almost impossible to stand up against. Whatever version of the prescribed path we follow, most of us just can't keep up with the demands and the hefty competition. We survive, but we don't do it well enough to measure up in the personal worth department. We're out. And with such a focus on the details of these tasks, the meaning and sense of a higher purpose will naturally slip into the background. Following the usual way means that the search for meaning will always continue. No meaning, no higher purpose, failing to measure up. These are the results of the usual way. Infuriating and frustrating, isn't it?

But we're not done. For not only are the *criteria* impossibly frustrating and lacking in meaning, but *how* we actually go about the normal tasks of living has bitter consequences. Here's one of them: we miss our lives. Let me explain.

Missing Our Lives

When we adhere ourselves to whatever version of the prescribed path we decide to take on, we are following the direction that it points to. And it points to the future.

The low pitched voice of "they" echoes hollowly towards us like those airport announcements, "You will have arrived successfully at your destination when you have fulfilled the following requirements..."

Arrival, "success," as it was defined in that one path at least, all occurs in the future. In high school, we're encouraged to think about and plan our futures. Then, once we slip into that steady job, even though it wasn't exactly what we had planned, we're already thinking about the partner we need to have. Then there's the next task and the next. Always in front of us is some major life project that we need to complete before we "arrive." This keeps our brains planted firmly in the future and the present is viewed as simply the means to get there.

The problem is that the future is always in front of us. We never to seem to "get there," at least not until the end of our lives.

We sit serenely in that rocking chair at first, sigh inwardly and think, *finally, I have accomplished all of the natural tasks of life.*

This is when we get a bit uncomfortable. An edge of discomfort will make us twitch a little in that chair. For we can look to the future and see only short expanse of time to enjoy the comforts and amenities that we have managed to gather around us. Then with a quick searing pang, we might just realize that "getting there" *was* the point. We might realize that our focus toward the future had the effect of stripping the present of its intrinsic worth. And the present is where the Sacred lies.

When our minds are constantly in the future, we are not living in the present. And when we're not living in the present, then we are literally missing our lives, missing the opportunities to Align ourselves with the Sacred that stands so boldly in front of us. It is not *this* moment or the Sacredness in it that gains our attention. What gains our attention is *the moment to come*. So what happens to this moment is that is gets missed in our experience. This is another sad result of following in the way of the flock. We miss our lives and thus we miss the Sacred.

It happens on the grander scale of our entire lives as we look to that next major developmental task to complete. It happens, too, in a smaller way, in the day to day experiences of living. We find that we are constantly looking to that next moment. The to-do list pops up on our mind's screen almost at the same time that the alarm sounds. (For some of us, the list might wait until after the coffee, but it still pops up.) It is as if someone opened the starting gate of the racetrack and we're off! We're running, running, doing, doing, accomplishing... We suck the air in, trying to take in enough oxygen to keep our reserves up long enough finish the race. And we continue to run.

You grab the dirty socks hanging over the railing of the balcony and call to your daughter to see if she has brushed her teeth yet. Glancing around you to see whether there are any other dirty clothes that may have wandered into hidden areas, you think about that check that you need to put in the bank and flash a look at the red numbers of the clock. As you pick up the syrup stained shirt wrapped around the legs of your daughter's chair, you think that you may have time to deposit that check before work. That is, you may have time, if you can manage to leave ten minutes earlier than usual.

Like that will happen, you think, but you yell a hopeful, "Hurry!" and "We'll be leaving in five minutes!" to your daughter anyway.

She is still brushing her teeth. You know because you hear the water running. Or maybe she just left it running. You walk into the bathroom to check and pick up the dirty blouse lying on the floor. Maybe during lunch you can pop over to the grocery for the milk that's missing from the fridge.

This person is not present in the moment that she is experiencing. She is not Aligned with the Sacred that is right under her nose. She is always one step ahead of herself. Her body is in the present. (Not much choice there.) But *her mind* is firmly planted in the future. We do

55

this all the time. We just keep running toward the future, whether it is the immediate future of the next thing on our "to do" list or the long term future of the prescribed path. No wonder we perceive so much black and white in the mundane daily activities of our lives. No wonder we whine so disdainfully with the voice of bitter betrayal when we finally do "arrive," only to look around us and find our lives filled with blanks. In living in the usual way, we have missed our lives, literally sacrificed the joyous and Sacred experience of the present so that we could "get there," only to realize that we missed the point entirely.

I need to tell you about a truth now, one that can be truly gut wrenching, once you come to understand it in a profound way. It's what makes the idea about missing our lives so sad. Here it is: There are no re-plays in life. What this means is that once a moment has passed, it has passed, and we cannot go back and play again in it. Missing the Sacred that lies within the moment, means that it is gone *forever*. Forever is a looooong time. It ranks right up there with "infinity." Almost unimaginable. Let the idea sink beyond your intellect for a minute and you will feel a poignant sadness begin to ease up.

That time you were caught with your lover in a weekend summer rainstorm held a series of moments to savor. It was supposed to be a clear day and you had planned a romantic picnic in a field. The sun had massaged warmth into your skin. Your lover's face had glowed with it. Small caresses and feeding grapes to each other warmed your hearts as well. The storm hadn't come in until you had almost finished those crunchy grapes. Within seconds you were mostly drenched and the wetter you got, the more irritated you became. Then, as you started to jerk up the basket and the grape stems, you felt a solid smack against your back. Whipping around, you see your lover standing there, legs apart in an attack stance, hair dripping and an impish look on her face. Then you notice her mud covered hand and realize that you have been hit with a blob of mud. Neither of you moves as the rain pelts your bodies. There is about thirty long seconds of hesitation. Then you decide. You walk slowly over to your lover with a slightly impish smile of your own and begin to hug her. Meanwhile, you slip one of your hands to your own back where that mud blob has been oozing slowly downward. You take a firm hold of it and then smear it into her hair. You step back to take in the visual effect of mud caked hair on her appearance. The laugh gives it away. She feigns anger and that's when the full blown mud fight begins. Never have you had so much fun.

Nice scene, isn't it? But what if the person in this scene had been mentally into the upcoming Monday morning events at the office while they were eating grapes? Then the scene would have been experienced differently. Let's step back into the mind of this person as it wades around in the future and see how we can miss our lives.

As you lie in the field eating, you wish it weren't so hot. *The heat makes it hard to concentrate. It's that meeting on Monday. I've been working all month trying to get a good presentation ready.*

"Grapes?" she says.

"Yes, please." *Now, let's see. It starts out with a general overview of the plan. No, no, the boss won't like that approach. He prefers a more creative bang.*

She's rubbing your hair and you look up at her face. *That's a nice smile, but even she's sweating. My boss will be sweating too. He probably won't even listen to the presentation. He'll just be watching the clients. Damn. It's raining. So much for the picnic.* You start to gather up the food.

"Ouch. What's that?" you say.

Mud. She's actually thrown mud at you.

"Now what did you have to do that for? The stain's not going to come out. Let's just go, okay?"

The two scenes don't even sound like the same situation, but they are. One of them is lived in the glowing color of the present, where the spontaneity and Sacredness lives, the other in the black and white of the future. Notice just how much is missed in that second scenario. And once the picnic is over, you can't go back and re-play it. That particular present is gone and so is the richness and Sacredness therein. It is no longer available to experience. This holds true, even if you were to plan another picnic in the same field on another warm summer day. For you wouldn't be able to plan the rain or the crunchiness of the grapes or those specific caresses or the unpredictable reaction of mud throwing. If you're not present for the experience when it happens, then you missed it. I'm sorry. There are no re-plays in life.

In each moment there is the Sacredness of life as the present unfolds before us and heaviness of death as the present fades to the past. Perhaps realizing the infinity of the death of a moment will help us to immerse ourselves in its life. This is the reason for telling you about that harsh no re-play rule.

When we follow the usual way, our focus seems always to be in the future, whether it is the smaller future of the rest of this day or the grander future of the rest of our lives. And when we're in the future then we literally miss our lives and all the Sacredness within those moments. Intense sadness comes rolling forward in our experience when we come to comprehend that there truly are no re-plays.

Being Reactionary

But we're not done yet. There are still more negative results to consider when we live according to the way of the flock. For, this way of living not only leaves us feeling inadequate as we fail to measure up to that success criteria, dissatisfied with the farce of meaning as we "arrive," and dry mouthed with the poignant sadness of having missed great chunks of our lives, the usual way of living will leave us reeling. We are constantly reeling because this usual way is a method of living that is reactionary. We become caught up in a continuous loop of reacting to the next set of circumstances that come up. A situation comes up and we swat at it with our best taking-care-of-it behavior. Before we're even finished processing that situation in our minds, another pops up and we find ourselves swatting again. Pop, pop, pop. Swat, swat, swat. It never seems to end. Life happens and we react to it based on the first inclination or emotion. This is a very tiring and not particularly satisfying way of doing life.

You're trying to make dinner and the dog keeps getting under your feet.

"The dog shouldn't even be in here now. The kids were supposed to let him out twenty minutes ago."

You put him in the other room with an irritated sigh and continue cutting the carrots. Your daughter pops in excitedly and starts to tell you something.

"Hey, Mom."

You turn in her direction and that's when you notice the paint on her face. The thoughts jab with a speed of light. *She shouldn't be painting now! I don't have time to clean her up.*

The thoughts don't even finish running through your mind before they start pouring out of your mouth. Loudly.

"You know you're not supposed to paint until Saturday when I can be with you. You *knew* that already. Why am I having to tell you again? You probably made a mess back there. I don't have time for this. Can't you see I'm in the middle of dinner?"

Your daughter's face has dropped and she is shrinking backwards towards the door.

You finish with, "Go clean your face and the paint you spilled."

As you're chopping the carrots now, you are reviewing the maddening injustice of her behavior. And you're still pissed at the dog. Several minutes later, your husband comes in and announces that he just got a thousand-dollar bonus. You wheel around and squeal with delight as you practically jump into his arms. On and on you go about how great it is, what you might want to do with it as the excitement reels up and takes over.

Swat, swat, swat. Whew! All that swatting drains this person's energy and moves her nowhere, except, of course, to the next set of circumstances to swat at. Life turns into an almost endless continuation of reactions as one situation bleeds into another. What is missing from this method is an awareness, an attention to the potential nourishment and evolution that each set of circumstances provides. Each situation holds potential for Aligning herself to the Sacred that is within her and around her, but Mom remains unaware of the beauty of these events or of what these events might be telling her about herself. There is potential for Alignment with the Sacredness of the present, which would nourish Mom's Soul. There is potential for evolution, too, a move that would push her toward restoration, but she is not aware of it. She's too caught up in the events themselves and her own reacting to do any real reflecting and learning. She reels from one situation to another, spinning forward into the future in her reactionary way. Exhausting!

Repeating Negative Patterns of Behavior

Did you think we were done? Nope. We don't measure up according to the "success" yardstick; the meaning slips away from us; we miss precious moments of our lives, and we exhaust ourselves with our reactionary methods. As if all this weren't enough, there is another most insidious negative process that occurs when we follow the way of the flock. It's the repetition that happens when we fail to learn and evolve. Already, with our reactionary Mom from above, we have seen how this usual way does not include an awareness of the potential for growth. There is no reflection about what the events in our lives mean, nor how those events could move her toward an Alignment with her Soul. Sure, we may occasionally stumble on some piece of learning, something that we suddenly understand, either about ourselves or our lives. There is some occasional movement toward Alignment through growth, but it is often staggered and random. And most of the time, it is done blindly.

Without reflection about the situations of our lives, without awareness of how life events can help in our spiritual evolution, then, we will most definitely tend to repeat the same problematic patterns of behavior. This is an insidious process and it can be infuriating. What happens is that some provoking situation occurs and we meet that situation with an automatic response, a pattern that developed a long time ago. Any similar situation will induce the same set of responses, the same pattern. It's infuriating because, even though it may repeat often enough for us to realize what the pattern is, we cannot manage to change it. The pattern is like some old habit that insists on staying around.

You're not sure why, but whenever anyone criticizes you, you become furious and always seem to end up exploding. In fact, anytime there is even the slightest hint of criticism, you explode. It's a pattern that repeats. Most of the time, we're not even aware that it's there. But even when we do know that this nasty pattern is poisonous to us and everyone else around us, we still do it. We can't seem to help it. Since learning is not a part of the prescribed path, we're not likely to actively pursue even the patterns that we *do* perceive. There are, after all, other aims to pursue. So we just repeat these automatic responses, again and again and again.

You are in the movie theater in one of those chairs that rock slightly. With a silly grin on your face, you try it out like a kid. You notice a bit of resistance when you push back, but just attribute that to the seat itself. Then as the chair suddenly swoops backward with your pushing, you realize that someone behind you had their feet on it. Before you can even turn around, the hiss of venomous words through gritted teeth are right next to your ear.

"Don't...do...that...again."

The words are simple, but effective. You look around to see the twisted face of a woman, outrageously contorted with anger. Your head snaps backward and then forward again as she slams her feet back up behind your head. The internal dialogue of your mind blows forth as you begin to argue with yourself.

It's your chair. Say something to her.

Well, she can have her feet up there. That's her right, too.

It's your chair and it rocks so that you can move it. She has no right to tell you that you can't move. That's absurd. Tell her.

But she looks so angry. Maybe we should just let it go.

Back and forth you go, two speakers in your head, vying for attention. In the end, though, you take no action. You never did like confrontations. So you sit through the movie trying not to move, very aware of her feet behind you.

When you get home from the movie, your wife tells you that her mother is coming for dinner. You cringe with this news and realize that your mother-in-law is starting to form a habit of eating dinner at your house every Thursday evening. It's not that you don't like her. She is actually quite easy to be with. And you do enjoy those political discussions you and she sometimes get into. But you don't like the commitment of the pattern of every Thursday. Still, you decide not to say anything, finding some mental justification for your silence. When your mother-in-law does come that evening, you tune her out and wander through distracted thoughts about subjects that you will not remember later.

Now, here's a person who does not like confrontation. In fact, he will do almost anything to avoid it. He will juggle thoughts around, come up with rationalizations; all aimed to justify avoiding a confrontation. This is his pattern, a habit or automatic way of responding. He takes it with him wherever he goes. At home, at work, at the movie theater. Confrontation occurs and he's out of there. If he is following the way of the flock, then he is not likely to be terribly concerned about this pattern or the deleterious effects that it has in his mind or his heart. Of course, without learning, he will repeat this same pattern in the next confrontational situation. This pattern, this repetition is something that gets in the way of Aligning with his Soul, yet he is unaware of the meaning of it and the consequences of allowing it to continue. The pattern is a barrier to restoration. Just one of many, as you have seen.

Our entire lives or lifetimes can be spent following a method of living that is filled with all of these negative results. This is the way of the flock. We can follow one version or another of the prescribed path, and hold up the trophies of comforts and amenities that we acquire along the way. We can taste the sourness of not quite meeting the criteria that are laid before us. We can live with the dissatisfaction of meaninglessness that eats away at us like a slow burning acid. We can listen to that now maddening voice that continues to say, "This isn't it." And we can unconsciously repeat our negative patterns, react to life's events and miss the moments of our lives until we run into the future, right into our graves. There may be some hesitation when we realize where we're running. Our eyebrows might rise in alarm at that last second panic when death begins to stealthily approach and we try to put on the brakes.

"Uh...What's this?...Whoa... But I'm not ready for..."

Of course, it doesn't work and we take our place among the gravestones. And then we realize that we *are* finally done. Pretty grim, ugh?

What makes it so grim is not the death itself, (although that can be scary enough to face). But what makes us want to turn away from these thoughts is the horror that when we come to our final hour, we might feel like we blew it. Horror is the right word. Because it would be a grating, jagged sort of horror, if during that final few moments, we realized that we missed the point of life so completely. With a stabbing jolt, we might realize that we had been exalting things that were so unimportant and failing to see the meaning in the moments of life when we could've been...well, focusing on Aligning ourselves with the Sacred, focusing on experiencing the nourishing peace of the Sacred and on evolving to the point where we allow Soul to direct our lives, moving toward a complete restoration to our original state. And, with the blood pumping so hard from the depth of this realization, the horror at that point would feel almost warm. I'm sorry. There are no re-plays in life.

Fortunately, however, there *is* a choice.

THE WAY OF JONATHAN LIVINGSTON SEAGULL

A Meaningful Way of Living That Focuses on Our Alignment to the Sacred

I will show you now a glimpse into meaning.
I will show you a new meaning of success
> *That has nothing to do with how much money you make,*
> *How much you own,*
> *How big your house is.*
I will show you that it is O.K. to be who you are,
> *No matter what choices you make in your life.*
I will show you what it means to breathe in the essence of the life,
> *Of the peace,*
> *Of the Sacred that surrounds you.*
I will show you the Sacred that is within you,
> *An honored place of infinity, peace and love.*
I will show you what it means to live from that place,
> *The place of the Sacred,*
> *The place of the Soul.*
Will you allow me to show you what I've found?

A New Definition of Success

Yes, there is a choice. We can choose a way of being that is different from the way of the flock, one that is saturated with meaning and higher purpose. We have seen the results of living like the rest of the flock. There is the dissatisfaction that inevitably swells because of the prescribed path. We either failed to follow it, which left us striking out in the worthiness-as-a-person department, or we somehow managed to follow it, only to be disappointed with the results.

"They broke their promise," we whine, "because there is no meaning here."

We are left feeling dissatisfied and frustrated. Then there is the pervasive sadness and angst when we realize that we probably missed some of the more precious moments of our lives because we were too busy rushing around, taking care of that "to do" list, our minds firmly planted in the future. We've got to deal with those pervasive feelings too. And the exhaustion of all that swatting at whatever pops into our field of awareness. The fatigue of this reactionary way of being can seep into the bones like an angry coldness. Then the frustration, or maybe exasperation revisits us as we repeat those insidious patterns that poison ourselves and others with behaviors that we can't seem to help. Clearly, the usual way holds much negativity.

All that negativity will provide a nice, blatant contrast to the brightness of the way of Jonathan Livingston Seagull. Here the primary focus is not on survival. Here, the primary focus is on Alignment of ourselves to the Sacred that is within us and around us, on our nourishment, evolution and restoration. Having this focus does not mean, however, that we do not focus at all on our survival, nor does it mean that we will not take on the normal developmental tasks that occur in a lifetime. We still focus on learning at school, finding a job, getting married (or having a partner / friend), perhaps having children, retiring and beyond. But the difference lies, once again, in *how* we go about our living and in the *criteria* we use for success. Now it's time for "compare and contrast."

We start again with the criteria used for success. Immediately, when we look at the criteria for success in the way of Jonathan, we see the simplicity and elegance coming forward. It's easy. Success = pursuing the Alignment of ourselves to the Sacred through the living of our normal lives. All this means is that we become aware that life as it is now, is teeming with potential for our evolving to a point where we allow Soul to direct our lives, for our experiencing the nourishing peace of the Sacred, and that we actively attempt to enhance this natural process. This definition might seem a bit redundant with what was written in the above paragraph, but that, in a way, serves to underscore the point. For, success here is really no more than returning to our primary focus, a focus on flying, or if you prefer, a focus on the Alignment to the Sacred that is within us and around us. In either seagull or human language, the emphasis is on the *process*. And simply engaging in that process is equal to succeeding in the way of Jonathan.

What this means is that there is no failure, not for even *one* of us. For, at some level or another, we are all making this Alignment. We are all learning and growing. We are all being nourished. Sure, the nourishment and evolution may be sporadic, unplanned and stumbled over. We may not hold a keen awareness of how this life works to educate and feed us, but, at some point or another in our lives, we all happen upon circumstances and situations that have these positive effects on us.

You're feeling really low, leaden with the negativity of that exchange you just had with your co-worker. You step outside into the small courtyard of that massive skyscraper in an attempt to regain your composure and your strength. *How will I ever be ready for round two?* Then it happens—the tiniest flicker catches your eye and you see it. A hummingbird has just landed on the smallest branch of the dogwood in front of you. Its chest is luminescent green. You soak up the Sacred beauty of it, but before you can take in the details of its head, it takes off. You expect it to fly away from you, so you're astonished when it doesn't. Instead it moves toward you and hovers just in front of you. If you reached out, you could touch it. You remain motionless and, as the seconds tick by, you are continually stunned by its continued presence. *Why would it stay so long?* For some reason, when it finally does fly out of sight, you feel full and content. Round two with your co-worker is not going to be so difficult after all. You're not sure why, but you feel refreshed.

Whether we are aware of it or not, all of us, to some extent are engaged in the process of Alignment with the Sacred. This is what it means to be alive. We may not be aware of it. The Sacred may catch us off-guard, but nourishment and evolution still happen. With this definition of success then, there is no true failure. Contrast that with the masses who fail according to the definition of success in the way of the flock. It's tough to be in that top percent of your generation. Most of us can't manage it. Here, in this way of Jonathan, being in the top percent holds no meaning whatsoever. It's the focus that's important.

Notice what else is missing from this equation of success. There is no "getting there." Success is not something that happens at the end of our lives when we sit back in that retirement rocking chair and survey our psychological and physical wares. Success here happens *every single moment*. Every moment that we are moving in the direction of Alignment with the Sacred, we are succeeding. The person in the above example with the hummingbird was completely successful in that moment. He allowed himself to slip into the experience and soak up that nourishment. In this way, we need not wait a half-century for success to enter into our lives. It happens now. And now. And now. Quite a difference from the way of the flock.

Our Unique Paths in Life

There is another major difference here, another lovely missing element. There is no prescribed path in the way of Jonathan. Looking at life from this perspective, a prescribed path just doesn't make sense. For the expression of each Soul is unique and has unique needs and no one path would suit massive groups of Souls. Whether we realize it or not, we are all wisely aware of what circumstances and situations we need for our nourishment and evolution. We are all naturally drawn to these needed experiences and crossroads of choice. And just as naturally, our needs are all unique. Thus, in this way of living, there are only unique paths, chosen by each of us to provide exactly what we need in our continuing journey.

The implications and effects of erasing the prescribed paths from our perceptions are rather exquisite. Having unique paths means that we are no longer engaged in that rancid, burning competition with each other. Gone are those furtive looks around to see how we compare to the rest of the generation. Comparison here holds no meaning.

Certainly, having been so used to doing comparisons, we might be tempted to point to someone and say, "Gosh, he seems so much further along in his evolution than I am. He seems to be so…so aware and accepting and loving and together."

And then we might feel the old hints of jealously or envy that were so pervasive in the usual way. But with a brief pause, we come to realize that the comparison is pointless. It would be like comparing a first grader who is just starting to work on addition to a fourth grader, who is delving into long division. Just because that first grader is not yet capable of long division doesn't mean that she's stupid, wrong or even behind. She is exactly where she is supposed to be on her unique path. To try to attempt long division before she is ready would not be wise. Similarly, the fourth grader need not entertain feelings of smugness or ideas that perhaps she is further along than the first grader. She just happens to be in fourth grade, that's all. She is exactly where she needs to be on her unique path. A comparison is meaningless.

Without the ordinary comparison that happens when we have those prescribed paths, then the usual scorn, disdain, gloating, feelings of superiority or inferiority, envy, jealousy are gone. This leaves a lot of space, space that can be filled with the natural effects of having unique paths. Here, in this method of living, for example, respect is not earned as a result of being in that top percent of the generation. *Respect is automatic. It comes with being human.* It is not a function of whether you are chosen first for a baseball team or whether you are a Ph.D. and loaded with cash. Respect is automatically granted. You can work at Microsoft, or in a bank or as a carpenter or in a bookstore or at a gas station and you still get it. You can be single, married, widowed, gay, lesbian and you still get it. Whatever path you choose is your path to choose. It is what you need to be nourished and to evolve. Your Soul is wise and knows this. How could anyone else know better? In this way of living, respect is automatically granted.

The void that results from that lack of competition also leaves space for some other lovely effects; namely, understanding and compassion. These traits can, in turn, lead to altruistic behavior. Envision this approach and you will see just how natural these effects can be. First we have the general perception and the assumptions. We are all here on this earth in these bodies to Align ourselves with the Sacred that is within us and around us, to be nourished, and to evolve. Each of us has our own unique path that we will follow to allow this natural process to happen. Then, we can elect to become aware of this process and in doing so, take action in our attempts to enhance our own Alignment. We engage in our lives, take on the developmental tasks, work on enhancing the process. Living in this way, we experience both the profound beauty of being as well as the wretched pain. Transitions can be particularly demanding and difficult. So now, with this perspective firmly intact, we look around at the rest of the folks in our generation and celebrate with them when they find glimpses of truth or experience beauty or growth. We take delight in their joy. And, it becomes automatic to experience compassion when we witness another Soul passing through a difficult period. The next natural step that follows from these feelings is to lend an empathetic ear or a helping hand. Once we remove the need to follow the prescribed path, once we hold true to our unique paths, then success and respect become automatic, failure and competition become obsolete and compassion blooms.

When we approach living in the way of Jonathan, the criterion for success becomes elegantly and simply synonymous with the approach itself, the primary focus of Aligning ourselves with the Sacred that is within us and around us. From this perspective, the potential for success occurs in every moment, and failure and comparisons become meaningless.

Alignment to the Sacred That Surrounds Us

It all sounds fairly positive and bright, doesn't it? Idealistic, perhaps? Through our living we can Align ourselves with the Sacred, be nourished, evolve and enhance the process. The ideas almost sound romantic. But they are still vague. Exactly *how* do we go about doing this? You have read about the criterion for success used in the way of the flock and in the way of Jonathan. You have read about the *how* of the usual way of living. Now it's time to delve into the *how* of the way of Jonathan and the results of this way. We begin with Alignment to the Sacred that surrounds us. We begin with experiencing the nourishing peace that the Sacred contains.

Here, again, the concept is not complicated. Nourishment comes from an immersion in the essence of life itself, the Sacred in the present moment. Before, in the usual way of living, we would carefully place parentheses around the moments in our lives that we considered special or meaningful, worthy of our attention.

"There's where the color lies," we would say, "over there in that corner, when I do yoga." As for the rest of it...well, the rest of it was perceived as the black and white of the mundane, something to get through so that we could move between those parentheses. And we were always left wanting more of the color. No wonder John Cougar Mellancamp's song was so popular.

"Oh yeah, life goes on," it says, "long after the thrill of living is gone." If you're going to live in the way of the flock, he probably has a point. But if we choose to focus on flying, well, then he's just plain wrong. For the minute that we begin to Align ourselves to the Sacred of the present, then some of the color and thus the thrill of living gets restored and we are nourished. We can learn to shed the parentheses that surrounded those chunks of life that we considered so special and look more closely at some of the other moments. We thought they were the black and white of the mundane, of the ordinary. We passed over them because they looked so dull. But as we lean forward for a closer look, we see...color.

You breathe in the scent of wood as the door to the cabin squeaks closed behind you. The air is cold, even for November, so the walk through the woods has left a chill. Scanning the cabin, you are already more at ease with this place, a place where you will be spending much of the next two weeks. You inhale deeply to catch the full pine odor before building the fire. The wood has been gathered for you for this first fire. How nice. You snap the twigs and place them on the cold andirons. Then the crackling fills the air as you light it up. Squatting on your feet, you allow the warmth to sink into the front of your body, layer by layer, until it reaches your skin.

This does sound lovely, doesn't it? Merely reading the description of this scene, we can sense the life and the Sacred fullness of the moments. There is "thrill" here. No, it's not the kind of roller-coaster-bottom-dropping-out-of-your-stomach thrill. But it's there. It's the quiet, nourishing thrill, a fullness that comes from an immersion into the Sacred of the present moment. All we have to do is *pay attention*. You'll be hearing a lot more about attention later, but for now, I'll simply say that attention is what makes the difference between seeing the color in a present moment or perceiving that same moment as black and white. This person in the cabin wasn't thinking about how far the cabin is from his car or if there are any bears in the woods. He is completely absorbed by the essence of life as it is in the present. All of his senses are alert and taking in the entire scene as each moment unfolds into another. With a quiet attention he allows himself to be Aligned with the Sacred of the present. And when we're Aligned like this, we can feel the nourishment. It's like our Souls are *finally* being allowed to click into place. Snap.

"Oooo…that feels good. Can we stay here awhile?"

Oh yeah. There certainly is thrill in living. There is nourishing color. We just have to be paying attention.

Notice another thing about this tiny scene. No moments are valued more highly than the others. All are perceived as equally elegant, equally colorful, equally Sacred, equally nourishing. (I used "equally" enough, didn't I?) Sure the warmth of that fire on the body feels great, especially if you've recently been in a cold forest. But the squeak of the door is charming, as is the heavy odor of pine. And all of these details are taken in with equal relish. When each Sacred detail of the present is perceived as relatively equal to the others, then what we have done is to remove those obstinate parentheses. And when we finally shed them, then we notice that *all* of the moments are full of color and depth. They really always were. It's knowing that each of them has that color and then paying attention to it. Removing the parentheses and *taking a closer look will almost always reveal the true nature of almost any moment: full, radiant, nourishing color.*

Nourishment for the Soul comes from immersion in the essence of life, the Sacred of the present moment. The idea is so simple. You'll find that most of the ideas in this approach to living are not at all complicated. It's the *implementation* that requires the effort. We'll probably have to practice paying attention to the moments so that we don't gloss over the potential nourishment that is inherently there.

This last point brings up a short digression. Certainly, we might want to practice immersing ourselves into the Sacred of a present moment that is *pleasant*. Warm fires in log cabins sound particularly enticing. We can readily see how these types of moments might be nourishing. But what about those moments that are not so pleasant? There are probably some moments that we'd might rather skip altogether — like the painful ones. These are the moments that are simply too painful to continually endure, those tragic times, when the pain seems to rack us physically. We get walloped and need to take a break. Well…maybe. Certainly, this is a choice that we can make. But, at least for some of these less pleasant moments, we might not want to miss the tepid beauty of sadness and pain. They, too, are full and Sacred and are a part of our experience.

The gray smoke from the candle that you just blew out circles upward in gradually widening rings.

"How appropriate, how symbolic," you say out loud to no one in particular.

You have extinguished the light on this chapter of your life. You will be moving across the country tomorrow. Each of your three best friends has taken a turn to tell you how the last twelve years of their lives has been affected by your presence. There were jokes that brought laughter and memories that brought tears. And your view becomes blurry again as you watch the smoke from the candle cease and you turn for hugs. Sure, moments like these are sad and pull at the bases of our hearts, but we might want to choose to stay in the Sacredness of the present for them anyway. Fullness, beauty and color are there too.

In this approach to living, we have the luxury of choice. We can choose to immerse ourselves in the Sacred of the present moment or we can actively choose to distract ourselves if the present holds too much pain. This freedom of choice comes to us because of our awareness, an awareness of where that nourishment lies. In the way of the flock, we were almost always leaning toward the future, gazing steadily toward the moment when we would finally "get there." This way of leaning seemed to be an unevaluated habit, just the usual way. Unless we stumbled on some beauty in the Sacredness of the present that grabbed our attention, we would tend to skip right over the whole present experience. Awareness and choice were not part of the method. Our guy in the cabin might have done this. He could have been thinking about how good the warmth of the fire would feel when it finally soaked down to his cool skin. He could have put those convenient parentheses around that moment of warmth and held them firmly in place until that time arrived. And certainly, the warmth of the fire *would* have felt great after all of that anticipation.

"Ah, finally," he could say, "lovely, nourishing color."

As for all the other moments leading up to that time? Well, they would have been perceived as black and white. We know what happens to these. They get missed. We also know that, with our minds continually leaning into the future, whole chunks of our lives tend to fall into this "missed" category. And remember, there are no re-plays.

But with this method of living, we don't have to worry so much about that harsh no re-play rule. And we don't have to worry so much about missing whole precious chunks of our lives either, because we can practice and choose to immerse ourselves into the essence of life itself. With practice, we can choose to gather the nourishing peace of the Sacred present moment at will. Not so much gets missed this way, our Souls are nourished and we can fully engage in life. Here, the death of a moment that we felt so intensely through that no re-play rule before, doesn't seem as poignant. For it is much easier to accept the death of a moment when we have fully been in its life. Go out and catch a few falling leaves in the autumn. You can do it with children if you need an excuse. You'll end up dancing beneath the falling colors of orange and red that the whooshing wind blows. It's fun. When it's over, you'll feel full and you won't have missed a thing.

Alignment to the Sacred That Is Within Us

That was all about Aligning ourselves to the Sacred that surrounds us and it will indeed nourish us deeply. Now it's time to explore a bit more about Aligning ourselves to the Sacred that is within us, about evolution and restoration. This is the other piece of the *how* we approach life in the way of Jonathan. But before we can delve into how we go about this evolution and eventual restoration, we need to be perfectly clear about *what* we are evolving towards. For the way of Jonathan is a way of awareness, a conscious attempt to engage in the process of evolution. In the way of the flock, any evolution that occurs is done blindly, since we are simply following a path that is laid before us, prescribed by the flock and since we end up bouncing off the circumstances of our lives in a reactionary, repetitious way.

We begin our exploration with two assumptions: that *there is a Soul within each of us and that it is possible to learn to eventually live from this center of our beings.* And I'll go ahead and make another assertion—that this Soul is composed of the highest vibrations of the universe, the vibration of pure love.

Given these assumptions, then, any beliefs, decisions, or actions that come from the Soul would only develop out of the purest love. The results would necessarily be imbued with love (obviously), compassion, serenity and wisdom. (If I left any goodies out, just insert them in your mind.) And don't we want more of these qualities mingling into our existence? Of course. So it would make complete sense to desire and seek an Alignment with the Sacred within us, with the Soul, thereby allowing it to show up more in our lives, to eventually even *direct* our lives.

Ah, here's where we come to the idea of restoration. Restoration is the perfect word. According to the often used source of definitions, (Webster's Dictionary, what else?) Restore means to bring back or put back into a former or original state: renew. Restoration is exactly what we attempt to move towards in the way of Jonathan. We actively pursue a spiritual evolution so that we can restore ourselves to our original state, a state of pure love. *This is who we are.* Gradually, through the process of our conscious spiritual evolution, we begin to Align ourselves more and more with the Soul. Gradually, the Soul and all its lovely qualities, begin to show up more in our lives, to direct our beliefs, decisions and actions. And who wouldn't want love directing? Eventually through our evolution, we are restored to our original state, a state of pure love. We are evolving toward becoming the Sacred within us. This is Soaring. Now you know.

(Sounds like sort of a hefty goal, doesn't it? A bit overwhelming or idealistic? Well, we can make the whole thing a little more manageable by remembering that restoration through evolution is an on-going process that occurs in a moment, so we can take it one moment at a time. Remember, too, that success here simply means engaging in the process, not "getting there.")

If the idea is to allow the Soul to do the directing of our lives, to allow some of that love, compassion, serenity and wisdom to begin to show up in our actions, then it would be quite helpful to understand just what has been doing the directing up until now. These introductions to the pseudo-directors are going to be brief for now. The general overview provides a foundation for an in-depth discussion later. These pseudo-directors can be clearly seen by observing our usual way of living, since we can be certain that the Soul is *not* directing when we engage in that pop, pop, popping and swat, swat, swatting of the reactionary mode, nor when we repeat some grand patterns. Let's take each of these troublesome aspects of the usual way one at a time, shall we?

In the case of our reactionary mode of being, we find that it is none other than the overwhelming velocity of our own thoughts and emotions that directs us. The thoughts and emotions push forward and plop themselves stoutly into the director's seat and conduct the drama of our lives from there.

"Oh, here, look at this situation," they announce candidly from that director's chair, "this calls for a little venomous anger, maybe a little revenge later."

And we react accordingly, leaving us no time to Align ourselves to anything. Do you remember the mom from the last chapter who reacted with her best swatting behaviors when all those prompting situations would pop up? First it was the dog under her feet, then her daughter with the paint on her face, then her husband announcing a bonus. Thoughts and emotions would bubble up into consciousness and she reacted based on whatever was there. There was no awareness of this process, nor any attempt to act from a deeper place. Her thoughts and emotions were given free rein to direct her life. Pop, pop, pop. Swat, swat, swat.

Now, how would this same situation play out if the mom was more aware of the reactionary tendency, if she was attempting to consciously let her Soul do the directing?

You're trying to make dinner and the dog keeps getting under your feet. You thought that the kids put him out twenty minutes ago. The irritation mounts, then you catch yourself in your emotion. *Irritation over a dog? It's not worth it.* You put the dog in the other room. With a smile, you continue cutting the carrots.

Then your daughter pops in excitedly and starts to tell you something.

"Hey, Mom," she says.

When you turn to look, there's paint on her face and hands. With a flash, the expected thoughts rush forward: *she shouldn't be painting; you don't have time to clean her up; she knew about the no-painting-until-Saturday rule already.* The thoughts are accompanied by a glowing anger. The anger and the thoughts are powerful and almost make it to your voice box, but you step out of the experience for a second and see these internal events objectively. They're still hot. You need a minute to let the chemical effects of the anger abate, but your daughter is waiting. She had followed your eyes to her paint covered hands and has watched your mouth open and close. And she must have recognized the contortions of expression on your face because her initial exuberance has melted somewhat.

She comes closer and says, "I know I'm not supposed to paint until Saturday, Mom, but I wanted to paint a picture for Dad's birthday before he gets home from work."

Having a fairly legitimate reason for breaking a rule always helps to mitigate a parent's anger. You'll need less time to calm down now. You squat down to your daughter's height.

"I guess I looked pretty mad when you came in just now." She nods and you continue. "So you remembered about the rule, but you decided to break it anyway because you thought you had a good reason?"

78

"Yeah, I just wanted to make sure that he didn't see the picture and if I waited until Saturday, he might have seen it or we might not have had time to go off by ourselves or something."

"That sounds like a pretty good reason for breaking that rule," you say. She beams at this thinking that she is off the hook. That smile fades a smidgen, however, when you add, "What do you think would be a better way of making that decision about breaking the rule?" There is a pause.

"Maybe I could...maybe I could ask permission first?" she says tentatively.

"Maybe you could tell me what you are thinking and we could simply talk about it. How would that be?"

"Great."

"Now," you say smiling and glancing around her at the clock, "Daddy will be home in about fifteen minutes, so, if you're going to keep your secret, you had better go clean up."

She jumps up and down in place with excitement.

You grab her hand and, with a twinkle in your eye, you say, "By the way, did you know that you have a bit of blue right...here?" You tickle her under the chin and she collapses giggling. After a few seconds of recovering, you tell her that the blue is really on her cheek and that she'd better make sure that it is completely clean so that her father will not guess what she's up to. She tries to scoot away again, but you stop her to ask if you can see the painting after dinner.

With a gleeful, "yeah!" she finally manages to scurry out of the room.

Again, you are left cutting carrots. A few minutes later, your husband does walk in with the announcement of a thousand-dollar bonus. Speculations follow closely on the heels of the excitement that swoons up with his announcement. You go with your feelings for a few minutes and fling your arms around him, but you keep your speculations to yourself. Instead you ask him about what he did to earn the bonus, about how proud he must be. You think that you'll ask him later how he wants to spend it.

What a difference between the mom in the last chapter and this one! Situations and circumstances pop up in her life prompting an automatic reaction of thoughts and emotions. But notice what she does here. She doesn't react based on the first thought or emotion that jumps up into her consciousness. The thoughts and emotions are not directing her responses; neither do the circumstances that prompted those thoughts and emotions. She is not a victim of either the popping or the thoughts and emotions. The winds of thoughts and emotions spurred and fueled by the spontaneity of life's events blow diligently against her and she manages to maintain her course. She manages to Align her thoughts and emotions with her Soul and then act accordingly. This does not mean that she denies the experience of her initial emotion. Certainly not. She would be missing some color that way. Yes, color. She experiences the original thoughts and the emotions to their fullest and then chooses to change them along with her actions. She is centered in her Soul and it is her Soul that is doing the directing.

And what a difference between the tone of this version of the scene and the version in the last chapter too! Right away, there is a lightness to living that comes through. Mom's not bothered by the dog. The exchange with her daughter, instead of being full of criticism and rancor and resentment, is filled with understanding and attempts to teach better ways of making decisions. The current scene is soaked with positivity and forward movement. This is what happens when the Soul is doing the directing. We get the benefits of all of the Soul's positive qualities reverberating around inside us and radiating outward as well. This is the way of Jonathan. The reactionary mode of the flock is replaced by an intentional effort to act from a deeper place, from the Soul. The initial thoughts and emotions are experienced, even enjoyed, but they are not given the power of directing. And the effects of love and wisdom are so much nicer than the negativity that often accompanies the reactionary method.

We can see how thoughts and emotions can take over and direct our lives when we give them free rein, causing us to be reactionary. But there is another way that we allow the Soul to be pushed out of the director's chair. It has to do with those insidious patterns of behavior that tend to repeat themselves in our lives. You remember those habitual, pervasive ways of behavior that we can't seem to stop. These habitual patterns have some deep roots, usually based in a series of past experience and, lying at the roots is the command center. This pseudo-director gets its own name: themes. We learn a way of behaving early on and repeat it again and again, any time a similar situation comes up. Since it is so automatic, so ingrained into our psyches, the theme seems like some ghostly director. We are sometimes hardly aware of its presence. Themes can be like ghostly currents of air that furtively control our behavior. They hover around under the surface of the subconscious subtly prodding us to think and behave in a certain way. A situation comes up that wakes the theme from its slumber and it starts nagging. And they are relentless.

"This is it! This is what we do in this situation. Go on! You already know. You've done it a hundred times. Just go on. Do it!"

And we do. We react according to our theme and then whip our heads around to see who was doing all that poking. But too late, the ghost wind has vanished. Themes are regular little dictators.

"Step aside, Soul," they demand, while giving a harsh shove to our delicate parts, "this is one of those situations that calls for *my* direction."

The example from the last chapter was the person who couldn't seem to deal with confrontation, either in the movie theater or with his mother-in-law. Somewhere, along in the experiences of his life, he developed a sort of anti-confrontational theme. Maybe it started with a series of confrontations with a controlling parent. He always lost, so he learned not to confront. Or maybe it was the series of losing battles on the playground that did it. Wherever it came from, it developed into a full-blown theme that automatically kicks in whenever he is in a confrontational situation.

Thus, part of our evolution means that we work on transcending our themes. The Soul will not direct if a theme comes in to take over, however temporary it may be. We don't want to be victims of a theme's direction any more than we want to be at the mercy of our own thoughts and emotions. Now, transcending themes is complicated work and there will be more said about it later. Generally speaking, though, we usually have to dig around in the past a bit and find where the pattern first shows up. This understanding alone helps to undermine some of the power that they have over our behavior. Then, of course, we have to practice changing the behaviors. After all, themes dictate patterns, which means that we've been doing them habitually for a long time. Practice is always called for when you're changing something that has a particularly long, well-established life. They just don't roll over dead. You have to work at them. Still, the idea is that we are clearing a path, deleting another dictator that stands in the way of allowing the Soul to shine right into our lives.

In the way of Jonathan, we are consciously attempting to evolve so that the Sacred within us, the Soul will come forward into our lives in the forms of love, serenity, compassion and wisdom. We work on decreasing the reactionary method of the flock and transcending some of the themes that prevent this from occurring. Gradually, we move forward. Gradually, we Align ourselves with our Souls. Gradually, we Soar in Life.

Now that you have an understanding about *what* we are evolving towards, it's time to return to the question of *how* we go about this Alignment to the Sacred within us, how we go about our spiritual evolution. And once again, we begin with an assumption: that who we are and what we need to know in order to evolve is reflected in the "world" of our lives. What we need to learn to further our spiritual evolution is right under our noses, *right in the living itself.*

It's in the brief encounter that you had with the mailman the other day. It's in the cello practice session and the way you became so frustrated with that one passage. It's in the interaction with your boss when she told you how slack you had become lately. It's in your inability to turn down a cup of coffee and your constant affection toward strangers. It's in your automatic, loving acceptance of other people's differences. It's in your relationships and your reaction to the flat tire. It's in the music you hear on the radio and the passage that you read in a novel. It's in your preference for the warm summer months. The messages and knowledge that we need to have in order to evolve to a point where we are Aligned to the Sacred within us, is contained right in the world of our lives. It lies around just waiting for us to pay enough attention to discover its presence and its message.

The problem is that we are often too caught up in the business of living itself to focus on the *significance* of the events of our lives. The cello practice session is perceived as just the way you become a better cello player. And, while this is true, there are other reasons for sitting down in front of that music stand. You might begin to notice, for example, that you prefer those practice sessions where there is a clear balance between how much you *work* at playing the cello and how much you *play* at playing the cello. You might also notice a definite lack of patience when you hit a passage that you cannot play. After all, you are an accomplished cello player. You ought to be able to at least understand what you're supposed to play. Your cello playing reveals a great deal about your expectations for yourself. In fact, if you're watching closely enough, you'll see how you have expectations of others as well. The encounter with the mailman would show you that, when you got on his case the other day for being one hour later than usual in his delivery. The messages that we need for our evolution are clearly in front of us. We only need to pay attention to their significance in order to start the transformation process.

This is how we can begin to move toward a complete restoration: by learning to perceive the messages that are contained in the living itself. This is how we can begin to alter that reactionary way of being and how we can avoid repeating those insidious patterns that were so pervasive in the way of the flock. The messages and knowledge that we need to start the transformation are all there. It begins with the assumption that this is indeed the case, then we learn to hone our attention so that we can see the significance behind the events.

Through our attention, then, we start to understand some areas where evolution is needed, where the Alignment to the Sacred within us is incomplete. At this point, it becomes natural to seek clarity about these areas, since the messages often seem hazy at first. For example, that cello player might begin to see her expectations for herself reflected in her cello practice, but these ideas and thoughts might be limited to that area. She might think that these expectations are only out of line when she's practicing. Later, though, if she's paying attention, she might also see how these expectations affect her relationship with her spouse. Now the issue has become clearer. She begins to realize that this issue might actually be a theme, something that runs throughout her life, like a complicated network of arteries. As her attention increases, she will notice more and more aspects about this theme. She will gain a certain clarity. Then, with a fuller awareness, she can decide how she wants to conduct her life with regard to expectations. What would happen to these expectations if the Soul were directing? That is the question and the message for her evolution becomes just a bit clearer. If she decides to make changes, then the next step is to begin practicing a different way of thinking and being.

This is a rather general overview of the process of Aligning ourselves to the Sacred within us and the process of our evolution. A major portion of the remaining chapters of this book is devoted to the detail of this process. In general, though, evolution starts with the assumption that what we need to know is reflected in our living. Then, through attention, the areas of potential growth become clearer and clearer until we arrive at that crossroads of choice. At that point, we can actively decide how we want to be, how we can Align ourselves to the Sacred within us, evolve, and take on the work of change.

* * * *

The way of Jonathan Livingston Seagull. A way of living where our own Soulful wisdom is acknowledged as we choose our own unique path. We know what circumstances will lead us toward our eventual restoration.

The way of Jonathan Livingston Seagull. A way of living where success is defined as engaging in the process of Aligning ourselves to the Sacred through nourishment and evolution.

The way of Jonathan Livingston Seagull. A way of living where we understand the preciousness and infinite life in a moment and can nourish ourselves by completely immersing ourselves into life's Sacred essence.

The way of Jonathan Livingston Seagull. A way of living in which we teach ourselves to allow the Soul to direct our lives.

The way of Jonathan Livingston Seagull. A way of living that is imbued with meaning and higher purpose.

(That might have been a bit dramatic, but a little drama can be amusing from time to time.)

The Transformation

Now, if we choose to begin to live in this way, then after awhile, we'll start to notice something. The Soul starts to direct our lives a bit more. As a matter of fact, we are so much more comfortable sinking right down into the color of detail in a moment. Those clicks when our Souls seem to Align with life's Sacred essence, come more frequently. Effortlessly, now, we inhale the sight of frost twinkling in the early sun of morning. We can be completely immersed and full. And the thoughts and emotions don't step into the director's chair so much anymore. Those situations that used to string our nerves taunt to the breaking point don't seem so potent over us either. We've managed to sift through a few of those themes too, so they don't assault us so often. After awhile, we realize that a gradual, lovely transformation *has* and *continues* to take place. The Soul radiates outward so much more of the time. We're maybe…even… Soaring a bit.

The Sacred has expanded in our lives and we begin to see the qualities of Soul that we have for so long allowed to be blocked by the pseudo-directors. The transformation is profound. You'll feel it on the inside. You'll see it on the outside. Peace, a profound serenity, will come with your Alignment to Sacred around you and you won't even have to go on vacation to feel it. It is almost always there in front of you, just waiting for you to recognize it, waiting for you to Align yourself to it. And this holds true almost no matter what is going on in your life. Love, the deepest sort of love, will make an appearance as well. You'll notice it in your thoughts, in your emotions and in your behavior. Love is a great companion to peace. They travel together frequently. Spontaneity and pure delight will also come forth. By-products of this transformation, these qualities are completely joyous. They tend to come from the freedom that you experience, for Soaring is setting your Soul free. (This paragraph only gives you a taste of the results of living in this way. There's a whole chapter on this later.)

As we come closer and closer to Aligning ourselves with the Sacred that is within us and around us, what we are really doing is *identifying* with the Sacred, *identifying* with the Soul. We are finding out *who we really are*. As we transcend the pseudo-directors, we begin to gain a clearer perception of ourselves and the view is magnificent. We come to not only understand that we are love, wisdom and serenity, we come to identify with these qualities of Soul. We will have a clearer view of who we are.

Yes, we'll have a clearer view of ourselves, of our Souls because of this transformation. But something else happens after we've been living with a primary focus on this Alignment to the Sacred through nourishment and evolution for awhile. We'll have a clearer view of others too. After all of this focusing on ourselves, thinking about *our* lives and *our* evolution, our view begins to naturally turn outward. And, without the tarnish of so many reactions, without the grime of so many themes, we can gaze into the eyes of someone else with an expansive view. Letting ourselves go for a moment, we can perceive that inner beauty of light that radiates around the core of their being. It's there. A tender, glowing light of love. Now, without so much grime around our own Souls, we can perceive it. And, with this expansive, clear, direct-shot view, we can see something else too. Something that will pull at our hearts. Pain and struggle. The inevitable, lovely turmoil of life. It's there too. The experience of negative perceptions and events tugs at their eyes, leaving a trace of pallid hollowness. We recognize it well.

We recognize it because we have lived it, are living it. What happens when this foundational recognition occurs is a profound blossoming. Compassion unfolds within us like those long petals of an iris. We feel it with our expansive gaze into someone else. The struggle that we know so well. It's there. Here is this ethereal being of light wrestling with the same harshness, struggling in the same way as we are. *Of course* compassion will rise up. And something else comes up too. We get a deep sense of connection. Suddenly, the separation of you and me, us and them starts to fade and we realize that we are all beings of light, sharing the same struggle. At this level of understanding, separating ourselves because of personality traits or skin color or whatever is laughable. The idea doesn't even get past the giggle test. The connection feels much too strong.

You have read about the way of the flock and know the results of living in that way. And you now have read about the way of Jonathan and know about that method. At the bottom of all this discussion, what we are talking about is ways of approaching life and living. How are you going to do life? There are two different ways here. At some point, we choose, *for even not choosing is making a choice.* I want to tell you a story.

Once upon a time, there was an intelligent woman who was troubled and struggling with her life. She was bold enough to step into the arena with the demons of her depression and found herself face to face with stagnation. She contemplated this particular demon for awhile and was beginning to slide into an understanding with him. The rationality of his arguments seemed to be gradually wrapping around her. Before engaging in the final dance with this particular demon, however, she decided to ask her friend. Her friend, who was shimmering with love for her, placed before her the antithesis of that demon stagnation. He positioned her directly in front of Aligning herself with the Sacred. With an open mind, she contemplated this. Then, with her sharp intellect shining, she asked her friend the question,

"But what makes Aligning myself with the Sacred any more valid than dancing with stagnation?"

"Nothing," was her friend's answer, "it is simply a matter of choice. The perspectives point toward different directions and end in different places. Consider the effects. That is all."

And the woman made her choice.

Now it's your turn.

THE BASIC POSITIONS OF FLYING

The Basic Perceptual Approaches to Life That Are Consistent with This Focus

You want to know peace,
* I teach you acceptance and meaning.*
You want to know peace,
*   I teach you just how precious and joyous*
*   The moments of life can be.*
You want to know peace,
* I teach you the value of pain.*
Will you listen?

Choosing the Glasses We Wear in Life

So maybe you haven't taken your turn and made your choice yet, but you're still reading. That's a good sign. Checking out the area, getting a full picture is always an intelligent approach. Taking flight before you're ready can lead to crashes and burns, after all. As a matter of fact, we're going to do some checking ourselves. We are going to check out the basic positions of flying that are consistent with Jonathan's way of living.

The basic positions of flying is just a cute way of talking about the basic perceptual stances that we take toward life, how we approach our lives and living, what we assume before we even start. When we think about living, when we get up each morning, we open our eyes and view our lives with certain perceptual positions already in place. They are like glasses that we wear for life. For instance, we may think of life as an endless series of activities, so that when we get up, we're already jumping toward the first one in our mind. *What's first on that 'to do' list today? Oh yes, the laundry.* And off we go. We're approaching life through this basic perceptual position. Or we may think of life as a long, painful struggle that "goes on long after the thrill is gone." In this case, the wake up call is going to be followed by a series of negative thoughts and "I told you so's" as we see the pain and struggle that we predicted come to us through our experience. The glasses that we start out with can remain steady throughout our living.

We all have basic perceptual positions that we have adopted somewhere along the way of our lives. The glasses that stay so firmly planted on the bridge of the nose, may have been passed down from our parents or from society in general. These positions are of the old-taped-up-chipped variety of glasses. They are worn out before we get them. We have already seen some of these. For the oldest and most often worn pair is none other than the glasses of the prescribed path itself. The flock provides these for us. We approach life with the developmental tasks to tackle, focus on the details of these tasks, try to stay ahead of a good percentage of our own generation and finally succeed. You know about these glasses already.

But there are others pairs of glasses that are more personal which we adopt. They come from our experiences themselves. Maybe something happened in the past that jolted us in a way that we will never forget. In fact, maybe the event was so stunning that we ended up changing our approach to life. We ended up adopting a new position. Someone who spends years being a doormat for a spouse, being mistreated by many people might adopt a new position somewhere along the way. That person might decide that "I must get what I can for myself." With this new position, this new set of glasses, she goes through her life and approaches situations from this stance. Her position comes from a response to her experience. She won't have that old junk happening anymore. She won't stand for it. As a matter of fact, she will scrounge for herself first, even at the expense of others. She adopts the new set of glasses. These aren't the hand-me-down kind. They are the kind that are intentionally adopted because of experience.

Now, if she wears these glasses long enough, as with any pair of glasses, they will eventually become invisible. Poof! Magic. They're gone. The position becomes assumed. This is exactly what happens to all of us. We have the positions that are passed down from our society, those positions that extend out of the prescribed paths. We have the positions that we adopt because of experience. After awhile, though, we forget that we have glasses on and the positions become assumed. This is quite natural. Indeed, they become so assumed that we are *no longer aware of their existence.*

This is when things can get dangerous if we are at all concerned about Aligning ourselves to the Sacred and about our personal evolution. Because, when positions become assumed, then we are also assuming that we're looking directly at reality, directly at our lives. But we're not, are we? We're looking at our lives through the filters of our glasses. So should we try to take off all of our sets of glasses and see a raw, True-with-a-capital-"T" reality? I'll be careful here not to get too philosophical, but I will say that we could never remove *all* of those glasses, all of those ways of perceiving our lives. In order to do that we would have to remove the biggest pair of glasses, *ourselves.* That's not going to happen. So we're stuck with some glasses and perceptions.

It seems, then, that we again arrive at the crossroads of choice. If we're aware that we necessarily adopt certain perceptual positions and that these positions radically affect how we live our lives, then doesn't it make sense to attempt to *choose* what glasses we are going to wear? How we choose to approach life, what glasses we wear, is going to infiltrate our thoughts, our relationships, our careers, our interactions, our experiences in the most pervasive way. It just makes sense then, that we would want to have a say in what these positions will be.

When we choose to live in the way of Jonathan, then we adopt a fundamental underlying assumption: that we are here to Align ourselves to the Sacred that is within us and around us, to be nourished, to evolve, to be restored. This assumption, in turn, points to the most basic perceptual position. Given this assumption, life becomes an extremely fertile slice of time that is solidly sprinkled with events for the Alignment to occur. Every moment, every event, every experience is precious and holds potential for nourishment and evolution. Should we choose to adopt the primary focus on flying, on the Alignment of ourselves to the Sacred that is within us and around us, then we start from this most basic position.

And, like the branches of a tree that shoot off from its trunk, there are other supporting positions, other perceptual stances that underscore the most basic position. That is what this chapter is about. Three basic positions are presented here that are consistent with the way of Jonathan. Here is the first one.

Viewing Life's Events With Acceptance and Meaning

Life appears to be a ride.

Seemingly random events sweep into our lives and stir us all up, leading to massive changes and transformations. Or maybe these events just leave us clinging desperately to our old positions, as, wild-eyed, we jerk our heads around to see what might be coming next. But we don't know what's coming next. There's no sneak preview. We can't prepare for or manipulate the future. The unpredicted events just keep coming our way. The idea that life seems to be in the driver's seat most of the time, instead of us, leaves us all twitching slightly. We glance around nervously and stand on our tiptoes, hoping to get a glimpse of the next part of the ride. Our egos don't like being a passenger. In fact, the majority of us will deny this most vehemently if asked.

"Who's in charge of life's events?" we inquire. A hearty response is more convincing, so the ego puts on its best deep voice and replies, "We are."

The ego, of course, is *not* in charge. But the denial continues, just the same.

Particularly in this country, the most common assumption about life's events is that we are in charge of them, that is, our egos are doing the driving. Of course, we don't often go around proclaiming loudly about this position. Indeed, some of us aren't even aware of its presence, so submerged it is in our psyches. But we can tell that this assumption is there, if we stop to consider how much planning of our lives that we do and the reactions we have when these plans don't follow our outline.

We begin planning our lives at a very early age, completely certain while we're doing it that these plans will come to fruition exactly as we have planned them, so long as we do our part. Somewhere along this planned path, though, we inevitably hit a bump, an air pocket, or we fly into a rainstorm. We want to become a doctor, so we take the college prep courses in high school, select a college that is known for its pre-medical program and even pre-select in all high hopes the medical school itself. Then there is the residency to consider and where in the country we'd like to live and we plan this too. Then life happens. An unexpected pregnancy. The alcohol problem we didn't know we had. The unexpected intolerance of dead bodies. Whatever the reason, the bump occurs.

And it's not just our careers we plan to this extent. We plan our families, too. Okay, let's see, we'll have two children exactly three years apart in age. That will give us plenty of time to get through most of the baby years of one before having the other. Perfect. Then, of course, it happens. Life again. After a month of pregnancy, we miscarry. Or we find out that because of some physical condition, we can't have children at all. The events of life happen in their unexpected way again and again, somehow managing to always interfere with our plans.

The extent of our planning is quite phenomenal. It not only covers the long term, big aspects of our lives, but also seeps into the more mundane daily aspects. We plan activities, meals, errands, but it seems, at least sometimes, that our plans get foiled. We want to go to the movies, make a selection from the paper, arrive at the cinema, only to find out that the movie was sold out. Lasagna was the plan for dinner because we were feeling particularly optimistic about our cooking skills that evening. We prepare half of the ingredients only to find an empty space in the cupboard where the noodles should be.

And then there is what we call the accidents. These are those events that we hadn't planned at all. What this twists into, though, is that we actually *did* plan. We planned for them *not* to happen. We are parked at a traffic light and some other car reams us from behind. We've already had two children and we're pregnant—again. Our child secretly climbs the tree we told him not to climb and he falls off and breaks his arm. The plant parked in the corner of the living room gets knocked down and dirt is ground into the carpet by the children before we realize what has happened. We hadn't planned on these accidents. There's that proverbial bump again and again and again.

The usual position of being in charge of life events shows up again in another way. It shows in our reactions to the foiling, the bumps, and the rainstorms. What do we do when life happens in a way that we didn't plan or anticipate? We yell. We curse. We scream. Maybe we become sarcastic or withdraw in anger to our private space in the basement. Or maybe we bitterly complain to our partner, verbally reviewing the disappointment over and over again. We balk and throw our hands up at the incredible injustice of the whole thing. If we wanted to be a doctor, but just can't do dead bodies, we ask, *how dare my intellect and my emotions betray me this way?* If our child breaks his arm, we ask, *how dare he climb that tree after I specifically told him not to climb that particular tree?* There should be lasagna noodles in the cupboard. They shouldn't have knocked that plant over. What we judge to be the injustice of life's events never ceases to astonish and infuriate us.

Or we react by digging ourselves into our rigid position. We will *make* our plan happen. And, despite multiple trips to the bathroom because those dead bodies incessantly evoke the gag reflex, we grit our teeth and hold our bile breath while hovering over the cadavers. We will get through this, by God! And miserably, we do. We didn't allow life to take hold of the wheel for long. Or we react to the unexpected events by bowing our heads in defeat. We slowly shake our heads in a tsk, tsk, fashion, reviewing the whole thing over and over again, vainly searching for where we went wrong.

Fury and astonishment. Forcing events to conform to our outlined plan. Bowing in defeat. These are the reactions that are dead giveaways to the position behind them. We assume that we're in charge. And the results of attempting to maintain this position? For one, we stay miserable. The fury is heavy and thickly loaded. We wade into the pool of misery and decide to stay and swim for awhile, all the time, sending out verbal lashings about our injustice to anyone who will listen. And there is that insidious anxiety that hovers just below the surface.

"I don't know what's coming. Do you know what's coming? If you do, tell me. I have to know. How can I know what to do if I don't know?"

This is the anxiety of our egos not being in charge. If we continue in our fury and anxiety long enough or react consistently to life events in this way, we will begin to suffer the physical ramifications of holding onto anger and anxiety. These are well documented. The ulcers, the headaches, the heart attacks. Non-acceptance is relentlessly painful, both emotionally and physically. Also, having this reaction means that we learn nothing. For, how could we possibly learn anything about our flying, about ourselves if we are swallowed up by our fury and injustice? It would be predictably impossible to learn much under these conditions.

Life seems to be a ride and our egos are not driving. For most of us, we're not too comfortable giving up the illusion that the ego is in charge of life's events. Sure, intellectually, we have no problem. The evidence is there with the logic behind it. The ego can't control life events. Of course we know this. But on some other level, (the level on which we becomes infuriated when life happens outside our predictions), the thought that we're not in charge leaves us feeling a bit woozy, like maybe we need to sit down for a second on our favorite laz-y-boy chair. Something familiar please. Yes, that's better.

Perhaps, with some practice though, we can extend that intellectual understanding to the part of us that becomes infuriated. Because these bumps, accidents and foiled plans are simply our Soul's way of inviting events into our lives that will push us toward Alignment with the Sacred through evolution. Our egos may not be doing the driving, but our Souls most certainly are. The Soul is wise and knows what situations and circumstances are needed to propel us toward Alignment through evolution. And, if this is indeed the case, then maybe we can learn to accept life events as they happen and delete the evaluation of them right out of the equation. Maybe we can even learn to see meaning in them. Viewing life's events with acceptance and meaning. We could learn to view the events of our lives in this way with practice. With this basic flying position, then, we would react quite differently when the ride of life took a sharp left turn in an unplanned direction.

Instead of dropping the jaw with that stunned look of surprise and stammering out, "But it shouldn't have…it couldn't have…how *dare* it?" we might react with something like the mild surprise of raised eyebrows and say, "Whoa, that was a sharp turn…looks like a new direction…wonder what I can learn *here*…?" Obviously different, eh? Let's look more closely at this reaction and where it leads us.

"Whoa, that was a sharp turn…" This is a clear acknowledgment that these unplanned events that can seem to occur spontaneously are sometimes painful. Just because we hold the basic flying position of acceptance doesn't mean that we don't feel the pain or disappointment. The unexpected pregnancy that essentially put a halt to the career we were planning still smarts. There is still disappointment, but it doesn't turn into fury that is fueled by thoughts of injustice. Instead, there is acknowledgment of the feelings as we fully experience them, then let them go.

Of course, the "Whoa, that was a sharp turn…" reaction is truly reserved for the sharp turns. Arriving at the cinema to find that the tickets are sold out, finding no noodles in the cupboard for lasagna, knocking the plant on the floor of the living room, don't even warrant much of a reaction at all. These are the incidences that fall into the small stuff department. And the old cliché does still apply. There's no point in sweating it. Imagine, after you've vacuumed the dirt off the floor from that plant that fell, thinking *Wow, that was difficult to get through.* Are you at least snickering now? Because the absurdity is funny. Dirt ground into the living room carpet is only going to have a major impact in our lives if we react in a way as to give that incident that power. It's just not worth the emotional energy. (Certainly, not sweating the small stuff does require practice. It gets one paragraph here, but it may require several chapters worth of attention in order to learn it. Practice is to be expected.)

"Looks like a new direction…" This is the piece of the reaction that underscores accepting the events of life as they come. Planned or unplanned, life is as it is. This reaction is only an observation of the new course that has been laid out as a result of the life event. There is no evaluation, no judgment about the new direction. It's just a remark. Acceptance is the position here. What this means is that we see the new direction and *go with the currents of life instead of against them.* If it's raining, don't go on a picnic. Forcing a picnic in the rain leaves us with the sour taste of soggy food and drenched clothes. Miserable. (Unless, of course, you'd enjoy slinging some mud at each other.) From Benjamin Hoff comes a shortened version of a story written long ago that underscores, well, several points, but you will see how it relates to acceptance of life events.

> An old man and his son lived in an abandoned fortress on the side of a hill. Their only possession of value was a horse.
>
> One day, the horse ran away. The neighbors came by to offer sympathy. "That's really bad!" they said.
>
> "How do you know?" asked the old man.
>
> The next day, the horse returned, bringing with it several wild horses. The old man and his son shut them all inside the gate. The neighbors hurried over. "That's really good!" they said.
>
> "How do you know?" asked the old man.
>
> The following day, the son tried riding one of the wild horses, fell off, and broke his leg. The neighbors came around as soon as they heard the news. "That's really bad!" they said.
>
> "How do you know?" asked the old man.
>
> The day after that, the army came through, forcing the

local young men into service to fight a faraway battle against the northern barbarians. Many of them would never return. But the son couldn't go, because he'd broken his leg.

Gone is the fury. Gone are the attempts to force the direction. Gone is the perception of defeat. The evaluation is deleted from the equation altogether. The old man here doesn't perceive the events of life as being "good" or "bad." They simply are as they are and he goes along with them. Next.

With the big curves that life tosses towards us, we can acknowledge how difficult they are and we can accept them and go along with their new directions. And when we view the events of life with acceptance, instead of astonishment and fury, we are leaving room to consider something else. Something important. Meaning.

"Wonder what I can learn *here*..." An unplanned, unexpected event inserts itself into our lives. No, we will not be the person we thought we would be. We will be transformed by the event. This is certain. But how we will be transformed is up to us. It is a choice, a choice that leads toward Alignment to the Sacred through evolution. That is why the event came into our lives to begin with. The frustrated to-be-doctor who ended up pregnant before graduation can view this event in a myriad of ways. The old way is to see it as a disappointment, a block in the plan, an injustice. What this means, though, is that in her pregnancy she will be miserable and will be revisited with bouts of fury as she thinks of the injustice. Also, she is probably going to resent the child for preventing her from pursuing the carefully outlined plan, even though it was she who became pregnant. Of course, resenting the child will have long term effects on both the child and their relationship. We can just imagine the extended negativity of this long harbored resentment.

She does, however, have another way of perceiving the whole unplanned event of pregnancy. She could start by simply acknowledging and feeling the pain and disappointment of the change that the pregnancy has brought. Then, of course, she could accept the pregnancy and the child that will be coming, all the while recognizing her full responsibility in becoming pregnant. This does not mean beating herself up mentally. It means acknowledging where the responsibility lies. That is all. In this way, the potential resentment toward the child is avoided and the relationship between the mother and child doesn't suffer from the tarnish of blame. As for meaning? Like the old man in the story, she doesn't really know whether this change in path is good or bad, so there is not much use in evaluating it. But she can look toward the growth that could occur, not just in spite of, but *because* of this pregnancy. Having a child may change the course of her life completely in ways that she may not be aware of. If she does only take a break in the path of her career, then there is no doubt that she will not be the same doctor she would have been without a child. How she views the world and how she behaves as a doctor will be altered by having a child. And, after the child comes, she could decide that she no longer wants to pursue that career, that somehow the child has altered her priorities, her way of thinking. And she goes on in another direction. She will be transformed by this event and evolution can occur, but she will have to leave the fury of the perception of injustice behind. She can choose to take a basic perceptual position of acceptance and meaning.

When we can manage to maintain this basic position, then even events that most of us would consider to be dire or catastrophic, take on a new face.

This is when we hear folks say things like, "If it hadn't been for my cancer, I never would have learned to cherish the moments with my daughter."

Or, "I know it sounds odd, but if he hadn't died, I never would have understood about giving."

Or, "My bankruptcy saved me from terminal stagnation."

Indeed, the most adverse circumstances can be the most growthful, if we can muster the strength to view it this way.

Jim Bedard recounts the twists and turns of his journey as he fought against leukemia in his book, *Lotus in the Fire*.

During one of his long stays in the hospital, someone comments about how accepting he is of his illness, that he seems to see it as part of his spiritual practice. He acknowledges that the illness was indeed a spiritual practice, as is anything in our lives that we experience, including health. Even enduring the horror of the suffering such as this, we can evolve and use the experience itself to help us Align ourselves the Sacred. Somehow, through the cutting and pain, vomit and diarrhea, Jim Bedard stayed with his practice and emerged as a weathered, but Soaring Soul. Because of his experience, he not only grew himself, but his candid written account of his journey through fire contributes to the evolution of others.

Notice too that adopting a position of acceptance and meaning for life's events leads to *peace*, a hearty, deep felt peace. For no longer are you fighting against the current of life, no longer are you spouting angry words about the injustice of it all, you are instead accepting what is happening and looking for deeper meaning. And *that*, my friends, leads to peace. Adopt a position of acceptance and meaning and you'll find yourself floating along in calm waters or holding on tight when you pass through some rapids. But you will have the peace that comes with going with the current instead of against it.

There is just one small caveat that I want to add in order to avoid any potential confusion. Viewing life's events with acceptance and meaning doesn't mean that we stop thinking of the future or planning altogether. We don't just sit back in those familiar, comfortable laz-y-boys and watch while life happens to us. We still plan our lives and take the active role of pursuing the paths that we consider to be growthful. Only now, we hold these plans more tentatively, knowing that what we have in mind is not necessarily what will occur. But that no matter what occurs, we can choose the perspective of acceptance and meaning which usually points in the direction of evolution.

"Whoa, that was a sharp turn…looks like a new direction…wonder what I can learn *here*…?"

Viewing the Moments of Life as Precious
— *So That We May Find a Nourishing Peace*

Every one of us has had the experience of a ruthlessly special moment. These are the sort that tend to stand apart in our memories. Way apart. If you dig around in that large sack of memory, somewhere you're likely to find one of these moments. They're actually easy to find because they are so brilliant and clear. We can pull them up on the video screen of our minds and watch them again and again, if we wish. Maybe it was a solitary moment of ultimate peace as you studied the way that water dances through a stream, bending and curving around rock and tree limbs with an enviable ease. Or maybe it was the time that you watched your child still sleeping, the contemplation of her eyelashes against her cheek in the rosy light of a rising sun making your love swell and reverberate throughout your entire being. Whatever the memory is, the details somehow remain intact, despite the passage of time. You can almost see the flashes of light on that stream as it incessantly trickles. And those eyelashes! Tiny dark lines stenciled against her cheek by the glowing sun. The memories of these special moments seemed to be etched onto the neurons. We all have these.

Then there are the other memories and the not-so-special moments. They tend to be hazy, dull and vague in comparison to the brilliance of the special ones. *Now, let me see*, we solemnly think as we scan that memory sack for clues to clarify, *was it once or two times that she fell out of the chair because of her absent-minded rocking? And that van we used to have…goodness me, we had it for ten years, but I can't seem to remember the color…Was it green?* All hazy and vague these memories are. What a contrast when we compare them to the special ones.

The special moments do stand out among the others in that sack of memories. But they also seem different *while* we are experiencing them. *Whoa*, we think while we are experiencing one of these special moments, *this is not the same old stuff of life. This is…different.* For one thing, the perception of time itself changes. Time, that old guy that seems to be speeding up with every passing year of our lives, suddenly pushes hard against the brakes. In fact, during one of these special moments, we might just get the impression that time…has…stopped. Just for a minute. Or two. Suddenly, seconds and minutes seem to stretch and get fatter. As you stare at your daughter's eyelashes during a morning sunrise, you become immersed. There is nothing else in the world right now, except this scene before you and the enormous beauty of it. You sink into the moment. Then the thought pops into your mind that you've got to wake her up and start the school morning routine. You glance at the clock with a timid anxiety and are astonished to find that only five minutes have passed. *That's odd,* you think, *it seemed a lot longer than that.* Time has somehow expanded.

But it is not only time perception that is altered. There is another quality that is more difficult to describe, an ethereal quality to these special moments. While we are immersed in one of these, *there is a sort of peace that floats through us, a joyous calm, a reverence and grace of being.* We feel moved. We feel profoundly touched. Here is when we feel the results of Aligning ourselves with the Sacred that surrounds us. Our Souls seem to click into place and relax into being. A serene, sighing sensation occurs. Here is the nourishment and peace that we long for.

It's bedtime and your son requests a few minutes of your company. You lie next to him and expect a long soliloquy of thought from him, which would be consistent with his usual active demeanor. Instead you are surprised by his silence and his stillness. You say nothing and begin to immerse yourself in watching him. He is watching you, too. He gently touches the bottom curl of your hair and follows it with his finger up to its origin. Then he decides to trace pretend glasses around your eyes, going behind your ears to make sure they stay on. Then he stops and stares directly into your eyes. He face is studious, pensive. You are completely absorbed by the beauty of his face, by his flexible personality. You can feel the infinity of the love between you.

Then he says, "I can see the love you have for me in the black part of your eyes. I love you too, Mama." The overflow of love comes in the form of tears.

No wonder we remember these moments. No wonder they seem different. For the time that we are having this experience, we are consumed by the detail in each second. For that expanse of time, however long it is, we are soaked to the marrow with the tiny events. It is almost as if we have merged with the present. Somehow the line between us and the object of our attention is not so clear anymore. But, if we don't want to go that far, we could certainly say that we are Aligned with the Sacred of the present. Completely. And the nourishment of peace fills us.

Generally, we don't tend to spend much time being aware of the Sacredness in the present. Our attention bounces around in the future or lingers in the past while the present slides by. Like a slow moving film, the present slides in front of us. As the frames flick by, we don't pay much attention. After all, we've seen most of this black and white stuff before. Nothing new here. Putting on clothes.

"Um-hum," we say with dull acknowledgment, our attention playing happily in thoughts about the future.

Those thoughts are so much more interesting than what is happening on that film. Walking in the hall.

"Yeah, sure." And so it goes.

Certainly, there are times when the film gets our full attention, times when a full-course drama unfolds there. Verbal battles, hot handed sex, hurts and injustices, major events. The drama will always capture and enfold us. But every so often, there will be something smaller, less dramatic, something even ordinary that somehow manages to quietly call and gain our attention. Somehow, this tiny detail that would usually slide on by these slow frames unnoticed, manages to pull our attention away from its usual displaced position. This is when you notice the eyelashes. Somehow, it is if you are seeing those lashes for the first time. Perhaps it is beauty that calls so seductively to us. Or maybe it is the warmth of love. Or maybe it is just that we are between thought segments and during the pause, we happen to do a double take at those frames that are endlessly flicking by. *Whoa*, we think, *there's some nourishing color there.* And the frames gain the full force of our attention. This is when we become immersed in the moment. That flash of color just caught our attention. *Those lashes! we think, I never truly looked at them before!*

This is the reason for this grand, blatant difference between the special and not-so-special moments. The special moments seem special because we are *in them*. It's quite simple, really. The special moments take on the radiance of full blown nourishing color *because we are suddenly paying attention to the Sacredness that is there.* The act of paying attention is what makes the difference between what is perceived as black and white and what is perceived as color. Paying attention transforms the mundane into the brilliant. Paying attention to that stream transformed it into the magical genie of dance. Paying attention to your daughter's eyelashes transformed her into a delicate, innocent angel. There is enormous power in paying attention. Paying attention transforms and injects nourishing color. We will come back to this idea again and again. For, like the stream, it dances through and around the way of Jonathan.

Now we have a reason why those moments are so memorable,

why they stand out so vividly from the rest. It was because we were completely Aligned with the Sacredness of the moments through our attention. And we can find ways to practice paying attention. (We'll talk about practicing just that a bit later. For now, we'll stick to the positions or perceptions). But the question remains, why *were* we paying attention during these moments? The circumstances and subjects of our attention were not particularly dramatic or extraordinary, after all. That stream that seemed so magical—you could have walked over it as you have done countless other times, over countless other streams. But you didn't. Your daughter's face— you have seen it for millions of seconds before. You could have just woken her up. But you didn't. What was it about these situations that captured us?

Well, maybe it was the quick recognition of beauty or a flash of color that caused us to do that double take at the frames. Or maybe it was something else. *Anticipation.* Sometimes we *expect* to find color. Sometimes we *expect* to feel that click of immersion, of Sacred nourishment, of deep peace that comes from Alignment with the Sacred. This works too. If you're looking forward to the walk in the woods and plan to just enjoy the experience, anticipate that you are going to see that lovely stream, then chances are, you will not be thinking about the office, your relationship with your children or that "to do" list. With the anticipation strongly planted in your mind, you are able to watch the water of the stream bend and curve around rock without thinking or being anywhere else. Your anticipation and expectation prepares your attention. The frames of experience flick by and you see them with your usual dull attention, but you look ahead to the upcoming frames. *Okay, here it comes. That walk in the woods is moving this way.*

"Ah," you say, as you take that first step on the path, "the nourishing color is finally here."

You *expected* the walk in the woods to be nourishing, so it is. Here we have those parentheses again. Remember these? We can look into the future for the chunks of potentially special moments and put our parentheses around these moments. We hold our breath and trudge through the black and white, all the while continually popping glances toward that hopeful color that is just ahead. We're waiting. Then it comes and we sink in.

"Ooo, this is nice."

But suppose we decide to extend this anticipation to *all* of the moments in our lives? Well, okay, as many as we can. If we anticipate the nourishing color to be in the moments whenever we happen to be paying attention and if we can use this anticipation to enable ourselves to become Aligned with the Sacred, then we have essentially removed the parentheses. And we can sink into the peace of the Sacred. Here is the basic flying position. We anticipate the Sacred that is intrinsically there in a moment. Those frames that flick by are really always full of color. Our attention is what is required to see it. That's all. And our attention can be prodded into alertness by anticipating that any moment we choose can be nourishing.

So this would, of course, include those moments that are ordinarily perceived to be black and white. You know. The mundane, the everyday, the ordinary. We can learn to *anticipate* that the ordinary contains full-blown nourishing color. And you know what? If we're paying attention, it will. The dinner fixing, the shower, the sweeping, even the toilet washing. With the fresh eyes of anticipation and attention, we can immerse ourselves in the nourishing color and realize that the moments are indeed precious. That just to be in them can be amazing. When we approach the moments of our lives, then, we can put on these glasses. We can adopt the position that all moments are saturated with the Sacred nourishment that we so desire and long for, and we can learn to anticipate the color to be there as much as we can.

Viewing the Moments of Life as Precious
– *So That Soul Will Direct Our Lives*

Jonathan wanted to learn to fly better. So what did he do? He observed himself. He paid attention to his own flying. When he moved a wing at high speeds, he would crash. Of course, he noticed this. How could he miss the bone crunching crash into a brick of water? He also noticed that when he moved only a small feather at this same speed, he would turn quite nicely. So at high speeds, he used the feather method for turning. There is an assumption behind learning this way. Jonathan was assuming that what he needed to know about flying was contained in the flying itself, that by observing his own flight, he could learn and evolve. The translation? What we need to know in order to Align ourselves to the Sacred that is within us, in order to evolve to a point where Soul is doing the directing, is right in front of us. In our lives. The messages that point toward growth and evolution leak out all over the place, through our own behavior and through the situations that we find ourselves in. How we think, how we perceive, how we react is all very telling about our living. If we're attempting to learn to decrease our reactionary way of being, then we'll be able to learn quite a bit by watching our reactions. And those themes that dictate those repetitive patterns of behaving — they'll come out too. All of our "stuff," the layers of grime that block out the Soul, will show up in our thoughts, in our actions and in the events of life. What this means is that the messages that point us in the direction of evolution are contained right in the living of our lives. And once again we find ourselves looking to those precious moments.

Your friends have been hounding you to get together for a social visit. You haven't seen each other in such a long time. So you finally decide to invite them over for dinner one evening. You suggest that they come at 6:00 p.m. Although they would prefer to arrive later to start the evening, they agree. You can tell after you hang up the phone that they weren't happy about it, though. Then, on the evening of the visit, they still haven't showed up by 6:30. Eventually, they arrive about 7:00. When you open the door to welcome them, they're talking over each other, stammering out incoherent excuses for their tardiness. Hum...interesting. You can't take in the excuses, though, because you're staring at the third person they have brought along with them. They didn't tell you about him. When they notice your steady gaze at their friend, they quickly stumble through introductions. *Just get them in the house,* you think. After the meal, you're sitting in the living room and listen while one of your friends tells you about car shopping. She says that she's been trying to select a car, but just can't make up her mind. So she's been going to quite a few dealerships recently. She laughs as she tells you how she tries to get a better deal. Apparently, dressing in a dumpy way and adopting a saucy street language is supposed to help. At least, according to your friend, it is. She goes on and on about it. You listen politely. They leave later than you had thought they would. You find yourself exhausted and facing a dirty kitchen.

Look between the lines of this scenario and we're likely to see some potential areas for growth. There's "stuff" leaking out everywhere, isn't there? For both the host of this social evening as well as for the guests. The actions of the guests are showing a possible way of approaching life. They came when they wanted to. They brought who they wanted to. They seemed to form the evening into what they wanted it to be. Their actions betray their position, which may be something like: "I must think of me first." Even the conversation about car shopping highlighted this approach. And while it is true that many of us hesitate when it comes to dealing with car salespersons, we probably wouldn't go to such lengths. But the host has some "stuff" too. Despite her misgivings about the whole situation, despite multiple incidences of being taken advantage of, she allows it to continue. This is one scenario, one event. But life is full of scenes like this. At home. At work. In a store. It becomes quickly obvious that opportunities for practicing Alignment with our Souls through growth and evolution are indeed everywhere.

So here we are again, tripping upon the idea of *anticipation*. For, if we assume that the messages that we need for our evolution are sprinkled through the moments of our lives, then we could begin to approach the circumstances, the moments with an eager anticipation. And wouldn't this change the view a bit? We don't often go around and see the events, circumstances and moments of our lives with these glasses on. We're not in the habit of actively looking for opportunities to use life's events to Align ourselves with our Souls. This is probably because we just don't think that the messages for growth will be there in the ordinary circumstances of our lives.

Sure, there are those times when a message slaps us hard in the face. We see these all right.

Like when your friend, out of exasperation finally comes out with, "Do you always have to perceive every comment as a criticism?"

Gosh, you had no idea that you did this, and indeed, you may not, but the slap will surely make you think about it. Usually, though, without those hard slaps, we don't anticipate learning much from our daily lives. That brief interaction with a co-worker doesn't point toward any wild insights. And your son telling you about how he did on his math test doesn't seem to qualify as particularly enlightening. The host in the above scene is probably not perceiving the evening as holding any particular messages about her growth and evolution. She's not likely to be thinking about how she allowed these "friends" to essentially mow her down. She's probably simply trying to get through the evening. But, of course, the opportunities are there. They seem obvious if we're watching the scene from the audience's point of view. And, if we approach the events of our lives with a keen anticipation that messages for our evolution are indeed there, then we are much more likely to actually perceive them. There's no need to wait for the slaps. We approach the moments with an automatic anticipation of being able to learn something about ourselves.

What this means is that almost any moment we choose can show us something about ourselves. We can pick almost any moment, approach it with an anticipation of gathering messages and we are likely to see a loud display. This holds true for all of life's events, even the ordinary and the mundane. Even in spilt milk. Your child spills the milk during dinner and it runs under casserole dishes in a narrowing stream to end by slowly dripping on the newly upholstered dining room chair on the other side of the table. Almost instantly, you feel the anger. Just as instantly, your child's face pops up to search your expression. He is expecting a reaction. And, judging by his serious expression, he thinks it is going to be negative. But, you manage to remind yourself that spilling the milk is not that serious. Definitely small stuff. You mentally wipe your brow and feel relieved to know that at least you're getting *that* message. While he is wiping up the spill with the sponge, you calmly tell him that he should've been watching what he was doing, that he should've been paying attention. You're watching him as you say this. A veil of guilt crosses over his face as the words are absorbed. You take this in and start to think. You think back to the morning when he put on a purple shirt with green pants and you told him that of course they don't go together. And you remember yesterday when he brought home the story that he wrote in school and you pointed out how he had misspelled the word "baseball." You seem to point out his failures. A lot. Um… You begin to wonder just how often you do this. Perhaps some further exploration is called for.

Spilt milk is most certainly not a slap in the face. We probably wouldn't even remember it the next day. The occurrence is mundane, ordinary. Yet, notice just how rich the ordinary can be. Rich with the potential for messages that can lead to growth. Odd, isn't it? Something as simple as spilt milk can lead this parent into thinking about a pattern of behavior that he might not have even considered, a pattern of behavior that is not necessarily Aligned with the Sacred within himself. But, in order to see it, the parent had to be open to the idea that even spilt milk will tell him something. He had to be anticipating an opportunity for his evolution.

Anticipating that the messages for growth and evolution lie in the tiniest events in the moments of life is the basic flying position here. And we can extend this anticipation into the rich arena of the ordinary. What we will find is that our lives are indeed sprinkled with all sorts of opportunities for learning about ourselves. But let's not get carried away. This position, as with any perception, could be taken too far. We could start to look for messages in every minute detail. Doing this type of obsessive searching would be maddening. Besides, if we're attempting to look for these messages in *every* second of our days, we wouldn't be able to keep up. So when we have a flat tire, we could just know that we had a flat tire. Or when your child responds to you with a head toss and that casual "whatever" for the first time, it doesn't mean that he is going through some transition or that you have somehow caused distance in your relationship. We must be careful not to go overboard here.

Actually, as we begin to anticipate the messages for our evolution, an interesting phenomenon starts to occur. We tend to pick up those messages that we are ready and willing to receive. In fact, the messages will seem to show up everywhere. Welcome to the world of Rorschach. We see what we need to see, what we're ready to see. The messages that we are ready for will show up in the dramatic circumstances of our lives, as with those harder slaps. And they will show up in the ordinary. Even in spilt milk. The parent in above example was ready to see the possible trend of pointing out his child's failures. It was ripe, on the tip-of-the-tongue, so when the smallest incident triggered any reflection at all, the thoughts about this trend came naturally floating up. Was the message really in the spilt milk? Nope. But the parent was ready to see this issue, so that was what showed up.

The same holds true for the flip side of this Rorschach coin. We will most certainly be blind to messages that we are not ready to see. There are almost always some things about ourselves that we are simply not ready to face. Maybe it's the self-indulgent attitude or the inability-to-say-no syndrome. Whatever the unpleasantness in our ways of living, we may not be ready to deal with that particular area of potential evolution. So, simply enough, we won't see it. The Rorschach phenomenon works both ways. We tend to see what we're ready to deal with and are blind to those problematic areas that we can't quite face yet. (No need to worry about stagnation for those blind spots, though. We'll just keep repeating them.)

We'll want to stretch ourselves, though. We'll want to attempt to see what we might have been blind to before. This is part of the value of evolution and restoration. We attempt to always maintain a position of readiness to perceive messages for our growth, even if they might be ugly or painful. You'll read more about pain in a minute, so let's just leave that where it is for now.

Up until this point, the emphasis here has been on approaching the moments of our lives with anticipation of seeing the messages that we need in order to Align ourselves with the Sacred through our evolution. In other words, we will start to pick up the *wise questions*. We'll begin to know what areas will need some attention and work. But, if we continue to maintain this basic flying position, we will also be able to pick up the *wise answers*. They are there too. Right in front of us, in our living, in the moments. Sometimes, these answers are all too obvious. You listen to your wife as she tells you that the mortgage check bounced. Quickly, the anger starts to rush up, but you manage somehow to avoid verbally spraying it all over her. Certainly, this is a wise choice. The answer seems obvious. Sometimes, though, the answers seem to come to us in an almost, well...mysterious ways. You've been grappling with a problem in your relationship. You've ruminated about it for two weeks and just can't seem to think of a plan of action. Then suddenly, while you are in the middle of pulling out those weeds around your favorite hickory tree, you know with honored certainty what to do about the situation. Here is the light bulb going off. How does this happen? We could speculate that perhaps the mind continues to work on the problem on the floor of the subconscious. Maybe. Maybe the Soul is accessing higher guidance. We really don't know. Still, the light bulb does continue to spontaneously go off. The answer suddenly comes to us.

And the mystery continues when we perceive answers in the events and situations of our lives. A song on the radio might prompt a memory that helps you somehow understand why you tend to react so quickly to criticism. Or a dream leads you to some insight about yourself. Or you simply overhear a conversation.

It was only a half-hour ago that you found that condom in your son's drawer.

"He's only thirteen years old!" you keep repeating to yourself as you drive toward the bowling alley.

You didn't want to bowl after you made that discovery. You wanted to stay home and think about how you are going to approach him later. But you had to keep your commitment. As you slide onto a bench to put on those rented shoes, you keep thinking about it. *He's only thirteen years old! What is he thinking? Is he actually having sex? Maybe he's just curious. Gosh, I'm gonna have to talk to him when I get home. What am I going to say? I gotta straighten him out.* Your anxiety and irritation come out physically as you jerk down to tie the shoes. That's when you hear the guys behind you talking.

"No, no. Not like that. If you get off the path you've got to walk on the leaves. Walking on the leaves makes too much noise. You might as well jog through piles of cracking branches. And that's gonna scare every living thing in the state! You have to be more subtle than that. Staying on the path means that you can look where you are going instead of thinking about what crunching noise you're gonna be making with those feet. Stay on the path and take it slow and gentle. Walk gracefully, even."

With the mention of the word 'graceful,' the two men, suddenly self-conscious look at you. You finished tying your shoes a long time ago and they know it. You have absorbed the words. *Stay on the path. Be gentle. Walk gracefully.* Mentally, you thank them for the advice. You have just received an answer about how to handle the sticky situation with your son from a man who was giving advice about hunting!

Is this woman seeing an answer simply because she is looking for an answer about the situation with her son, or is the universe or God mysteriously providing one? Does it matter? Indeed, we may have stepped back into the world of Rorschach. But it probably doesn't matter. The point here is that the woman now has a wise answer about how to tackle that tough situation with her son. She had to be open to perceiving it as an answer, though, didn't she? We can adopt the basic position of anticipating both the questions and the answers. We can anticipate growth and evolution from the events and circumstances of the moments of our lives. By now, we're not too surprised that the moments are so precious.

Crashes as "Golden Cockroaches"

Nowhere are the messages for evolution so dense, nowhere are the opportunities for Aligning ourselves with our Souls richer than when we crash. This is when we decide to fly lower to the water, but for some reason, perhaps fatigue, perhaps distraction, our attention flags for a second. Due to the slip in attention, that tired wing tip dips into the water. You can see the crash coming, but, by that time, there is nothing that you can do to stop yourself. You recognize the familiar pain as your body strikes the water.

Invariably there will be times when we crash. These are the times when we lose it. You know. When you shake your child. Or scream at your husband. Or yell at your co-worker. Or throw that toy train across the room. Or maybe you find yourself in a power struggle that more closely resembles two children arguing rather than an adult talking with a child.

"You will pick up that toy."

"No I won't."

"Yes you will."

"No I won't."

Need we continue with this one?

Or you threaten to abandon your child as a way of attempting to control behavior. Maybe you don't go so far as to say that you will leave her forever if she continues with that behavior, but the message that you send with your rejection may be exactly the same. You decide to go to your favorite bookstore for coffee and some quiet time reading books with your son and daughter. You read to them for awhile, then you let them graze through some books while you get that coffee you so desired. A couple of hot sips and you glance at your watch. The relaxed idle state you were relishing turns into a rush of mild panic. You realize that if you don't leave right away, you'll be late for their ball game. Swiftly you glide through the racks toward your children. Despite the rush, you calmly tell them the situation and ask that they quickly put away their books and prepare to leave. So far, so good. Your son gets up immediately and asks you to help him find where the Clifford book goes. By the time you return, you're expecting your daughter to be up and putting the books away. Instead, she is still grazing. Irritated, you restate your request and the reason. She doesn't even look up. Being ignored is one of those trigger points for you and you become angry. With clenched teeth, you take her arm and the request now becomes a demand. Meanwhile your son is twitching with impatience, but is waiting, watching. You don't want to physically force your daughter out of her chair, but you decide to tug her arm again. When this has no effect, you lean close to her ear. You say that you are leaving and when she is ready to go, she should call you at home. As you walk toward the door, you glance back over your shoulder, see her face suddenly register your words and in an instant, she is crying, scanning the store for you and running toward the door. She can't see you over the racks, but you can see her.

As she rounds the corner of the shelf, she is still crying and calling, "Momma."

Your first angry thought is something like, *Good, let her suffer. She should've listened to begin with.* Then you observe this thought objectively and for a moment you are shocked at yourself. You acknowledge the thought as probably coming from the "child" in yourself and accept the thought, all the while knowing that this is not the way you want to be. All of these thoughts have occurred in a few seconds as the child runs towards you crying. You watch the depth of horror on your child's face and feel it full force within yourself and know that you have made a serious mistake.

Yep. This is what a crash looks like in a parent and child interaction. There are, of course, variations on this crash behavior between adults, but *the effects* of the crash are the same. Emotional bloodletting. Feeling literally warm and frothing with anger and a sense of being wronged. It's all harsh and sticky.

And how do we ordinarily react when we crash? Usually, we blame. We can direct that blame outwardly, inwardly or both. We blame the situation or the other person. The toy wouldn't still be sitting there if it had been put away the first time the child was told to do so. If the toy had been put away, the power struggle wouldn't have occurred. Thus, it must be the child's fault. Or your co-worker knows that you hate to be interrupted while you're trying to talk on the phone. You have told her countless times in the past about this, so when you yell after slamming the phone down, she should understand. After all, you are right. Your yelling is justified and she is to blame. When we react in this manner, what we are doing is putting the responsibility of our behavior onto someone else. This pushing off of responsibility doesn't enhance our growth or theirs.

The other mode often taken after a crash is to turn that blame inward. True, this is taking responsibility for our own behavior, but we are taking it a bit too far. Suddenly the fury that we blew out at the world is now directed inward as we berate and judge ourselves with the harshness of sandpaper on sunburned skin. Given enough time, we delve into our guilt, allowing it to absorb us, as if, by doing this, we are somehow absolved. After a period of time of feeling bad, we resolutely tell ourselves that we will never, *never* allow this to happen again. Of course, it will happen again. And the cycle repeats itself, each time with us feeling more and more guilt and less and less positive about ourselves. The perspective here is that we messed up—big time.

All that blaming only perpetuates the emotional bloodletting, as we end up either slicing more pieces out of ourselves or someone else. The blame simply doesn't lead us anywhere positive. So let's just give that part up and recognize that we are *practicing*. We can be sure that we are not going to glide silently and peacefully all the time. We will certainly crash. It happens. If we can take the position of forgiving ourselves or others, as the case may be, then we can finally move on to our evolution. And when this value becomes the focus, then we are moving in a positive direction.

With this focus and perspective, then, crashes become the golden cockroaches that they are. Foul by nature, they are, nevertheless, rich with opportunities for practicing our Alignment to the Sacred within us, to our Souls, through evolution. The parent in the bookstore can view this incident from these varied perspectives. She could say that the child is to blame for her own suffering because she didn't respond to the request to leave. This is throwing the blame outward. Or she could, as she did in the example, recognize her mistake. Always a good start. But then she could ruminate about it and wonder how she has psychologically damaged the child and her relationship with that child. Or she could perceive it as a crash and an opportunity. A sort of golden cockroach. If the parent chooses the latter viewpoint, here is what could happen. First, she recognizes the mistake and lets go of the rising judgments, knowing that they will only get in the way of any Alignment that she is attempting. (Judgments don't come from the Soul). The parent at this point also lets go of the idea about getting to the game on time. The priorities are outlined by the clarity of mind that comes with letting go. Being late for the game is definitely less important than learning a lesson about flying. It's a no-brainer.

She holds the crying, panicked child and says, "I'm sorry. What I said about leaving you here was wrong. You're really scared that I would leave you, but I will never leave you. I shouldn't have said that. I was angry that you were ignoring me."

Still having residual feelings of fear, the child slowly calms down upon hearing these words. The parent admitting being wrong is powerful. They continue to hug for awhile and the mom thinks that they will stay in this store, hugging for as long as it takes for her daughter to feel level again. To her surprise, the child pulls away in a few minutes.

As they are walking out, the child says, "I guess we both had lessons to learn this time. You needed to learn not to tell me that you're leaving me and I needed to learn to pay attention."

At this point, they go on to talk about what they will both do the next time in a similar situation. Obviously, this is a child that is used to dealing with situations in this way. This daughter is used to practicing a focus on flying, as her observations indicate. The parent and the child have successfully used this crash as a growing experience. They are both flying better and their relationship is even closer. These are the results of perceiving crashes as golden cockroaches.

Viewing Pain as a Transient Signal Towards Evolution

Most of the time in our lives, we fly along fairly smoothly. To be sure, if we are focusing on flying, our attention on Aligning to the Sacred that is within us and around us will be relentless. We will fine-tune here and refocus there, but most often we won't be flying into dense confusing fog. Except for the times that we do. Occasionally, we will fly into the thick of some major transition, hurdle or theme. And it is like flying into some heavy fog. At first we might experience a sort of restlessness or discomfort. *What is this?* It is like that itch in the upper middle part of the back that won't go away and can't be scratched. Or it is the sense that something is missing from our lives. Thoughts keep popping in our minds about how the relationship with our partners is somehow lacking or the relationship with our children has somehow turned negative or how our job is not as satisfying as it used to be. The thoughts keep niggling us until we have to pay attention and become fully aware of just where that itch is. Then comes the realization of the fog; that is, that we're in one. Confusion might come up, as we look around us, unable to discern where the ground is anymore. And we get a clear picture of the density. We begin to truly know the largeness of the issues involved. Our relationship with our partner may be dying and the itch has turned into a full awareness of the fact that neither one of us is being emotionally nourished by the other, that we have become roommates. Or we begin to realize that every time we interact with our children, we are yelling or angry or unhappy. This is the point at which we may choose to become ostriches and love the sand surrounding our heads, because it is at the point of full realization of the situation that we also become fully aware of the pain.

I walk through the desert of our relationship
And scan the horizon for any living signs,
But the only green I can see is the cactus,
Which, by its very nature causes
Pain to the touch.

I walk through the desert of our relationshi
And am scorched to the base of my soul with its vast non-being
In the distance, I see an oasi
And run towards it with the grace of desperation,
*   But the closer I come, the farther off it seems until,*
*   With a screaming pain,*
*   I realize that it is only a mirage of my memory.*

I walk through the desert of our relationship
And stare at the sands of death beneath my feet
And wonder just how deep its infertility extends.
Hope and sadness drain out of me in sweat and tears
*   As I angrily plunge towards the ground,*
*   Clawing with all of my strength*
*   To find that idealistic, rich, depth of earth*
*   That can grow anything.*

Could it be possible that the sand is not so deep here?

Could I maybe plant a new beginning?

Emotional pain like this is hardly tolerable. Thus, it is hardly surprising that we would run from it with the gusto of all of our strength. And this is what we ordinarily do. We run as fast as we can. We avoid it. We repress it. We act as if it doesn't exist. Even the writer of this poem could not tolerate it long enough to finish without some infusion of hope towards the end. We are constantly seeking ways to avoid this pain. We may try to ignore it and hope that it will go away. The relationship is not really *that* bad. Or we may try to intellectualize it with some mental gymnastics so that we can temporarily feel better. *She stills cares about me; it's just that her work is so hard for her right now. Once the work is less stressful, she will come around.* There are a number of ways to avoid the pain and we, as humans, can be quite creative about this. But by avoiding, what we are really doing is procrastinating. The pain is there. Running from it will not make it go away, as the child deep inside us, desires so badly. In fact, the pain

118

will only increase in density from our denials and our failures to address the situations. Then, of course, it becomes long term, chronic. *Won't this fog ever dissipate? When will I be able to tell where the ground is?*

We are used to perceiving the pain as a sizzling emotional burn to run from. It hurts, by definition. But maybe in our harried bolt away from the pain, we are doing quite a bit of forgetting. If we are bolting away so quickly, then we are forgetting the transient quality of pain. It won't last forever. Nothing does. Certainly, there are circumstances where the pain is so intense that we become completely immersed in it. At these times, the pain seems to swallow us until we cannot foresee ever coming out of that thick density. But, eventually, sometimes with great effort, we do emerge from the fog. We can see the ground again. Eventually, the pain does dissipate.

We may also be forgetting, that, at least in some circumstances, pain may be serving a function. When we were little, our moms told us not to touch that hot stove. But it wasn't glowing red anymore. It didn't look hot. So we touched it and when we did, there was a clear sensation of pain. The pain served two purposes in this situation. Because of the pain, we didn't linger with that curious touch. We quickly removed our finger which prevented a severe burn, then we probably started crying. We also learned something: that stoves don't have to be red to be hot and dangerous. Pain was the beginning of our learning about the hot stove. Sometimes, the pain is providing a clear, very loud, not to be mistaken signal that a situation or theme needs to be addressed. If the relationship with the spouse is not going well, then a bit of pain will have the effect of sounding a gong that this aspect of our lives needs some attention. Bong.

"Pay attention over here," the pain screeches, "see this problem?"

In circumstances like this, choosing to ignore the pain is much like leaving that finger on the stove. The burn deepens. Ouch. Now it really hurts. Now the relationship is so stagnant and we have been hurt for so long that any remaining hope for reconnection wisps away with a soft wind. We have ignored the function of that pain for so long that we have a third degree burn or a festering, pus seeping hole in our psyches that would take monumental efforts to transcend.

But perhaps we could learn to view the pain as the signal that something in our lives warrants attention. We could learn to listen to that gong before it becomes the pus seeping, irreparable hole. In other words, we could *allow the function of pain to work.* When the initial prick of pain occurs, we don't dodge or run as usual, but instead turn our full power of attention towards it. *Now, why did that smart so much?* we wonder, as we turn around for the full view. With the full view, then, we can go ahead and address the situation before it withers into the dried, caked hardness of lifelessness. That relationship gets the attention that it needs to stay fresh and vibrant long before this happens, if we can manage to perceive the pain, particularly the early smaller jolts of pain as a signal to pay attention. We can remember the function of this type of pain.

And, if we can remember that pain is transient and that it can be a signal that points toward a troublesome area, then we can remember that this type of pain is likely to lead to growth and evolution. In other words, it will point us to an area where we are not Aligned with the Sacred, where our Souls are not running the show. Usually, on the other end of pain is some sort of change. Small or big transformations have occurred, perhaps in a grand sweeping way that is obvious to everyone. We got a divorce. Or perhaps in a grand sweeping way that is not so obvious. We stayed married and reconnected with our spouse. If we are focusing on flying and thus have an active hand in the transition that follows the pain, it will most likely mean more than simply change. It will mean coming closer to Alignment with our Souls.

Now, if we put these pieces of this perception together, what we get is: Viewing pain as a transient signal towards evolution. That is, the emotional pain that accompanies the daily circumstances of our lives is a temporary sensation that serves a purpose. It calls attention, sometimes in a prickly sort of way and sometimes with a blast. It signals us that there is work to be done. This type of pain, therefore, is just the beginning of our Alignment with our Souls. And this type of growth isn't something to run from. This type of growth is something to embrace. Does this mean, then, that we embrace this pain? Not hardly. But we can view the pain with the half smile of understanding. We can know on the front end of the transition, that the pain won't last, that it points our way, that it is just the prelude to evolution. We can anticipate the joy that comes on the heels of that growth. If, instead of getting all caught up in the intensity of that pain, in the density of that fog, we can look ahead with the wise eyes of experience to see the growth that is coming as a result of this pain, we may even begin to view the pain itself with a certain amount of joy. Because, eventually, the pain will simply translate into that anticipated joy of a closer Alignment to the Sacred within us. That is, viewing pain will come to actually mean the joy of evolution that is likely to follow. Sounds a bit odd, doesn't it? Pain becomes joy? Well, pain doesn't exactly *become* joy. But we can learn to view the pain in a way that takes into account the joy of our Alignment to our Souls. And in this way, pain and joy can hold hands without embarrassment.

What this perception does, is to take some of the sting out of the pain. If we can remember to view the pain as temporary, which it is, then just knowing that it won't last forever inoculates us somewhat from the intensity. And, if we can get to the point that we remember the eventual joy of our evolution, then the pain deflates even more rapidly. But this perception does something even more powerful. It returns our power to us. When we view the pain of transition as a signal that points toward the troublesome area, we are using the pain. We are acknowledging the function of that pain and using it to aid us in our journey. We no longer allow ourselves to be swallowed whole by its intensity or catapulted towards avoidance through fear. We are no longer running from it, but we are instead using it. The power is returned to us. And the sting, at least some of it, is taken out. How nice. This is what the perception does for us. So with a cunning nod and a half smile of understanding, we respectfully acknowledge the sensation of the pain and follow its transient signal toward evolution.

* * * *

These are the perspectives, the Basic Positions of Flying of Jonathan: Viewing Life's Events With Acceptance and Meaning, Viewing the Moments of Life as Precious, so that we may find nourishing peace, so that Soul will direct our lives, Viewing Pain as a Transient Signal Towards Evolution. All of these basic positions are extensions of the core value of focusing on flying. There is always a keen eye, whether blatant or more obscure, toward the Alignment of ourselves with the Sacred that is within us and around us.

Life appears to be a ride and our egos are not in charge. We can choose our perspectives to be those that will point us toward meaning and restoration. So, did you make that choice yet?

Reading and References:

Bedard, Jim. *Lotus in the Fire: The Healing Power of Zen.* Shambhala
Publications, 1999.

Hoff, Benjamin. *The Tao of Pooh.* E.P. Dutton, Inc., 1982.
   A book of perspectives and ways. Refreshing. Lovely. I read it
   every year or so, just as areminder. Highly recommended.

Hoff, Benjamin. *The Te of Piglet.* Penquin Books, 1993.

WINDS THAT CAN BLOW US OFF COURSE

*An Exploration of the Interfering Effects of
Thoughts and Emotions Run Wild*

Would you like to know why
    Your path is so difficult?
Would you like to know why
    Life seems so empty sometimes?
Would you like to know why
    You react so easily to life's situations?
Would you like to know why
    You miss the essence of life itself?
Would you let me show you some reasons?

Whirlwinds of Thought and Blasts of Emotion

Now we need to take a more intimate look at the winds that can blow up and knock us right off course. For, if our intention is to focus on flying, to focus on Aligning ourselves to the Sacred that is within us and around us, then we'll need to have an altogether intimate understanding of the culprits that can frustrate our efforts. We'll need to know about the little hindrances that can keep us from immersing ourselves in the Sacredness of the present and soaking up that nourishing color. We'll need to know, too, about the scoundrels that provoke a reactionary response or that hide the light of our Souls. You probably remember these guys. You have been introduced to them before. There are the themes, those furtive, old dictators that slide into the director's chair whenever one of those repeating situations prompts an appearance. And then there are the thoughts and emotions that will jauntily snatch that director's chair right out from under us, almost any chance they get. As for the themes—they won't get much discussion here. That's because they get their own chapter later, so dense and entirely sticky they can be. For now, we're going to be focusing on the whirlwinds of thoughts and blasts of emotions.

Thoughts and emotions. They are such an elementary part of our experience. We are never without them. And we wouldn't want to be. Our thoughts and emotions are central to our experiences and perceptions. They penetrate the molecules of our lives. Imagine just how *truly* black and white our experience would be if we deleted thoughts and emotions. It's difficult to go there, isn't it? But being without thoughts and emotions might seem similar to being a robot. Devoid of the capacity for spontaneous thoughts and emotions, that robot would be limited to the zeros and ones programmed in it. You, the robot, scan the room and take in the plant sitting next to the window. You take in the sun shining on it. The data are noted and you move on. Gone is the perception of gracious beauty. Gone are the associations that naturally come up when thoughts and emotions are present. There are no thoughts about how that plant reminds you of the one that your mother gave your father for their first wedding anniversary. There are no emotions of angst and romantic serenity that ordinarily come with such a thought. As a robot, you would just take in the data and move on. No, we'd rather not be the robots, thank you.

Yet it is the parade of thoughts that can distract our attention away from the Sacredness of the present, and prevent us from getting that nourishment and from recognizing the messages for our growth and evolution. It is the piercing scream of emotions that can overwhelm us and cause us to react before blinking. Yep. This is a problem. But the problem does not lie within the qualities and characteristics of thoughts or emotions. There's nothing inherently flawed about them. Thoughts are thoughts and emotions are emotions. They are fine as they are. The problem is that we sometimes give our thoughts and emotions *free rein*. Perhaps without knowing, we open the gate and these wild winds rush forward, completely ready to take over and dictate our behavior.

Whirlwinds of thought can spray into consciousness and dominate our attention to the point where we're not even sure of where we physically are. And blasts of emotions can so destructively blow us off course that nothing else seems to even exist in that snapshot of time except the emotion pulsing through our veins. When they are allowed free rein, thoughts and emotions are powerful crosswinds that can blow us completely off course and keep us from dancing in Sacred of the present or gathering the messages for our growth or choosing our actions. Our Souls can stay buried beneath these layers. We've got no chance at restoring the Soul to its central place, the director's chair, if we allow thoughts and emotions to overtake us. Because thoughts and emotions can be so powerful, we need to bring the wild winds into the full bright circle of the spotlight so that we know just how they can blow up so quickly and take over so completely. Those prancing whirlwinds come first.

The Whirlwinds of Thought
The Lure of the Past and the Tug of the Future

Let's face it. The present is sometimes boring. At least without the fresh eyes of swollen attention, it is. If there's not much happening at the moment that is new or exciting, some event that causes a quick inhalation, we typically think the present lacks the flair to warrant even a blink of attention. Sweeping the floor is not going to cause the heartbeat to speed up. Inserting the numbers for that monthly report doesn't exactly stimulate us. We've been there and done that. That this recently hatched cliché is so often used, points to the very perception that I'm talking about. The present seems boring. Most of the activities that we will do today, we have done already. In some cases, millions of times. Well, at least hundreds of times. Brushing the teeth. Taking a shower. Breathing. Driving to work. These are the mundane activities that fill our days and nights.

Sure, there is the occasional spark of some unfolding drama. We like the dramas. They're more interesting. Like when there is a disagreement between you and your boss over how to approach the next project. Or the romantic dinner with a new romantic prospect. Now that's more exciting. But there just doesn't seem to be enough of these interesting little dramas and we find ourselves once again immersed in the drab, everyday stuff. There just seems to be so much black and white, doesn't there?

"There's not enough color here," we whine.

So we go out looking for some. In some way or another, we attempt to spice up the seemingly dull present with some flair, some drama, some activity that seems fresh to us. We want to be captured by the present, so, in our creative ways, we attempt to inject some of the nourishing color that we perceive to be missing. Of course, how we go about attempting to make that injection of color will vary. Some of us seek out adventure in risky ways. We look for the thrill of living through activities that jolt the adrenaline. Bungy jumping, skydiving, hang-gliding, swimming the Atlantic, diving from cliffs. The list goes on. Some of us choose a less risky approach and simply increase the drama in our lives by ruffling the feathers of the people around us. We might decide to let it slip to the boss that our co-worker is planning a presentation to the owner, a presentation that might make the boss look bad. Oops, it just slipped out. Now let's see what happens. And, with a Grinchy smirk spreading over our faces, we sit back and watch the theater unfold.

Without a doubt, we humans are diverse and creative in our ways to inject that color. But there is even a more subtle, more common way to spice up the present. If the present seems dull, we can simply turn the dial to automatic and allow the mind to play. So many of the activities that we do each day, the showers, tooth-brushing, sweeping and all that, require the smallest fraction of our brains to do. Fundamentally, we don't have to think to breathe. (Thank goodness for this, or we wouldn't be able to do anything else!) We don't have to concentrate on that shower. The shampooing and soaping can be done automatically. And, since we've done this so many times before, the automatic mode becomes automatic. What this means, then, is that there is a large chunk of our minds that is free to wander.

And wander it does. There is the lure of the past that calls to us. Past experiences come up on the video screen of our minds to be reviewed. Some past event will come up and we'll be swept along in the mental video of it. A pleasant experience can be a lovely excursion away from a present that is perceived as humdrum. You step out of the blandness of the shower, into a memory of a summer hike through the woods. You can smell the earthy odor of soil, watch the sunlight dancing through the leaves, hear that sort of grunting, chirping noise that squirrels make, all the while rubbing the shampoo in the hair. Of course, the video of the mind is not always so serene as this. Sometimes, an anxious or negative memory haunts us and, despite our best efforts to push it off of that screen, it continues to come back up for review. We still rub the shampoo in the hair and our minds are still mostly in the past.

Or the future may tug our attention during the more mundane aspects of the day. A mental review of up-coming activities may emerge on that mind screen. Or some fantasy, real or contrived, slides onto it. The fantasy is about what could happen. We've all taken these interesting little mental trips. They can be fun, especially when we're not limited to actual events. After all, the future is unknown. The fantasy about the potential dinner conversation with that new romantic interest would be soothing. Not to mention a fantasy of what could happen after dinner. Not exactly soothing. Definitely entertaining. Of course, sometimes, these future fantasies are not so fun. You've got an important meeting tomorrow morning at work, so you're planning to swing by the cleaners this evening to pick up the dress you wanted to wear for that meeting. They were supposed to have mended it. Standing in the shower, you're picturing yourself going through this errand. You can see yourself standing in front of the counter at the cleaners and being told by a man that the dress could not be repaired. That's right. The dress that you were counting on. You can see your anxiety rising as you stand there in the fantasy cleaner. The anxiety causes the fantasy trip to the cleaners to fade, only now, the anxiety has stepped into the present, in that shower with you. Maybe you'd better go check on that dress this morning before work.

This shower has lasted far too long and we've never had cleaner hair, so we will get out now. Being the victim of all these mental excursions into the past and the future means that you probably *did* stay too long in the shower and you're now running later than you had planned. (Maybe you won't have time to stop by the cleaners, after all.) Okay, we really will leave the shower behind now. The point is that the mind easily takes us for these rides into the past and the future. We are seemingly entertained and we leave behind the dullness of what we may think of as a black and white present. This is one of the ways that the whirlwinds of thought can blow us off course and take us away from the Sacred moments that make up our lives. This is one of the ways that we miss whole chunks of life, and whole opportunities for Aligning ourselves with the Sacred that is within us and around us. The lure of the past and the tug of the future. My, how our minds like to play.

Mind Rolls

And here is another way: mind rolls.

Our minds are spectacular. (That we can consider our minds to be spectacular is spectacular.) All those neurons sitting up there, interconnected in ways that are more complicated than the Internet. No doubt this is why we can free associate so easily. Those neuro-chemicals jump the gaps of those synapses with a graceful ease. The idea of chocolate turns into cafe mocha which turns into Barnes & Noble, then to reading and bedtime chapter books to the kids, then to Captain Underpants. Really, now. From chocolate to Captain Underpants? The capacity for association is truly amazing. This ability to associate a myriad of ideas is probably responsible for at least some of our creative talents and problem solving feats. Both of these are rather lovely effects of the seemingly endless interconnections.

But this same ability to associate is responsible for distracting our attention away from the Sacredness of the present. When thoughts are allowed to associate freely without choice or interference, they can become the whirlwinds that obscure our living. This is when we miss our experience. The associations of the mind begin to roll with the speed of a jet and before we become aware again, before we can catch ourselves, the experience is over and we weren't present for it. And remember, there are no re-plays. Unless you're using the mind roll in some way, as in the creative process, they are as useless and silly as chocolate to Captain Underpants. Somewhat entertaining in a humorous sort of way, but not too useful. When you're in one of these mind rolls, it is as if the automatic pilot button is pressed and you dive into a sea of thoughts, wholly unaware of what is happening around you.

You are walking in the woods on an autumn day. The crispness of the air reminds you of the winter that will follow. As you push the flannel collar of your coat up further around your neck, you wonder how much it will snow this winter. *Last December it snowed only three inches and that was a week before Christmas. Was the snow still on the ground for Christmas? Think so. Just a few patches. Still it qualified as a white Christmas. Some people have already done their shopping by now. Haven't even started thinking about Halloween, which is only two weeks away. Wonder when to buy that candy. Maybe tomorrow. Tomorrow, after work – oh yeah, the appointment with the dentist. Maybe we can swing by the store. We need milk anyway. Wonder if there is enough milk for tonight?*

What happened to the walk in the woods? Stepping into the rolling mind of this person, we might not even know that we're in the woods at all. Indeed, we are *not* in the woods. The body is there and is taking in the stimulation through the senses. The body hears the rustle of the leaves, the crunch under the boots. The body sees the sunlight and the colors of fall. But without *attention*, we are not present and have missed the experience. Instead, the mind roll has lead to an existence within an illusory world of thoughts. When we are caught up in the whirlwind of thought like this, we are living in our minds. And while this type of existence can be somewhat entertaining, it is removed from the reality and the Sacredness of the present. If we are especially taken by the roll of association, we might even unwittingly perpetuate it by giving it attention. And, if our aim is not creative or bent in the direction of problem solving, if we simply perpetuate the whirlwind because we like it, then this is nothing more than unintentional mental masturbation. We would just be letting thoughts take over. They would have free rein.

Getting caught in the whirlwinds of thought means that we have missed the immediate present experience of one or several of those precious moments. And they don't get re-played. Of course, we have also missed any messages held within those moments. But added to this is a subjective sense of dissonance, as our minds and bodies are in two different places. Living, breathing Picassos, we become. Our feelings right afterwards will sometimes underscore the dissonance of these blank sections of our lives. We may end our walk in the woods feeling disconnected, distracted, and maybe even a bit stressed out about all the things we must do over the next day or two. And when we arrive back at our car or our doorstep only to realize that we just missed our walk, we glance backward with regret. We feel out of sync, unfulfilled. Blank. These feelings are the results of allowing ourselves to miss the Sacredness of the present and they are probably all too familiar.

But what about thinking and planning? In all fairness, we do, at some point need to think about whether we have enough milk in the refrigerator for dinner. There are times when we need to plan our shopping time or consider whether we are going to eat before or after that dentist appointment. The problem comes in when we tell ourselves that we are going for a walk and we end up planning our careers instead. Or ruminating about a disturbing conversation. Or speculating about the viciousness of the Portia spider that we read about in the National Geographic. Our intention is to take a relaxing walk and we end up going on an unintended trip to another land of mindplay. But we can deliberately decide to plan when we are going to pick up that milk and what we are going to have for dinner. And while we are planning, planning is what we are doing. That is, our attention is deliberately focused on this.

Split Attention

Here is another Picasso in action. Split attention. One type of split attention happens when we're attempting to think about or do two things at the same time. Your focus bounces between one subject and another as you try to attend to both. We are enamored with our capacity to juggle in this way. We flamboyantly attempt to juggle two, three or four subjects at one time, all the while feeling quite pleased with ourselves that we were able to accomplish so much in so little time. You can talk on the phone to a client overseas and write a note to your secretary at the same time. No problem. You can make lunches for your children and help them with their homework at the same time. It's not that difficult. And you can even make those lunches, help with the homework and have a relatively decent, though somewhat sporadic, conversation with your spouse. This is doable.

Yes, juggling is doable, but is it satisfying? Is it nourishing to the Soul? There is no real reason to answer these questions, is there? If you think back to a time, probably in the past day or so, when you were juggling two or three subjects and consider how you felt while you were bouncing around between those subjects and how you felt afterwards, the answer is evident. You start the water for the children's bath. They run in when you call them, already taking off their clothes. You gather the clothes to put in the washer, but as you're walking by the trashcan in the kitchen, you notice that it is full, so you put the clothes on the counter for the moment to empty it. While you're emptying the trashcan, one of the kids calls to you, so you scurry to the tub where one sorely complains that the other one took her toy. You guide them through settling the disagreement, then go ahead and wash their hair, since you're already there. Now, what were you doing before? Oh yes, the clothes. You leave the kids in the tub and go around the house collecting the dirty clothes to put in the wash. You might as well get most of them to wash. As you're bending down to get the underwear that someone threw in the corner, you notice that the giggling from the bathroom has gotten a bit gleeful, so your antennas go up. They've probably started throwing water on the walls to see the pattern or something. So, clothes still in your arms, oops, you dropped a sock, you rush back into the bathroom to see what the damage is.

Are you feeling tired yet? The above scenario is linked to home and children, but we could easily translate it to an office environment. Juggling is a common malady of the office. No matter where it takes place, though, splitting attention between two or more subjects is not particularly satisfying. While we're going through it, we feel like a pinball, pushed in this direction, then pulled in that direction. After it is all over, most of us walk away feeling a bit disjointed and irritable, or at least tired, sometimes even exhausted. We have been caught up in the juggling game, seduced by the thought of accomplishment.

Admittedly, accomplishment is indeed seductive. We do feel satisfied at having gotten so much done. And there is that slightly swollen pride at having actually been able to pull it off. *That was pretty impressive*, we think. But, at least in some cases, logic tells us that no more has actually been accomplished. Not really. Making lunches takes a certain amount of time. Helping with homework takes a certain amount of time. If we decide to do these activities by juggling and bouncing back and forth between them, we haven't actually decreased the amount of time they take. It still takes ten minutes to make the lunches. It still takes twenty to do the homework. The half-hour is the same whether we decide to do one thing at a time or juggling our bodies and our minds in trying to do two. And we already know which method is more satisfying and more nourishing.

Of course, occasionally, we actually do accomplish more with the split attention, juggling method. The parent in the bath/clothes scenario was probably able to take advantage of some lag time. That is, the children would probably want to sit in the bath and play for a few minutes. If the parent could just squeeze in some clothes gathering while they were contentedly playing, then there would be less to do later. True. But, strictly from a feeling point of view, was it worth it? The feelings that we're having during and after the Tasmanian devil, juggling behavior should weigh heavily into the equation of whether it was worth it or not. Certainly, you get to decide.

There is a second type of split attention that blows up. This one is more subtle, more passive, almost unnoticeable, unless we're paying attention. This is when your mind is hovering and buzzing around one subject while the present is demanding your attention. You don't realize that you're not fully present. You're not really aware that your mind is distracted. You're just sort of halfway there. Your child has just come home from school and wants to tell you about the stamp that his friend gave him. He is animated and wants to share his excitement with you. You look at him while he is talking, but your mind is thinking about dinner.

"It's such a cool stamp, Dad. See, there's a smiley face and it lights up on top."

You're thinking about how tired you feel. *Don't feel like cooking. Maybe we could just have soup?*

"...gave it to me, even though it was her favorite!"

Then you realize that you missed the name of the friend who gave the stamp to your son. In fact, he just got up and left. As you hear him calling to his sister to tell her about the stamp, you wonder if he picked up your half attention. Probably. And you find yourself regretting your lack of presence. And dinner is still not planned.

This sort of distracted split attention is insidious. It sneaks up on you. Neither subject area gains the benefit of your energy and attention. In this case, the son probably feels unheard and dinner is still in the same state as before. Frustration mounts as a result because nothing has been accomplished. And the dad in this situation likely feels dissatisfied with the interaction and maybe even a bit guilty. Nothing positive comes from this. Once again, we're caught in some hazy wave of thoughts that serve to distract us from being fully present in the Sacredness of the present. Not exactly nourishing or peaceful.

The Blasts of Emotions

Those whirlwinds of thought can blow up in a sneaky sort of way, can't they? Seamlessly, we go from interacting in a conversation with someone to speculating about what we'll have for dinner. We weren't aware that we were no longer paying attention to the person. At least, not until they ask us a question—for the second time. We lay down to sleep in anticipation of a deep, satisfying rest. Of course, we are completely surprised, when, one hour later, we're still awake, our minds buzzing down some free association stream. Irritated that we've been gypped out of that full night's rest, stunned by the subjects that our mind seems to find fascinating, we roll over and sigh miserably. But when did that mind roll start? We're not sure. The whirlwinds of thought are like that. Sly ones, they are. They start off with a small, seemingly innocuous puff, then build up to gale force without our even noticing. They can blow us off course and slide right into that director's chair in a gradual, building way.

But emotions are not always so sneaky. Emotions are volatile. Yet they, too, can start with a tiny puff. The puff can then swell into a tumbling blast or it can simper back to that initial puff that merges back in with the air. You let your eyes scan the racks of socks at the local Target store. It may be silly, but you have a certain kind of socks that you like and you won't buy anything else. Therefore, focused scanning is required to find these particular socks. In fact, you are completely absorbed in the search, so much so that you fail to see your friend right away. You only notice that there is a person out of the corner of your eye. You have no clue that he is your friend. But that much proximity has violated the social codes and so, just for a second, you are irritated that someone could be so bold as to get that physically close. The irritation mounts. Then you look up and see your friend beaming at you, obviously enjoying the play of waiting for you to notice him. Instantly, the irritation is gone. That was the puff that merged back into the air. Now the irritation is replaced with a swelling of joy, for this is a friend that you hold close to your heart, one of those few extraordinary people that come into your life. Joy and love swell instantly and you warmly embrace this life long companion. You are filled with these feelings. This is the blast of emotion. In this case, it is a positive one. We like the positive ones, don't we?

Positive or negative, emotions can be not only volatile, but quite powerful and intense. A blast of emotion can smack against us so hard that we can be overwhelmed and even crash before we are truly aware of what happened. Whoa, what was that? Within a few seconds we can become livid with rage, raw with sadness, seething with lust or manic with elation. The right stimulus and our count to ten can find us swimming in an emotion that, ten seconds ago, seemed as far away as infinity.

You bounce into your wife's office at quitting time, excited by the surprise picnic dinner you have planned. As you fling open the door in greeting, you see her sitting behind her desk as you expected. Her neck is tilted and her eyes are closed because her co-worker is bending over her from behind, nuzzling her neck. Of course, he pops up rather quickly when that door hits the wall. But not quickly enough. It only takes a few seconds for the emotions to swell. Anger, a sense of betrayal. The list expands as the intensity builds and pretty soon, you're slamming the door closed, a lot harder than you opened it. Expressions like "seeing red," and "being beside yourself," were coined for these occasions. And the intensity is not just reserved for the negative emotions. Realizing you just won three million in the lottery would probably leave you feeling "beside yourself" with something like rapture rather quickly. Positive or negative, the blasts of emotions can be so powerful and smack so hard that we feel astonished and disarmed. We *have been* disarmed, robbed of our choice about acting from that deepest part of ourselves, the Soul.

We found out about this intensity of emotions quite early in our lives. It must have felt even scarier then, to feel so intensely when we're so little and unable to understand these blasts. We probably don't remember our personal introduction to the blasts of emotion, but we can certainly observe them in our own and in other people's children. The toy is snatched and the injustice soaks through in a few seconds. When the fury peaks at the end of that crescendo, it splashes forth with a slap. Of course, the child who did the slapping is pulled away, but the fury continues in the form of a fist swinging, foot kicking, crying tantrum. Wow. That must feel bad.

The blasts can be so intense and so sudden that we are entirely overwhelmed. At this point, we "become" the emotion. It seems to swell and overtake our consciousness. Being consumed like this, whether the blast is positive or negative means that the wind has indeed blown us off course. For, no longer are we aware of thoughts when we're soaked through with emotion, no longer are we aware of our surroundings. Our awareness is limited to the emotion and perhaps the stimulus that caused it. That is all. The bull has entered

136

the china shop and plows through, oblivious to the fine crystal and that delicate vase it just shattered. Becoming an emotion has the effect of blinding us to the rest of our experience. It makes absolutely no difference whether the emotion is positive or negative. We are blinded either way. The same bull can be blind with rage or rapture, but he is still blind.

But what's even scarier is that we're no longer running the show. The emotion has taken over our consciousness, all right. And our behavior. Temporary insanity is a part of the law. It certainly feels like insanity, at least for the few seconds or minutes that we are overcome with that blast. We don't always know what we're doing. It seems that someone else is at the wheel.

Skin Stealer

This evening I unzipped my skin
And carefully unscrewed my head,
Exactly as I always do
When I prepare myself for bed.
And while I slept a coo-coo came
As naked as could be
And put on the skin
And screwed on the head
That once belonged to me.
Now wearing my feet
He runs through the street
In a most disgraceful way,
Doin' things and sayin' things
I'd never do or say,
Ticklin' the children
And kickin' the men
And dancin' the ladies away.
So if he makes your bright eyes cry
Or makes your poor head spin,
That scoundrel you see
Is not really me—
He's the coo-coo
Who's wearing my skin.

—Shel Silverstein

Nope. It's not us doing all that absurd behavior. That behavior is most certainly not coming from the Soul. It's the blast of emotion. Some coo-coo who's wearin' our skin. Here is where at least some of our reactionary way of being begins. That reactionary swatting sometimes starts with the swelling of an emotion.

Emotions are volatile, intense and can blast us off course within seconds, sending us into reams of behavior that we never even thought we were capable of. It's that coo-coo again. He's doing it. We don't like that coo-coo. And we don't particularly care for the unpredictable, volatile nature of emotions. Perhaps this is why we're afraid of those blasts, particularly the negative ones. We're never entirely certain what will trip them off, when they'll be coming, how intense they will be or how we will react. It's unnerving. Anxiety mounts as we attempt to peak toward the future in anticipation of these blasts.

"Is it coming now?"

The anxiety transforms quickly into fear when we actually do see one of these wild emotional winds coming. The fear emerges because we feel helpless against the power of the blasts.

How We Ordinarily Deal With These Blasts of Emotions

We needed to do something to tame the wildness of these emotional blasts. We couldn't just go around becoming our emotions and behaving like that coo-coo, now could we? So we learned various methods for the taming, early on in our lives. For the negative blasts, we learned more "appropriate" ways of expressing the powerful knots that rushed so quickly upon us. Of course, what was seen as "appropriate" was set by the family and the environment. Let's take a more common, garden variety of a negative emotion as an example. We all have been intimate partners with this one — anger. The little red guy. In some families, you could let out some of the anger by hitting, at least in some circumstances. Like you could hit when you were hit. Except, of course, if you had been hit by your parents. Then you couldn't hit back. Or maybe hitting was never okay, but yelling was "appropriate," so you gripped your fists tightly at your sides and screamed until your throat hurt. Or maybe you were only allowed to say "in a normal voice" what was bothering you, so through gritted teeth, you ground out your complaint. Or maybe you had to stifle the anger back, so you choked the neck of your little red monster and tried to stuff him back into his box. It took a lot of energy, though, to keep him there, what with all that squirming to get out. We all had our unique "appropriate" methods, but they all seem to leave us feeling a bit dissatisfied. We couldn't do what we really wanted to do. So we had to swallow whatever portion of anger that remained, whatever piece was left unexpressed. We had to keep that little red guy in his box with the lid tightly closed.

The story was much the same with the other negative emotions. Hatred, greed, envy, jealousy. For every one of these negative emotions, we were taught an "appropriate" way of expression or non-expression. Indeed, some of these we weren't even supposed to feel at all. Hatred, for example, was probably one of these for most of us. We're not supposed to feel hatred. What this meant is that we couldn't even allow a smidgen to come out of our box, not even a little screech. The box would bounce and tumble with that thing seething to be felt. And we would perch ourselves squarely on the lid in order to keep it on. Arms crossed, heads shaking, vehemently denying even the slightest hint of that emotion. Meanwhile, though, our bodies are rumbling with the movement of the box. And even when the "appropriate" way does allow us some expression, there always seems to be a bit of residual emotion to stuff back in. Not only are we left feeling dissatisfied, we are left with the battle of the box.

We seem to constantly be battling against our emotions, against ourselves. Our civilized self brandishes its rationality and the emotional self picks up the nearest blunt object that might serve as a brawl starter. And all of this fighting and stuffing and denying takes continual surges of energy. We sit there, on top of that nasty hatred box, smile plastered on through gritted teeth, hair stringy and disheveled. Bouncing from the movement of that emotion jostling for expression, our eyes dart around nervously at the other boxes that are beginning to rumble. Too much energy it takes just to keep this lid on and the anger box is twitching violently. Of course, after a while, we can't do it anymore and some lid pops off. Then the emotion overtakes us. We become it. Then we crash.

With the negative emotions, then, we attempt to keep a close watch on those boxes. We want to allow just enough emotional steam to escape through our "appropriate" methods. This way, we don't have to let the lid come off completely. And we can be safe from the terrorizing effects of an unleashed emotion. Well, we can be relatively sure. Well, some of the time. Hum... This is how we ordinary deal with the wild winds of negative emotion. We'll look at some alternative ways of taming them in the next chapter, but for now, let's consider how we ordinarily deal with the blasts of positive emotions.

Do we need to even address this? Positive is good, right? It feels good to be consumed by elation, joy, happiness, no? Certainly, there's no denying the pleasure of positive emotions. Most of us would swell with a euphoric elation at winning a lottery. The giddiness would gradually work its way into a sort of manic rapture. We would likely be completely overcome with this swelling. Nice, right? Well, we've already talked about how being overwhelmed with emotion can blind us to other aspects of experience. You remember the bull in the china shop. Blinded by being overwhelmed. It didn't matter what the nature of the emotion was, positive or negative. You've just found out about that money from the lottery, when your son arrives home from his last baseball game of the season. He is sad because his team lost the championships. But you're overcome with rapture and barely even process the words as he tells you about that loss. In fact, you're impatient because he seems so slow.

"Wait a second, honey. Where's Daddy? I've got to tell him..." Your voice trails off behind you as you swish past your son toward the door. Your son losing the championships is just as important to him as your winning the lottery is to you. Of course, if you're blinded with rapture, you're not likely to catch any of this.

How we ordinarily deal with positive blasts of emotions is that we embrace them. We give them a hearty hug. Enjoying the swelling of a positive emotion is truly a lovely experience, one that we will absolutely want to be paying attention to. The trouble comes in when we are not content to ride the swelling and eventual ebbing of a positive emotion. The trouble comes when we attempt to extend its life. We start with a hearty hug and when the time comes for the

140

natural loosening of the grip and the dropping of the arms, we do exactly the opposite: we tighten our hold and cling all that much harder. After we've experienced the sort of giddiness and rapture that comes with an experience like winning the lottery, we oftentimes cling to it, try to expand its life. We want to make the feeling last. In this case, we might review over and over again that enticing moment when we learned of our winnings. We could at least recapture an aftertaste this way. We cling for as long as we possibly can, desperately trying to expand the feeling. The struggle here is to keep the positive emotion out of its box. We are still battling to keep the lid on, but this time, it is to prevent reentry.

"Oh no," we say, "you're staying out here with me."

We're sitting on the lid of the box again, only this time, the box is silent because it is empty. The positive emotion is out and we don't want to let it back in storage. This time we perch on the silent box and watch for any furtive attempts for that positive emotion to slip back in. Like trying to keep the lid on the negative emotional box, attempting to expand the positive emotion by blocking its reentry, requires energy. Eventually, of course, the elation or the happiness or the rapture will slip back in, stealthily, like a shadow. And then we're disappointed.

"How did you get back in there?" we exclaim in surprise. We thought we had all of the corners covered, but somehow, that positive feeling just faded back in.

And when we're not clinging to a positive emotion, we're trying to create the circumstances that will bring it about. We do whatever it takes to entice our happiness right out of its box. Hum, let's see…perhaps the right car or the right wife or the right beliefs or the right career will induce that elusive happiness out. As we manage our lives to fit into the "right" circumstances, we peek back over the shoulder to see whether happiness might have quietly slipped out. Of course, if it does ease out of its box, we slam the lid shut and resume our perch to extend its life, starting the whole process again. With positive emotions, we're just not content to enjoy them while they're out and allow them to withdraw at the natural time. We want to pull at them, seduce them, tug them out of their boxes if necessary. And all of this pulling and tugging requires much energy. Energy that is wasted, because, somehow, the emotion gets back in anyway.

Try as we might, we just can't seem to manage those emotional boxes as well as we'd like. The positive emotions seem to stubbornly want to return to their box. And the negative ones seep out constantly. In fact, despite our best efforts at preventing it, some of those negative lids pop right off. This is when the blasts of emotion hits us with such intensity and suddenness that we are caught off guard, become overwhelmed and turn into that emotion. And with that coo-coo bull in charge, we're blinded to the rest of our experience, not to mention that our behavior might be less than civilized. The brawl starter got the helm when that lid blew off. We could probably have predicted the upcoming collision, that is, if we had been aware enough of what was happening. But we weren't, so with a thunderous roar, we crash. The emotional blast has blown us off course. And with this blast we are far away from Aligning ourselves to anything Sacred within us *or* around us.

Fear

Here's an emotion that gets its own section. Fear. But I'm not talking about the kind of prickly, goosebumpy rush that would drive over your skin if you heard the roar of a grizzly bear behind you. No. That kind of fear belongs in the section with the rest of the emotions. It sets among the boxes like any other intense emotion. The types of fears we mean here are the Fears with a big "F," (although you might think that grizzly bear warrants a big "F" too.) These Fears get that big "F" because of their power: they are capable of completely halting any movement toward Aligning ourselves with the Sacred within us, toward our evolution. They are actually capable of moving us toward stagnation. And the stillness of stagnation breeds the putrid perceptions of black and white and meaninglessness. Not a particularly warm and welcoming place. We'd rather not go there. So we need to be aware of the Fears that can propel us in that direction.

Fear often begins, oddly enough, with the first signs of growth and evolution. You wouldn't think so, would you? You would expect the first signs of growth to be accompanied with relief or joy, or some other positive emotion. But, Fear will often make a small polite appearance at the beginning. Take one step in the direction of learning to live in a better way and a Fear is likely to jump up and remind us of something, something about the direction that we're heading that we're not likely to enjoy. Recently, you've been thinking about your relationship with your wife. Something's wrong. You're not sure what it is, exactly, but the relationship feels cold and stale. You've talked several times with her and it doesn't seem to help. You're thinking of taking the next step and asking for outside help. Marriage counseling.

"Um, excuse me," the Fear of pain pipes up, "I just wanted to point out that if you go in that direction, you're gonna experience pain. And pain feels bad. You're gonna be churning up an awful lot of crap by doing that counseling thing. It's gonna hurt."

At this juncture, the Fear of pain might throw in a memory of some past pain to remind you just how bad pain does feel. Like you need reminding.

Then the Fear of change sings a chorus with the Fear of the unknown.

"You keep going like that and you will have to make some *changes*. Why would you want to do that? Why go stirring things up? You like things as they are. It's easier to just let it go, really. Do you really want to go through with this? You don't have any clue about where you'll end up if you keep going. You could end up separated or worse. You don't know how it's going to be. It could be worse than what you have now. You just don't know."

With the prodding of these voices, of course, the fueling of these Fears begins. Part of us, somewhere, thinks that maybe, just maybe, they have a point. Maybe we could just accept the status quo of the relationship. It's not that bad. We've been living like this for years. We've gotten used to it. Yes, it's unhealthy, but at least we know how and where we fit in. The fuel continues and the influence and power of the Fears increase. And we begin to hesitate in our movement towards growth. A pause. A pause that turns into a longer pause, longer and longer until we find that months have passed and we still haven't moved. The Fears have fueled an avoidance or denial. Only now the situation is worse. Because now, it takes massive amounts of energy to continue to deny or avoid the problems in the relationship that we are already aware of and that we are reminded of, by the intimate details of daily living. And the Fears continue to build. For now, our avoiding behaviors fuel the Fears even more. By avoiding or denying we are even more convinced that the Fears are legitimate. After all, we're expending massive energy to avoid the pain or the changes or the unknown. So those pains and changes and unknowns grow in our minds. *It's got to be bad if I'm running so hard,* we think. Then, of course, the Fears grow even more and we redouble our avoiding or denying efforts. The cycle of Fear is insidious and self-feeding. What started out as a few sparks of fear turns into a roaring bonfire of Fear.

If the treachery goes too far, we can actually start to Fear our own Fear. This is when things get truly strange. Now the Fear has become so powerful that the experience of *it* is painful. Fear is not a pleasant emotion. The early, candid, polite appearance has now turned ugly with intensity and spite. With this new development, we start to fear our next experience of Fear. Here is where things get a bit mushy, as the cycle implodes on itself. For now, we are facing a pain that is somewhat useless and is far removed from the original problem, the problem that, ironically, we were avoiding tackling because of the Fear. The Fears have us totally immobilized at this stage. And if we stay immobilized, then we are well within sight of stagnation. The Fears will gladly make an introduction to stagnation.

"Well, well, well, so wise of you to finally come to your senses about this whole relationship thing. Stay right where you are. That's right. By the way, let me introduce you to a friend of mine..."

Fears with the big "F's," quite powerful they can be in blowing us off course and preventing any movement toward Aligning ourselves with the Sacred within us and around us, toward nourishment and evolution.

The Swirling Interactions of Those Whirlwinds and Blasts and the Effects That They Have in Our Lives

Thus far, in talking about the whirlwinds of thoughts and blasts of emotions, I have mostly attempted to separate them in hope of being clearer that way. But they are rarely, if ever, truly separated in our experience. Those mind rolls are never purely just thoughts. There are almost always a few emotions sprinkled in. The same holds true for our thoughts about the past and future as well as the juggling and distraction modes of split attention. Emotions are right there along with the thoughts and visa-versa. Thoughts reflect emotions and emotions reflect thoughts. One mirrors the other. With any contemplation at all, this becomes quite obvious.

You're at work, attempting to keep up with the rapid pace of the data coming up on your computer screen. The swirling interaction of thought and emotion might go something like: *Wow, that one is selling fast. Wonder if I can get it…* Tension, slight anxiety. *There! Got it before it went too high.* Relief. You haven't had a free moment to get your habitual cup of tea. *This stuff is just not letting up at all this morning.* Feeling tired and irritated. *Can't even get my tea.* An acquaintance, someone you only occasionally speak to, shows up at your desk with your tea. You thank him and as he walks away, you think, *Wow, that was so considerate. Gosh, I hardly even know him and he went out of his way to get me the tea.* A touched, tender feeling comes up. *He must have been watching me get my tea in the mornings since he knew what kind I liked.* Feeling special. *But that means he's been watching me.* Curiosity. *Maybe he's being more than just nice. Maybe he's interested in going out.* At this point a quick fantasy comes up of the two of you walking side by side. You're trying it on to see how it fits. You're not gone too long on this trip though, because the blinking screen in front of you reminds you of where you are. *Oops, look at that. I missed one.* Disappointment, followed by a sense of resolution. *I'll think about him later. Besides, the boss will be by soon to get this report.* Irritation, slight anxiety.

To be sure, our experience is not as staccato as this scenario. It is usually smooth and seamless. Real life is more legato. In fact, sometimes, we have trouble finding when the thought begins and ends and the emotion begins and ends. There just doesn't seem to be the jerky lines between the mirror images of the two as there are here. But the example does help to point out that thoughts and emotions reflect each other.

This is not really news, though, is it? Of course thoughts and emotions reflect each other. Just the same, the point needs highlighting because it is this reflecting quality of thoughts and emotions, this sort of combined wind power that can blow us off course, causing us to be reactionary, causing us to act from a place other than Soul. This is when the reflections turn into fuel that perpetuates wherever the wind might be blowing. And when they fuel each other without interference from us, when they are given free rein, then these reverberating thoughts and emotions can roll into some enormous misinterpretations.

Misinterpretations

The snowball effect. We know about this, where you start with some small emotion, which is then fueled by a thought, then another emotion, another thought until, presto, instant snowball. What this means is that where we started is likely far away from where we end up. The woman who received the cup of tea from an acquaintance at work started off by thinking about how considerate the guy had been to do this. These thoughts and accompanying emotions then eventually lead to a fantasy where she contemplates how well they would fit together as a couple. She is interrupted at this point. But what if she hadn't been? The reverberations could have continued. She could have fantasized about a date in great detail, the mental images, nicely interwoven with swells of romance and lust. She could have visualized how the future weeks unfolded into a loving, warm relationship. Then, with all this seemingly solid fantasy behind her, she could have contemplated a potential plan for communicating her romantic interest and finally asking him out. She starts with some positive thoughts about a person because she received a cup of tea and within fifteen minutes, she expands it into a relationship with the guy. Wow. What a snowball.

This is how the reverberations of thoughts and emotions can blow us off course. There is no way we're responding from the Soul at this point. For, the thoughts and emotions have fueled each other until the ending point hardly even resembles the beginning. You misinterpreted, misunderstood, or just missed it altogether. It makes you think of that game that we all played sometime during the elementary years, where you whisper a sentence to the person next to you who whispers it, in turn, to their neighbor and so on. At the end of the line, you all laugh at the sentence that is announced because it is nothing like what you said. Somehow it changed.

The snowball changed too. It got bigger. Now it has turned into a major misinterpretation. The result can be that we're not only blown off course, but blown away. It can be embarrassing. The woman whose thoughts and emotions started with tea and gradually echoed into a relationship, is going to act differently around that acquaintance now. She's going to communicate romantic interest in every way. Through her body language, through her frequent presence at the coffee/tea table, through her solicitous words. And these communications will work fine if the guy happens to be receptive. But what if he's not? What if that tea delivery was nothing more than just a kind gesture? Well, then that woman is likely to be standing at the bottom of the hill when she realizes the snowball she has created. And she's likely to be flattened by that rolling boulder. Once the realization hits, she'll wither rather quickly. Nothing for her to do now, but shrink down and slink away in embarrassment, try to save face as best she can and disappear. Don't you hate it when this happens? Misinterpretations and the myriad of nasty effects that follow them are often the result of the reverberating, self-fueling process of thoughts and emotions. They fuel each other until some swollen illusion stands boldly in the place of reality and we believe it, only to suffer the effects of being flattened by disillusionment.

As if misinterpretations weren't enough, this self-fueling can lead us to other nasty places. For instance, thoughts can fuel an emotion until we are overwhelmed with it. And we already know where this leads. You're on the highway and someone cuts in front of you. It's a sudden, swerving sort of cut that makes you put on your brakes. There it is, a spit of anger. Then the rush of thoughts come. *Look at that fool! What a stupid thing to do! I would have hit him if I hadn't slowed down. Oh, jeez, look at this. He's doing it again. Someone's gonna hit him. He's so stupid. They shouldn't just let everybody have a driver's license.* On and on and on. The spit of anger gets fueled by the thoughts and now we've got waves of anger. The driver here is no longer concentrating on driving, either, so focused she is on the injustice of being cut off and on watching the other car. Consumed by the anger, she is missing other aspects of her experience, in this case, at great risk. Being consumed by an emotion can cause crashes, literally and emotionally.

Echoes

Misinterpretations, being overwhelmed with emotion and crashes are some of the results of allowing thoughts and emotions to fuel each other without interference. But there is another sort of debilitating consequence that happens when this type of free rein swirling occurs. The residual effects of thoughts and emotions from one situation can infiltrate the next situation. It is as if the echoes of the thoughts and emotions of one situation linger and silently vibrate into the next set of circumstances. They echo in the distance, affecting the flavor and outcome of the current situation.

Remember the husband who walked in on his wife being nuzzled on the neck by a co-worker? Well, let's say that before he left to surprise her at the office, he noticed that the trash needed emptying. Usually his wife does this, but she must have forgotten that morning. He's on his way out of the door, picnic basket in hand when he notices this, so he experiences a mild twinge of irritation. The twinge is small and passes. He simply empties the trash and gets in his car to leave. When he arrives at the office and sees his wife, he is not likely to still be feeling the irritation from that trash. The situations are separate. There is not much residual echoing from one situation to the next. But what if he notices this trash after he *comes back* from his wife's office? He's just seen his wife being kissed on the neck by another man. He has been seething with thoughts and emotions all the way home and then he walks in and notices a full trash bin. Whoa. Watch out. There is likely to be trash propelled throughout the house. The entire place will reek by the time she gets home. Was the trash worth this kind of explosion? Of course not. He's just still reeling from the constant review of that office scene. All that emotion, all the echoes carry over from the office to home.

This is an example of a negative echo. There are certainly those positive echoes as well, like when the woman received the cup of tea from her co-worker. Perhaps, instead of her snowballing it into a misinterpretation, she stops at the "how considerate" phase. She might then hold this positive feeling until the next interaction, say, when her boss asks her for the report. The usual haughty flinging of the report disappears and is replaced with her smiling gently and simply handing him the report with full eye contact. Gosh, what a difference and all because she was still feeling the effects of that considerate guy. The echoing effect from one situation to another can be positive or negative.

So now, what we have when we step back and contemplate the circumstances of our lives is that thoughts and emotions are continually swirling and interacting with each other. Sure, sometimes thoughts seem to dominate consciousness, as in a mind roll. But emotions are always there, contributing their little reflections. And sometimes, it is the emotion that seems to be at the helm, yet we can be certain that there are thoughts bouncing around somewhere too. We have seen how they can snowball into mammoth sized misinterpretations when allowed to swell unchecked. And how they echo from one situation into another. The swirling never ceases.

No. The swirling never stops. The whirlwinds of thought and blasts of emotions and the swirling interactions of these two, just keep right on blowing. The winds blow into gusts that we weather and gales that we don't. (At least, not without crashing.) And we're blown along, reacting in our reactionary way, as best we can. The gust of a mind roll sneaks up on us and whoosh! We're gone. That was kind of an interesting trip, but, um, what was it about exactly? And within seconds of that mind roll, we are prodded into splitting our attention between two or three or more demanding circumstances of thought. One situation prods us and we whip our vision and attention in that direction, ignoring the other area, until…poke, we whip around in the other direction. Back and forth, until our necks and minds are sore. Aimlessly we can drift in and out of past memories and future fantasies. We are sucked into these mind trips during the drone of the humdrum. And our emotions. Those blasts. The lid pops on one of those negative boxes and before the next thought turns the corner, anger is pulsing in our veins, spewing out through spit and venomous words. Whew. That was powerful. The reflections of thoughts and emotions. The self-fueling into misinterpretations. The lingering effects of this swirling as they echo into the next situation. The winds continue to blow and we continue to be blown off course.

A friend of yours, George, sees you in the grocery store and stops to tell you that the speech you gave last week was magnificent, that he felt deeply moved by your words. The interaction concludes and you feel pride and a quiet sense of joy swelling. As you move through the isles of the grocery, half-scanning for your needed items, you review the conversation you just had over and over on that internal screen. *Wow. I really made a difference. At least with George. Maybe what I say is pretty wise. I guess I do know a few things.* The black olives that you needed for the pasta salad that you planned come into the scanning view. *Yes. Black olives and what else? Oh, yeah, Italian bread. Right. That goes well with salad. Maybe some roasted garlic to smear on the bread. That would be good. Just like that restaurant over on Sixth Street. What was the name of that place?* You wander toward the produce section where the garlic is, forgetting for the moment about the bread. Don't worry. You'll remember the bread in a minute. Probably after you get the garlic.

You hover over the garlic, trying to pick out one that is suitable, when another friend comes up to you, (you tend to see many friends in the grocery, don't you?) It's Sidney. He wants to tell you about a traumatic situation in his life. You listen and confidently decide to say some risky, but potentially changing words. After all, George was deeply moved by your words and you're a pretty wise person. With these affirming thoughts, you go for it. Sidney listens with the attention of desperation to your inspiring words. His eyes still reflect the sadness that he brought with him to the beginning of the conversation, but he has a half-smile as he walks away. And as you look down at the garlic, you feel even more confident warmth surging through you. Now you're just looking for the next opportunity to scatter some compassion and inspiration. You're pumped. You think that maybe you could even extend your talents and begin to fantasize about exactly how you would go about doing that.

The fantasy continues until a woman utters a polite, "Excuse me." It seems she wants to get some garlic, too.

Oh, that's right, garlic.

I like this example. It's just so full, isn't it? There are all sorts of swirling happening. Pricked by George's verbal affirmation, our guy experiences the swelling of some lovely emotions: pride and joy.

150

Then the lure of the past snags him as he continuously reviews this conversation. Of course, he does this to expand the life of these pleasant emotions. He's trying to keep that lid closed so that the emotions stay out with him. And his thoughts about himself fuel the pleasantness. In doing this, though, his attention becomes split between his shopping and his reviews as he continues to scan the isles for the items. And, if he's reviewing this conversation over and over, then he has successfully spiced up the humdrum of shopping with a pleasant mental review. It's not hang-gliding, but it works in the grocery store. Seeing the black olives brings his full attention back to the present. He doesn't stay long, though. Within seconds, he's off on some mind roll about bread, garlic and a restaurant whose name he just can't seem to recall. When Sidney comes up, our guy is still feeling the echoes of the previous interaction. Those feelings of pride and joy, the thoughts about his wisdom and ability to make a difference linger, echoing into the interaction with Sidney. The results of this echo are that our guy takes greater risks in his response to Sidney's tale of woe. And he is indeed inspiring. The echo here is positive. The swirling continues with a brief fantasy about how to extend his talents. The future has successfully tugged at him until he is transported back to the present with an "excuse me," from a fellow garlic searcher. Oh, that's right, garlic. All sorts of winds are blowing here. There's practically a whole list. And this is only during a simple shopping trip in a grocery store. This is how the whirlwinds and blasts can swirl, combine and blow us off course. And if we allow this to happen, then we've missed the fullness, the Sacredness, the peace of the present moment. If we allow thoughts and emotions free rein, then we are not Aligned with the Soul.

The Power Behind the Winds

The grocery store example is fairly typical of our lives, isn't it? The winds swirl and blow up and we go right along with them, caught up in their currents. We seem to be at their mercy, don't we? We go along in whichever direction they take us, as much victims to these winds as an autumn leaf. And victim is the right word. Like our guy in the example, we're not aware of these winds even as we are spinning along on their currents. Sure, there are times when we put up a fight, when we balk because we don't particularly care for the direction or the bumpiness of the ride. We might try to go against the current for awhile if the ride becomes too unpleasant, but we still seem to get caught up in the wild swirling. Our thoughts and emotions may take us wherever they go and wherever they go, we end up there with them. Depending on where they end, we're either rejoicing in the pleasantness, or wallowing in the unpleasantness. We are victims of our own internal experience.

But what we are actually doing is *allowing* ourselves to be victims of these winds. For, if we look a little closer, what we find is that *we* are the ones supplying the power. There is no mystical man behind the curtain. So when we, like Dorothy, run towards the curtain suspiciously to see who is doing all that huffing and puffing, what we will find is our own reflection staring back at us. Our egos are the ones providing the power allowing thoughts and emotions to sit in that director's chair.

The biggest way that we contribute to the firing up of this power is that we simply don't recognize that *it is just the wind*. That is, we get caught up *in* the winds, instead of being aware that the wind is blowing. **We *identify* with the wind instead of identifying with the Sacred that is within us or around us. We Align ourselves with the thought or the emotion, instead of Aligning ourselves with our Souls.** We're instantly in the whoosh of thoughts of the mind roll, instead of being aware that we're *on* a mind roll. Instead of, *Gosh, my thoughts seem to be taking off right now…*, we sprint forward with, *That cup of coffee was too strong…now I'm not going to be able to sleep…gee, did I make the bed this morning…well, it doesn't matter, the whole house is a mess.* And, like our thoughts, we get caught up in an emotion, instead of recognizing that it's just the experience of a strong emotion sweeping over us. Enveloped by a current of anger, we are unaware that it is just a current. We could take each of the winds and find that simply being caught in them gives them more power.

Since we're caught in them, identifying so completely with them, we are necessarily focused on whatever is in front of us. So, what we end up doing is feeding the winds even further with our attention. When we are caught up in the air current, spinning off on some future fantasy, we are focusing on all of those interesting thoughts. They can be so entertaining. They stimulate and provide the drama that we're looking for. We're not aware that we're on a mental trip and we perpetuate it with our attention. You fantasize about a date. *We could start with a walk in the woods. Ummm. That sounds nice. The day is sunny, but not too hot. She would like that. Hand in hand, just being quiet together, listening to the gentle rustling of leaves and the crack of twigs under our feet. Yes, a tender beginning.* The fantasy, of course, goes on from here, fueled by your thoughts and emotions. We won't go that far. You get the point. Our attention feeds the winds.

And, because we're *not aware* that we're identifying with something that is *not who we are*, but is only *an experience*, we're not likely to try to do much about our thoughts and emotions. More than likely, we're going to give them free rein and just go along for the ride. When you give something free rein, especially something so fluid and limber as thoughts and emotions, they will naturally get a little wild. Kick up their heels a bit. Show off their talents. The thoughts take off.

"Yeah, baby, saxophones to pubs to beer to hangovers to coffee to chocolate to Barnes and Noble to reading to, (oh no, not again!) Captain Underpants."

Pretty impressive. Do it again. But the emotions won't be outdone.

"Watch this," they say. "We can go from livid to lusty in five minutes flat." Then they do their little performance.

Of course, the thoughts come back with, "not bad, but get a load of…"

Thoughts and emotions can be wild and with free rein, they're going to test the limits. We give them power this way, too. We fail to see that we are caught up in a wind, some current of our own making, powered by us. It is a self-perpetuating cycle. So, yes, we are victims, but we are allowing ourselves to be victims of our own internal experience. We are the ones who supply the power behind the winds.

* * * *

Life is a ride, remember? Our egos are not in charge of the events. That alone will make us feel a bit sheepish. But when we stop to consider that maybe we're allowing ourselves to be victimized by our own internal experiences of thoughts and emotions, we truly shrink.

Who's in charge anyway? Our bold deep voice from the last chapter is smaller now, but we manage to timidly squeak out, "We are." But are we? After taking a longer look at the swirling winds that we unintentionally fuel, that blow us right off course, well, no, we're not.

But we could be.

We could choose to Align ourselves with the Sacred within us, instead of identifying so completely with just one aspect of our experience. We could choose to allow our Souls to be in charge. And if we can learn to do this, then thoughts and emotions and all of their effects would simply become the fascinating *parts* of our experience that they are. We could choose when we want to let our thoughts run free and when we want them hauled back in, for our purposes. We could choose when we wanted to settle into a strong flavored past memory or enjoy the haziness of a future fantasy. Or not. We could decide when we want to juggle several activities at once and when the taxing act of juggling is not worth it. And, instead of becoming an emotion, instead of being overwhelmed by the waves of intensity, we could follow the ride without being affected. Or we could decide to go ahead and jump in a joyful emotional current, allow it to overwhelm us a bit, all the while fully aware that we're in a current, fully capable of deciding when to get out. Our emotions don't have to dictate our behavior. There is no need to give the power away. It is fortunate that our peak behind the curtain of power revealed our own reflections. We can choose to respond from our center of being, the Soul. Unlike Dorothy. She got stuck with some quacky professor from Kansas in that director's chair.

You may be tired of the grocery store by now, but I thought we could review that scenario one more time, just to see what it might look like if the winds weren't in charge, if our guy could manage to stay Aligned with his Soul. Well…at least some of the time. (And this example will give you a glimpse of what's coming in the next chapter as well.)

Back at the grocery store…George bestows the sprinkling of compliments about your speech. You listen and thank him before he walks away. Then you watch yourself as the positive feelings of pride and joy emerge. It's a warm glow that you decide to let linger for a few minutes. Then you simply watch the feelings as they start to dissipate. You don't attempt to catch or hold onto them. They just emerge, you

154

feel them, let them linger and then they fade. You're moving through the isles trying to locate the black olives that you needed for the pasta salad when your mind reviews the smattering of compliments. Once again, you experience the pleasant feelings. *Maybe what I say is pretty wise,* you think. *Perhaps,* you tell yourself, *or perhaps I just like those feelings. The only way to know is to see if that speech made a difference in other people's lives as well. And I'm not likely to take a poll here.* You smile to yourself and redirect your attention to your search for the black olives. *Yes, there they are. Black olives and what else? Oh, yeah, Italian bread. Right. That goes well with salad. Maybe some roasted garlic to smear on the bread. That would be good. Just like that restaurant over on Sixth Street. What was the name of that place?* You wander toward the produce section where the garlic is, forgetting for the moment about the bread. Don't worry. You'll remember the bread in a minute. Probably after you get the garlic.

When Sidney comes up to you, you are just thinking about which garlic to pick. That is all. You turn your full attention on Sidney and listen intensely to his recent trauma. You are completely with him and respond to him based solely on where you believe him to be in his path and what you think he is able to hear at this moment to help. Compassion is what guides you.

This time our guy has the same emotional reaction as before. He still feels the pride and joy, but he lets the swelling of these emotions go. He doesn't fuel it with thoughts. At least not right away. The review comes up, accompanied by the feelings that go with it. Then there is the thought about being "pretty wise" that comes up to fuel the feelings. Our guy *is* wise, here, though. He recognizes the potential fueling and counters it. Then he redirects his attention to the moment. Oops, he still takes a short mind roll. Well, he's not perfect is he? Still, when Sidney comes up to leak out his recent trauma, our guy is poised to fully listen to him. He is in this position because he is not caught up with his own feelings about being wise. Our guy is *clear* to take in Sidney's plight. There is none of his own lingering mass of emotion or thought to cloud his judgment in responding to Sidney. Clarity and compassion are his guides. We can see who's in charge now. It's not the thoughts or emotions or that wacky professor from Kansas. It's Soul.

What freedom.

PRACTICING STAYING ON COURSE
The Methods and Techniques of This Way of Living

If you will let me, I will show you
  A practice,
  A path of conscious living,
  A path of peace and love.
Walk with me now,
  Into awareness,
  Into the consciousness that attention can bring.
Walk with me
  Into peace as you become aware of the Sacred around you.
We can both let go of the old ways that lead to meaninglessness.
We can both learn to embrace the clarity of objectivity.
We can both learn to see from Soul.
Will you walk with me?

The Role of Attention

Now, with a firmer understanding of the winds that can blow us off course, that can prevent us with Aligning ourselves to the Sacred that is within us and around us, we're ready to take back some of the power that we may have so casually tossed into the winds. We're ready to learn some of the methods that can be used to consciously Align ourselves to the Sacred that surrounds us and feel nourished, to consciously Align ourselves to our Souls. The process for beginning to consciously identify with who we really are and take back that director's chair begins with the simplicity of attention.

If you've ever been involved with real estate, whether you've bought and sold property or just know a real estate broker, then you've probably heard what makes property valuable. In fact, you've probably heard it three times, because it is rarely said only once.

Location. Location. Location.

The three times is a cute way of underscoring the importance of this factor. And when we consider it long enough, perhaps a second or two, we begin to realize that the location is what the property is. By definition. Thus, it's not so shocking to learn that location is sort of the central factor to consider in the real estate business.

Here, we are talking about the business of living, and, in this business of living, we also have a central factor, one that underpins the whole affair. I'll repeat it three times like the real estate people do so that it gets the weight that it deserves. Here it is:

Attention. Attention. Attention.

Actually, that attention is central to the business of living should not be too much of a surprise because "the business of living" is simply a rather boring way of saying "focusing on flying," or "focusing on Aligning ourselves to the Sacred that is within us and around us." And the word "focus," at the very least, implies attention.

If we are focusing on flying, then we are *necessarily* paying attention to our lives. By definition. So, in a sense, paying attention is central to the "how" of the way of Jonathan. Our lives reflect in them what we need to know in order to Align ourselves with the Sacred. It's all there, right in front of us. Every event, situation or circumstance holds an opening, an opportunity for our nourishment and evolution. What is required, at least in the beginning, is our attention. We need to be able to slip into the Sacredness of the present for our nourishment. We need to be open to seeing the growthful messages that surround us. It starts with our attention. Attention allows us to become immersed in the present. And it is through our attention that we can become aware of our thoughts, our emotions, our interpretations, our perceptions, our reactionary tendencies, our themes. Attention will bring it all to the surface and clarify it.

Then, with the clarity that our attention brings, we will be able to choose how we live. Ah, we have once again arrived at the crossroads of choice. We can be grateful for this freedom of choice, grateful that there is no longer a withering into being a victim of our own internal experiences, grateful that we can choose to live from Soul. For, it is through attention that we can choose whether to jump in the current of a mind roll and simply go along with that flow, or whether to skip that mind roll and immerse ourselves into the present. And it is through attention that we can choose to ride a blast of emotion without allowing it to overpower us completely, (or at least not without our permission!)

Attention will highlight our way of living, show us ourselves so that, if we dare, we can stand psychologically and spiritually bare naked in front of the mirror that life holds up for us. The exposure will be revealing. Attention will allow us to see who or what we happen to be Aligning ourselves with at the moment and then we can make a choice about how we want to live and how we want to be. I'm assuming, of course, that these choices are geared toward restoration. The ideas sound alright, but how it all looks in real life might be a bit hazy, so let's make it more concrete by example.

The mind stirs from that dreamy place and you roll over on this first morning in May to gaze out the window, check the weather and check your mental pulse. It must have rained. The creamy dogwood petal just outside your window testifies to this fact, through the intermittent falling of droplets of water. You focus on the dripping, the silkiness of the texture of that petal and how the appearance of sunlight has transformed the water into silver drops, like mercury. Taking in the sight of this petal is a lovely way to blend into the beginning of the day and you throw the covers off to embrace the coolness of the night air.

Then you remember. The nasty exchange that you had with your spouse last night comes up in your mind. With full volume, you can still hear how loud you actually got with one another, not to mention how negative.

"You can't just go spend 110 dollars to buy something, something that you're not even sure we really need, without at least letting me know!" she said.

"And you can't tell me what I can and can't buy. I don't need your permission. Just because we're married doesn't mean that you can control me!" you threw back.

"Don't be so small minded. I'm not trying to control you. I just want you to be considerate. We should make big purchase decisions together," she countered.

To this last statement you had responded by boring into her with that evil eye look of yours. You followed this glare with an exit that closed the subject for the night. The review in your mind brings back an echo of pain and anger. After the video gets rewound and goes through a second viewing, you become aware of the repetition and you become aware of the lure of the past. It's the pain from the exchange that prompts the review. So you remind yourself that the argument brought out some differences that you truly wanted to know about, that, although the next few steps are likely to be painful, you will be moving toward growth. You and she need to have some understanding about how you will spend money. No, you can't see at this moment how your two positions will be reconciled, but you console yourself with the thought that you will eventually work out some agreement. And your relationship with your spouse will deepen and broaden as a result. The pain won't last forever, you think. You decide that more reviews of last night's scene aren't necessary and look over at your spouse who is still sleeping. As you soak up her peaceful image, you think of the depth of the love between you and the future growth and evolution. One last glance and you head for the shower. There, you concentrate on how it feels to rub shampoo in your hair. It has the effect of massaging you awake.

Later, at work, your boss pops in and asks to speak to you for a minute. Uh-oh. The antennae go up. He doesn't usually ask. He usually just starts talking. You are instantly aware of this small formality and his awkwardness. A confrontation is coming. He tells you that your recent equipment purchase for the plant was questionable, not to mention more expensive than it probably had to be. While he acknowledges your keen ability to assess needs and fill them, he would prefer to be informed ahead of time about the decisions that involve that much money. All the time he is talking, you feel the anger mounting.

He ends with, "just be considerate and let me know. The big decisions we should be making together." He pauses, then adds, "Now I have to defend this purchase to my superiors and I'm not sure what to say."

This last part you barely even register into consciousness because you are struck solidly by the similarities between what your boss said and what your wife said last night. It's almost word-for-word, you think. After a pause, you notice that your boss is still looking at you, waiting for a reply. You put away your observation about the two conversations and respond by giving him some ammunition for defending the purchase and by suggesting that the purchasing issue needs to be discussed further at a later time. He agrees and leaves the office. Now you have something to think about. The similarities are uncanny. At lunch, you begin to think about the issue more.

Sifting through that purchasing issue at lunch was tough, and the afternoons work activities proved challenging, so you're tired when you arrive home. Your wife is preparing dinner and you decide to open a bottle of wine. You pour it into the glass, watching the redness splash up the other side and settle towards the middle. *We all settle towards the middle*, you think and snicker quietly. Settling. *Would I be settling and giving in to talk to other people before buying things?* you wonder. Then you stop yourself and realize that the free associations have brought you back to the issue that you were mulling over at lunchtime. Your mind is sore from thinking about it and you realize that you need some space away from that problem, so you refocus on the redness in your glass. Anticipation floods your mouth as you tilt the glass back. Then the wine floods your mouth. Abruptly, you spit it in the sink. Vinegar. *How old is this damn thing anyway? Why do we keep such old shit around here? I can't even come home from a hard day and enjoy a glass of wine. I bet there's not even another bottle in the cupboard, either.* A pause in thoughts gives you the time to notice where you're heading. You decide you really don't want to go there, but you still have the residual swelling of the anger of injustice. You can watch it, you think. So you get out of the kitchen where your wife is, just in case the anger gets too heavy. A few minutes later, after that decrescendo, you can remind yourself and believe it, that a bottle of vinegar fits neatly in the small stuff department.

Here are some snapshots of a relatively typical day for this person. In a typical day, there is the mundane and a bit of drama sprinkled in. We have both here. And there is much else, all of which is underscored by attention. Within these snapshots we can see a focus. To begin with, we can see a general focus on flying, a value that lies behind the circumstances, behind the perceptions and interpretations. The guy is aware of the moments, both in their potential for golden immersion into the Sacred and in their potential for growth and evolution. This focus or value then spreads into the individual snapshots, like roots growing through the earth. Let's look more closely at these scenes. (You knew we would.)

He starts off by noticing the dogwood petal outside his window. It's a detail that would have been glossed over without the spotlight of attention. He then makes a choice to linger on this detail, immerse himself in it. Immersion in the detail of a moment *is* a nourishing way to begin a day, an early click of the Soul's Alignment with the Sacred. Already there is color seeping through the moments, a color that is underlined with attention. This is the effect that attention has on the moments. It spotlights the color. Even in the shower. In fact, once we discover that the color of life surrounds us all the time, that attention is the method for seeing the splendor of the moment, we can become quite intoxicated.

"Honey, what are you doing just staring like that? I thought you were making a fire."

"I was, but just look at the lines in this wood. So delicate and hard at the same time. Amazing."

Attention allows us to realize that the moments are precious.

Attention allows us to be fully aware of them. Attention allows us to realize the full, multilayered radiant color of the Sacred that was always there and immerse ourselves in it. And, each moment that we do this, we are centering ourselves in our Souls.

Then, in this day-in-the-life, we watch the guy go through a couple of reviews of the conversation, argument? with his wife. He notices that his mind is reviewing the exchange. It is his attention that is doing that noticing. Once he catches the rehashing of the situation, he can then choose whether or not he wants to see it again. This is a case where he chooses not to go through it again, since, at this point, the reviews serve no purpose. He can't see a solution yet, so they are only dishing up unnecessary emotions. In this way, his attention has given him the power of choice and in that choice, he is freed from the painful, useless reviews of the exchange with his wife. Without catching the fact that he was reviewing the situation, without attention, the stinging mental rewind button might have gotten stuck for quite some time. Maybe during the shower, at breakfast and on his trip into work. The reviews could have continued indefinitely, sucking up his mind's mental and emotional energy until he was distracted by something else. Allowing this to happen would have meant that our guy was Aligning himself, identifying completely with the thoughts and the emotions. But this didn't happen. It didn't happen because of his attention and his conscious choice to move on. So much for the lure of the past.

And, stepping away from those reviews, he is able to remind himself of the potential outcome of all of this uncomfortable discord. He thinks of the future growth of his marital relationship once the issue is resolved. Here, we see a basic flying position. Pain is a transient signal towards evolution. He recognizes the pain from the argument and the upcoming discomfort of the future attempts to come to some sort of agreement, but he is consoled with the certainty of growth. His attention made him aware of those reviews and freed him to make the choice of a more positive perception. In other words, he chose not to fall prey to the winds here and consciously chose a perspective that would free him. Attention was the start of this process.

Later in the day, while at work, the guy was able to pick up some cues from his boss that a confrontation was coming. He was paying attention to the details again.

And it was attention that allowed him to catch the similarity between the situation at work and the one at home. Admittedly, the similarity was rather bold. It did sock him between the eyes, didn't it? He was right, his wife and his boss almost used the same words. Yet, even though the similarities may have seemed obvious, they might have been missed if he had not been paying attention. And again, there is evidence of another basic flying position. He is looking for the *significance* behind the similarity. He is seeking to get the messages that are in front of him. Next, he turns his full power of attention on what he thinks of as an issue. He spends his lunchtime exploring and sifting through this potential issue which may turn out to be a theme. Thus, it was through attention that he was able to pick up the potential issue or theme and through attention that he began processing it. Attention seems to be everywhere. But we're not done yet. The day is not over.

It was the attention that allowed the guy to catch himself early in a mind roll, the free association that occurred while he was pouring the wine. "Settling" to the middle. And attention was the method for checking his reactionary potential when the anger swelled because of the vinegar discovery. He was paying attention to his thoughts and saw what was happening. A bottle of vinegar does fit neatly in the small stuff department, and attention allows him to choose whether or not he will sweat it. He decides not too. Attention monitors that anger and takes him out of the room where reactions might spurt out on his wife. Again, he pulls out of the winds and moves toward a more centered position. Again and again, we see our guy pull himself out of the winds and Align himself with his Soul by using attention. Attention. Attention. Attention. Focusing on flying. Focusing on Aligning ourselves to the Sacred that is within us and around us, on our nourishment and evolution. Attention is central to the way of Jonathan. There is a story as told by Harry Moody in his book, of a wise master of living named Ikkyu. One day a man asked Ikkyu to write something simple about living wisely, something that most everyone could understand. He wrote the word "attention" on a piece of paper and gave it back to the man.

"'Is this all?" asked the man, unable to hide his disappointment. "Can't you add something more illuminating?"

Ikkyu took the paper back and wrote the word "attention" twice.

"Really," the man said, "I fail to understand the meaning of what you have given me."

At this Ikkyu wrote the word three times: "Attention. Attention. Attention."

Immensely irritated, the man shouted, "What does this word 'attention' mean anyway?"

Ikkyu answered gently, "Attention means attention."

No doubt the man walked away feeling at least frustrated by this exchange and most certainly bewildered. Well, if he had been paying attention, he would have been aware of the thoughts that were probably feeding his emotion of frustration and perhaps he could have just watched that frustration come and go, thereby leaving him open to understanding. At any rate, the point is made again. Attention is the foundation to the whole business of focusing on flying.

Paying Attention

Since attention is so integral, since it is the launching point, we will take a longer, more intimate view. From a wider angle. Or from different angles. Either way, we'll put a spotlight on the whole process of attention so that we can see it clearly.

Simply put, paying attention means being completely aware of where we are. This translates to being in the Sacred present. And what *this* means is that we are aware of what our bodies and its senses are doing, of the thoughts we are having, of the emotions that are swelling, and of the events. Being aware of our bodies and its senses, we can choose to immerse ourselves into the Sacredness of the present and wallow in its peace and its beauty. Being aware of our thoughts and emotions, we can allow the Soul to direct our course. Being aware of events, we can learn about when we are allowing Soul to guide us and when we're not. Meaning and color surround us. We just have to be paying attention.

Being Aware of Our Bodies and Its Senses

You might be wondering about what silliness I have in mind with this topic. Being aware of what our bodies and our senses are doing? Certainly, we always know what our bodies are doing. Right? Well, not always. Our bodies and senses are often put on automatic pilot. We don't have to think much about the ordinary tasks of the day, the ones that we've done so, so many times before. Opening a door, putting on our clothes, eating. None of these tasks requires any of our thought power. So we flip the dial to automatic. Of course, this automatic mode of being occurs more and more as we get older, because we have had much more practice at many more activities. Now, not only can we shampoo and shave automatically, we can also fill out that report at work automatically. Filling out the report is a more complicated task, certainly. And it required our concentration when we first started doing it. After several hundred repetitions, though, we could switch to automatic. The result? We have removed ourselves from the Sacredness of the present and into our worlds of thoughts or fantasies or whatever. (We are thoroughly familiar with the winds, aren't we?) To be sure, there will be less color and nourishment in our thought created world. By removing ourselves from the present with our bodies and senses on automatic, we have stepped into a black and white reality. Stay there too long and we begin to feel the itch of dissatisfaction and vague longing.

And, as a brief digression, being on automatic can be dangerous. Physically. Like when we drive automatically. *It must have been a green light. After all, I went through it.* As we toss a glance in the rearview mirror, we're hoping like hell that it actually *was* green. Smaller, non-life-threatening accidents occur in the same way. You reach up to put the glass in the cupboard, only to miss by an inch. The result is at least a chipped glass. Maybe even a broken one and a curved line of blood on your palm. Or we trip over that ill-placed toy. With the body on automatic, mishaps do occur. We're not paying attention.

Losing the potential peaceful nourishment in a moment and having accidents are the consequences of allowing our bodies and senses to go on automatic. There are probably others. But let's not linger on these. Let's think about how we are going to Align ourselves with the Sacredness of the present, how we are going to regain that nourishing color, how we are going to see the mundane with freshness. Well…we pay attention. (Okay, Okay, I'll explain a bit more than that, although I still believe that Ikkyu truly covered it all.)

Through our attention, we can take each sense of our bodies and flip that switch to manual mode. In this way, we can become aware of ourselves in the present and we can Align ourselves to the Sacredness, the peace, and the beauty that are inherently there. You have heard the saying, "see as if through the eyes of children?" Just so. Children see with fresh eyes because they are seeing much for the first time. They seem to soak in their surroundings through all of their senses. Children constantly remind us of this fresh perspective and, because they are so uninhibited and spontaneous, their joy is blatant. The first time they get up on a swing and the glee of the motion blooms on their face, their rapture is our rapture. They are giving us a gift and teaching us simultaneously. They are reminding us about living in a way that captures the fresh perspective, the perspective of the first time. We will do well to imitate them.

You can notice the color of the Sacred present during a "mundane" activity by fully paying attention to one of the senses of your body and then moving around to the other senses. You can attempt to soak up all of the details of one sense before moving on or you can bounce around between senses. Focusing on the detail is the important part. Like the guy who took in the details of the dogwood petal. In this manner, the experience of watering a plant in the July heat turns into full-blown radiant poetry. It is the poetry of the Sacred.

The heat of the sun drenches the top of your head and massages the muscles of your back. Penetrating heat. Your fingers lightly hold the sprinkler. Cool, smooth metal. The sunglasses resting on your nose are smooth too, but they feel warm. They slip down your nose every minute or two because of the sweat. You push them back up. The water spraying out holds the fresh scent of recent rain. Close your eyes and the odor could convince you that it must have rained recently. You hear a dog barking in the distance. Your eyes open at the sound. Jets of water sparkle from the intensity of the light. Drops jump the space between the sprinkler and the plant in an arc. The water lands with a small, gentle popping on the leaves and twinkles while it runs to find its settling place. A clear undisturbed drop of water magnifies the veins in one of the leaves. Variations on the arc of water are made by moving the sprinkler. You make a jaunty movement now. A giggle escapes.

You're just watering the plant, right? Ordinarily perceived as a boring task of a July afternoon. But when we open the gates of our senses through our attention, we can fully understand why our children jump up and down in front of us begging to take over the sprinkler. But maybe this time we'll keep it awhile.

Switching the dial to manual for our bodies and our senses is a way of guiding our attention back to the immediate experience of the Sacredness that is right in front of us, in the present moment. And when we Align ourselves so completely with it, then it doesn't take long before we become aware of the brilliant color that stays so imbedded there. The problem is that we don't stay in the present long. Even in a peaceful, uneventful, undramatic scene like watering a plant in July, we lose attention. Quietly and stealthily, our minds start to wander away. Some inane subject drifts through or the future tugs at us. And the present gently fades to black and white. It shrinks to the back of the stage. There are no fireworks of drama when we're watering a plant, so our minds are free to play. The thoughts take some light emotions along with them and before we know it, our full attention, our being is somewhere else.

The winds. They're back.

Being Aware of Our
Thoughts and Emotions
– So That We Can Choose Our Course

We knew the winds would be back. It was just a matter of time, usually a short time, seconds, or maybe minutes. Only now we have some armor, the armor of attention. For, ironically enough, we can take back the power that we may have thrown carelessly to the winds by being aware that *there is a wind,* by being aware of whether we are currently *in it or not,* and by knowing that it is *just* the wind. Translated into spiritual language, we can take the power back by being aware that the thought or the emotion is happening. We can take back the power by being aware of whether we are currently Aligned with the thought, the emotion or whether we are Aligning ourselves with our Souls. We can take back the power by being aware that this thought, this emotion is *not who we are,* but simply *one aspect* of our experience. And with this awareness, we are freer to choose our course. We are freer to choose to Align ourselves with our Souls. After the last chapter, you may have been wondering when I would be getting to this point. Well, here we are finally. And it is none other than attention, which gives us the power and thus the choice.

We begin by simply "catching" ourselves.

"Pay attention," your first grade teacher would say through pinched lips.

Of course, you would modify the amount of attention you actually paid, based on how pinched her lips actually were. But what she was doing was catching you wandering off in your mind somewhere and bringing you back to the lesson she was attempting to infuse into your brain. She knew that an infusion of information would not happen without attention. So she prodded you every so often to make sure you were doing your part. That teacher was a master at noticing the cues that let her know when you had slipped away. You had hardly even gotten through trotting outside in your mind, you hadn't even reached the monkey bars of your imagination, before she was calling your name, forcing that fantasy to disappear. How did she know? You were just sitting there quietly. You weren't even looking out the window. How did she know you weren't mentally there? Well, maybe she was paying... it's not even necessary to say, is it? Invariably, she would catch you and bring you mentally back to the lesson.

Well, we don't have that teacher mentally poking and prodding us any more to pay attention. (Thank goodness, she was a bit of a nuisance!) No one is calling our names to bring us back to the subject at hand. So, we have to learn to do it for ourselves. If we are not going to be blown away by the winds by Aligning ourselves with these pseudo-directors, then we will need to catch ourselves and direct our attention and our course as we choose. And "catching" ourselves is actually no more than realizing what our thoughts and emotions are doing. This is the first step in pulling in the reins. We need to know what they're up to.

Now, in order to do this, we must step out of our ordinary position of observation. Ordinarily, we view our lives and our experiences from one position. The position of inside looking out. We're in here, in these bodies, feeling these sensations, having these thoughts and emotions. And, from our ordinary positions, we peer out on the world of events and other people. Us and everything else. We found out about this position when we were babies and we kept hold of it. It's comfortable. We like it.

But, in order to catch ourselves being swept away in a crosswind, we must temporarily give up this position and view ourselves from a new position, from the outside looking in. Mentally, we step outside ourselves and peer back in. The idea might sound a bit weird at first, but it's not much different than doing a mental review. And we do these all the time. We think about how we did during a confrontation with a friend. We can review the confrontation, see ourselves and then consider what we could have said that might have been better. We review how we charmed our date with tantalizing dinner conversation. We step out and look back at ourselves, as if we were watching someone else. When we do this, we are beginning to Align ourselves with the Sacred within us as we move away from our usual identification with the thought or the emotion.

When we step out and look back at our thoughts and emotions while we are having them, we are catching ourselves, which allows room, room for choice about what we are going to Align ourselves with. You're at your best friend's house, listening to his band do some jazzy improvisation and the thoughts start rolling in their free associating way. Bass guitar, that strange bass player with the green hair from the group you saw last week, the pub on the corner, that woman wearing that teeny tiny shirt, being hot-hot-hot, being cold. Then you catch yourself. You step outside and look back. What you see is a short mind roll. Instantly, it stops. Once aware of the roll, you can choose to continue it, which you might want to do, if the present music curdles more with every note, or you can choose to redirect your attention to the sonorous melody pulsing from the guitar. You decide. You have taken the role of that teacher now and prodded yourself back to attention, only you get to decide whether you are going to follow the music or not. The point here is that catching required realizing that the mind roll was occurring by stepping out of that ordinary position of observation and viewing it from the outside. By stepping out, we can be aware that there is a wind and simultaneously be aware of whether we're in it or not. Choice follows.

This "catching" process works magnificently with the winds that are dominated by thought. It works quite well for those past situations that lure us and those future fantasies that tug at us. Catching ourselves does wonders for the mind roll and split attention winds. There is a reason for this. It is extremely difficult to be in the position of observing ourselves and be thinking at the same time. Imagine watching yourself while you are on the free association trip of a mind roll. Or continuing to have a fantasy about a future event once you've realized that you're having a fantasy. You would be thinking about your thinking while you're thinking. Sounds confusing, doesn't it? Well, it is. And most of us can't do it. Because the moment you step out into the position of outside looking in, the thoughts stop. Of course, you could easily slip back into the mind roll or that fantasy, but, for the moments that pass in the observational position, the thoughts do not continue. Said in another way, we can't hold two observational positions at the same time. You cannot be inside looking out and outside looking in simultaneously. At least, most of us can't.

Thus, we can use this fact to our advantage. We can stop the winds that are dominated by thought by the simple act of catching ourselves in them. Once we step out, we get a pause or a space between thoughts. And that space can be long enough to make a choice of where we want to put the attention of our minds. Do we want to remain in the present or shall we just continue in the mind? The second our jazz listener from above, caught the mind roll, it stopped. There was a space. Then he could decide where he wanted to put his attention. Catching is how we create those spaces. How nice. Now we have room for choices.

This is not to say, however, that once we've managed to pay attention, once we've caught ourselves in that wind, that it stops forever. Anyone who has had several sleepless hours can testify to the power of a nighttime mind roll. The mind just seems so agitated. The frustration is followed by sighs, which is followed by vows not to look at the clock. Then you sneak a peek at those red digital numbers and sigh again. The whirlwinds of thought can be powerful. They are not to be underestimated. Yet, the process of catching ourselves still works wonders. We might just have to do it more than once. In fact, we might have to do it, well, a lot. Counting the number of times you catch yourself is not likely to be an enticing activity. It's not something you would want to do on a Saturday evening. But we know that some of those whirlwinds are strong enough to warrant multiple "catchings." Our jazz listener's mind roll wasn't that powerful as to warrant an extended effort on his part. Once he caught the mind roll, he could choose. But let's say that the one of those associations, the woman in the teeny tiny shirt, prompted some of the emotional boxes to start jumping around. Now what he would have is a mind roll that is fueled with emotion, perhaps lust. Just a bit more powerful than before. In fact, it might turn into a lengthy self-fueling fantasy. If our jazz listener did want to listen to the group, then he might have to catch himself several times in order to cool the heat.

The process of catching a thought essentially puts an end to that thought as long as we remain in the observational position of outside looking in. From this position we can easily pick off any thoughts that wander in. It doesn't always go so smoothly for emotions, however. Wouldn't you know it? They can be just a bit stickier, a bit more heavy handed than the winds that are dominated by thoughts. This is because it is entirely possible to observe yourself feeling a blast of emotion *while* you are feeling it. Just the act of observation does not put an end to that emotion. Unlike those winds that are dominated by thoughts. You can be seething with anger, be acutely aware that you are seething with anger and still be a victim of the blast as you behave consistently with that emotion and perhaps crash.

No, it doesn't put an end to the emotion. But catching ourselves, stepping into the observational position of outside looking in and watching an emotion, does do something. It does make a deep gash in the power of that blast. Catching ourselves may not obliterate it, but it does affect it. Because, once we catch ourselves in the emotion, we are that much closer to gaining the perspective that this is *just* a wind, a state of being that comes and goes. The emotion is *not who we are.* This perspective can be valuably potent. True, the heavy blasts don't just melt away with this realization, but we are less likely to become victims of them. What we are experiencing is an emotion. It is just a state of being. One aspect of our experience. It is no more than an feeling that will come and go. That is all.

Do you remember when you were little and your mom tried to help you "gain perspective?" She asked you to tell your father that dinner was ready. But when you started jogging in the direction of the den, your brother looked at you with that narrow gleam of competition in his eye and sprinted toward the door. Of course, he got there first and made the announcement, despite your best efforts at yelling over his head. When you complained to Mom, she tried to give you some perspective, saying things like, "Now, honey, it's not the end of the world." The first time you heard this, it wasn't a cliché and it probably made you think about the end of the world. (You hadn't known that the existence of the world was an option.) Mom was attempting to help us gain perspective on the situation and our feelings. Although it was poorly done by the mom in this example, the attempt was made because Mom likely realized that once we put it in perspective, missing our turn would not feel so bad. Well, when we step out of our usual position of observation and see our blasts of emotions, even those heavy ones as just one aspect of experience, we are making deep cuts in the power that those emotions have over us. From the outside looking in, we gain perspective and see the emotion for what it is. Just an emotion. Just a temporary state of being. Just a wind. *Not who we are.*

By catching ourselves, that is, by becoming aware of the swelling emotion, we know what is happening and where we are in it. With this infusion of strength, then, we can take the next step and remind ourselves of how this experience fits into the big picture. When we can see ourselves from the outside looking in, we can put the emotion into its proper place: an emotion, one aspect of experience. Thus, the catching process coupled with the perspective helps us to avoid inflating the thing to abnormal proportions. And when that wind that is dominated by emotion is in its usual proportions, it is easier to experience the emotion without being overwhelmed.

But sometimes, catching the emotion and gaining perspective is only the beginning. This is what makes emotions a bit stickier. They tend to linger even while we watch them. They hang around, loitering in our bodies and minds. The chemical version of these blasts can continue to pulse in our veins long after we've realized that we've been caught in the wind. But that's okay, we can hang around too. We can practice maintaining our position of looking back at ourselves, we can practice maintaining that perspective and just watch the full life of that emotion. We get to outside looking in and stay there for awhile, just watching. No need to worry. The blasts won't last forever. In fact, most of the time, they are actually short-lived. That is, they are short-lived as long as we're not fueling them somehow. The emotion will swell and then dissipate. And we can hang around and watch the whole process.

Do you remember the incessant pushing and pulling of the struggle with those emotional boxes from the last chapter? We sat on those emotional boxes, putting our full weight on the lids. We were hoping to keep the negative ones from escaping. Slick little devils. They would always get out when we weren't on guard. And we were hoping to keep the positive ones out and with us. We thought they were our buddies, but they would somehow sneak back into their boxes. All of that struggling, the worthless hoping, (it never did do much good), the attempts to force; all of that took so much energy and left us reeling with disheveled minds. Always breathless and worried is how we found ourselves, regularly glancing around at the myriad of boxes scattered along the floor of the subconscious. We were ready to pounce when necessary. But we always seemed to miss one, then we would become the victim of that emotion, get caught in the blast and suffer the consequences.

Well, breathe deep. We can afford a deep breath now, because we can take some of that power back. Catching ourselves in the emotion reminds us of its limited power. We can get the perspective. Just a state of being. Just an emotion. And maintaining the position of outside looking in will allow us to watch the emotion come and go. Now, we don't need to expend massive amounts of energy anxiously surveying the floor of the subconscious, looking for any telltale signs that a box is about to blow. Now we can turn our attention elsewhere, to, say, watching our senses in the Sacred present. Maybe checking out that dogwood petal. So, when one of those positive emotions comes out to shine brilliantly, there is no need to sneak over and park ourselves on the lid to prevent reentry. We can just watch. And when one of those negative boxes start to rumble, when one of the lids steams up, we won't need to run over and throw ourselves on the lid. We just watch. Yep. There it is again. Our old friend. Anger. It swells and threatens and we just watch. We're not impressed. Without feeding it through the energy of our resistance or the fuel of thought, it withers much more quickly and slinks back into its box. There. Done.

It's Christmas season. Despite your October promises, your procrastinating side won and you are shopping during that last crammed period. You've been spinning through stores for two hours, brushing by people in the packed aisles and standing in lines that start so far away from the register, you're not even sure where the register is. You're in one of those lines now. As people step forward, a woman takes advantage of your slowness to move and steps in front of you. Thinking that she may have misunderstood about where the line started, you point it out to her. Even though you were polite and gentle, she glares at you with an affronted stare and lingers in this confrontational eye contact for a full minute. Well, it feels like a whole minute. Then, without saying a word, she simply turns her back to you. She did not move from the place in line. You felt the heat increasing during her look, that old friend anger pushing its way out of the box. As she turns her back, there is that familiar rush as the anger settles in the forefront of experience. Your civilized self won't allow any physical behavior, so your mind jumps forward. Different fantasies pop up. You visualize yourself pushing her out and toward the back of the line. Or whipping her around by the shoulders and screaming obscenities a few inches from her face. You can see the spit flying in that one. Or whipping her around and back-handing her across the face while forcing her to listen to a soliloquy about being so self-centered that taking advantage of people is a way of life and that she needs to do something about her Miss Entitlement complex.

Then, you catch yourself. *Whoa, that is red-hot anger gushing through my mind and body. Powerful stuff.* You step away and become aware of the intensity of the anger from an observer's point of view. For two seconds, maybe, you maintain the position, then you're back in. A few of the fantasies jump forward for a quick review. You're halfway through the spitting one when you catch yourself again. Again, you remind yourself of the perspective. Just a passing state. Intense, but temporary. And again, your mind blows up another review. After all, she is standing right in front of you. *It would be so easy to…*again, you catch yourself. The thoughts jump in for a bit of fuel. *How bold do you have to be to march plainly up to the middle of a line and step into it? At Christmas time too! So much for spreading good cheer and warm feelings. Maybe I should just spread out my arms and pop her on the...* Yet again, you catch yourself. *Gosh,* you think, *this is so strong.*

You realize that you need to do something else. The waiting for the anger to subside just leaves too much space for those fantasies and thoughts to come back up and fuel it. Especially with her still standing in front of you. You think about the whole situation. How it seems somewhat silly. The woman broke in line. Small stuff. She did it and she's not moving. That is how it is. *But she was rude about it! Like she had a right to jump in anywhere she pleased. Miss Entitlement, I'm telling you!* The thoughts seem so incessant about this, you think as you catch yourself again. You don't want to spend your time swathed in anger. After all, you want to enjoy your shopping. Maybe refocusing on the Sacredness of the present will help. So you decide to try to redirect the subject of your mind and think of the gift you're buying. Your nephew will adore Woody from that *Toy Story 2* movie. You do an internal check. Nope, anger is still pulsing as you glance at the back of her head. You need something more direct, more related to the situation. So you start to speculate about what sort of desperation might lead the woman to act so inconsiderately. Now you use your jaunty imagination again. Only this time, you are imagining some potential situations that would lead to such rudeness. Maybe she's late for something. You can see her rushing from the store to the restaurant, where her dinner date is currently pacing the lobby, a scowl marking his forehead. Then you imagine that she is late for church and she is the minister giving the sermon. No, neither one of those scenes work. She's not dressed nice enough for a restaurant or a church. In fact, her clothes are rather worn, you notice. But it doesn't matter, because already, you can feel your anger fading. You glance at the gift she has in her hand. Buzz Lightyear. Oh. She's buying for a child. You make one last internal check to see what's happening with the emotions. You're not completely sure, but you do feel mostly clear. You wait another minute and nothing comes up.

So you bend around to the side to get her attention and say, "I see you have Buzz Lightyear."

Not quite sure that you're talking to her, she does a double take in your direction. You're looking straight at her, so now she's sure, but she hesitates. In a flash, she is trying to read your face, a lightening search to see whether you might be opening to another confrontation. You are clear, so your face is clear.

She answers with a stumped, "Well, yes..."

You fill in the conversation. After a couple of minutes of going back and forth about the toys and the movie, there is a lull. She stops and looks down, fiddling with the wings of the toy.

You think she's going to apologize and she even starts with, "I'm..." But then there is a pause. You don't say anything. Just a moment longer, she hesitates, then she continues.

"I'm in a rush because I've got to get this in the mail. They told me that if I got it in the mail by 3:00 this afternoon, it would reach my son by Christmas. It has to be there by Christmas. It just can't be late because, well, it's all he'll be getting from me."

Son? Mail? Sending her *son* a gift in the mail? The only thing? There are too many implications in this to absorb quickly, but you realize that there is a whole history here and it's likely to be a sad one. Of course, you had no idea. Histories don't show on the outside.

You give her a quick squeeze around the shoulders and lean in to say, "That sounds like a pretty good reason to...be in a rush." You were going to say "break in line," but changed your mind. As you glance up from your watch to tell her that she is going to make that deadline, warmth and gratitude are written on her face.

When you get home, you have a few minutes to think back about the whole situation. When the fantasies come up now, they almost seem comical. You stifle a giggle. *Now*, it all seems like such small stuff. All of that struggle and emotion over a woman breaking in line. It's kind of odd, isn't it? Having such strong feelings, such violent fantasies over a trivial incident? You begin to consider some potential contributing factors. Yes, you were tired. And being surrounded by crowds depletes your reserve of energy, so you would expect to have less patience. But fantasizing about backhanding someone? This is not typical of you. Now you wonder why. You pour back over the whole situation. It was more than the simple injustice of breaking in line. What was the trigger? You were losing out. You were being taken advantage of — again. You begin to think that maybe this needs more exploration, that maybe there is a trend.

The example speaks for itself. I like examples that do their own speaking. But, as you might expect, there are some points worth underscoring. Notice first, that the person here had to catch herself several times and even employ some other strategies before the wave of emotion had less of an influence on her. This is to be expected. She is practicing. But the catching allows her, temporarily at least, to step out of Aligning herself with her thoughts and emotions. It gives her space for choice.

What is absent in this example are negative self-judgments about having to catch herself more than once. She doesn't complicate the situation by filling up her head with a bunch of "shoulds." *I should be able to get control of my thoughts. I ought to be able to let go of this anger. This shouldn't be so difficult.* All of this is missing from the above example. Instead of confusing the situation with "should," the person simply deals with what comes up. Acceptance is the underlying assumption.

Notice too, that the negative fantasies that first served to let off some of the steam of the anger end up fueling it. Here, we have bumped into one of those fine lines. Because physical aggression was stifled by the person when the lady broke in front of her, the aggression found another, more acceptable outlet: the fantasies. The fantasies worked well initially, didn't they? They allowed that anger some way of letting off some built up steam. The lid could safely slide off the box this way. But then, after a while, the same fantasies had the effect of maintaining the anger. They ended up being the fuel. It's difficult to pinpoint exactly when the same fantasies stopped being the steam and started being the fuel for the anger. Hence, the fine line. We probably won't be able to find exactly where that line is, no matter what the circumstance, but we can continue to catch ourselves. In this way, when the emotion has steamed off somewhat, we can be ready to catch it before it turns into the fuel. The person in the example does exactly this. The fantasies start and she catches herself in them. They come up for review. They're not done yet. She catches herself again. At some point here, the fantasies turn into fuel. But she relentlessly continues catching and eventually tries other methods. Her efforts undercut the fueling capacity of the fantasies and thoughts. Then the anger dissipates. She had to hang in there for quite some time though. She had to get through the fine line that real life makes blurry. We don't have to know where the line is. We just keep on practicing.

This whole idea about letting off the steam vs. fueling the emotion, brings us quite nicely into the next idea: that of release. Releasing is just another way of saying, "letting go." If we're fueling the emotion, or allowing fantasies and thoughts to swirl around with our emotions essentially fueling each other, what we are actually doing is holding on to the whole mess. Such a tight grip leads to nasty places. And we can bet that if we're holding onto this whole mess, then we're not Aligning ourselves with our Souls. In fact, holding onto the whole thing means that we're actually Aligning ourselves with the thoughts or the emotions.

What we choose to Align ourselves with most definitely affects the outcome of the situation. If the person in our self-speaking example had done absolutely nothing about the anger and the fantasies and the thoughts, the scene would have played out quite differently. The person would have felt that anger for longer, been miserable the whole time she was in the line, even if she hadn't taken any action. There would have been no connecting interaction between the two women. The person would probably have made her purchase, seething all the while and rushed on to the next activity, anger dripping from her psyche, ready to splash onto someone else. The drive home would have been infiltrated. And there would certainly be no reflections about why her reaction was so out of proportion to the scene. Of course, this means that she would have missed that message, a message that is likely to lead to a theme, then to potential growth and evolution.

In fact, she probably would have continued to fuel the anger, allowing it to echo right into the evening meal. Dinnertime would be the perfect opportunity to gather some support for her feelings of injustice from the other members of her family. They would, of course, nod their heads sympathetically upon hearing of the bold break into line. And, predictably, this retelling would have the effect of bringing it up all over again. So the anger, fantasies and thoughts would spring to life *yet again* for more reviews. This is holding on. It has the effect of drawing out the negativity, of allowing it to echo into the next situations, of preventing an immersion in the Sacredness of the present, of obscuring messages for growth and evolution. To be sure, eventually, she would release the whole scenario, along with the thoughts and feelings. This would naturally happen, because some other event would jump up to take its place. And the whole cycle would begin again. We've seen this before. Reactionary.

So, when it is time, when the emotion has expended its life, (and only you will be able to say when *that* is,) we let go and glide back into the main current of balance, where no one aspect of our experience dominates. Here is the steady, gentle breeze of the Sacred present. Ooo...that's better. And letting go means that we have regained our perspectives, literally. In fact, we can actively attempt to release the hold that the wind has, by trying to regain perspective. Yes, this does mean that we attempt to realize that the wind is *just* a wind, a state of mind that won't last. We've been over that.

But it also means that we remember the perspectives that underlie the entire approach. These are none other than the basic flying positions. Remember them?

"Whoa, that was a sharp turn...Looks like a new direction...Wonder what I can learn here..." (I know it's been awhile, so I thought the memory might need prompting.) Then there's viewing the moments of life as precious so that we may find a nourishing peace and so that Soul will direct our lives. And there's pain as a transient signal towards evolution. These perspectives, too, are inconsistent with the imbalance of being caught in a wind. That is, it is difficult to be caught up in some swirling emotional/thought current if we are maintaining these perspectives. Therefore, when the time comes for release, we can actively embrace or remind ourselves of these underlying perspectives and thereby regain balance and steadiness.

The person in the Christmas shopping example made several attempts to remind herself of these perspectives. When she says, "Gosh, that was strong," it translates into "Whoa, that was a sharp turn...," an acknowledgment of how tough this is for her. This is the beginning of accepting the event. She tries to take the next step toward acceptance and put the incident into the small stuff department where it properly belongs. It doesn't work. (We'll get to why it didn't work in a minute.) If she could've managed to view the incident with this perspective, she would've been far along in releasing the emotion. She makes the attempt, but it doesn't work and the thoughts pop right back up. And we can see her reminding herself that she doesn't want to spend her time being laden with anger. Behind this thought is the value of the moment as precious. This reminder, too, could have the effect of moving her toward release, but it doesn't. She manages to finally release herself from the winds by another method, specifically, fantasizing about possible legitimate reasons for the other woman's behavior. She is looking to compassion to help her move away from those persistent thoughts and emotions. *And compassion resides in the Soul. Using a quality of that most Sacred part of ourselves to gain some perspective will also move us in the direction of Alignment.* If, somewhere earlier in the long chain of thoughts and emotions, she could have regained some perspective, then she could have more easily released herself and glided out of the wind.

Throughout this whole section on emotions, the concentration has been on the winds that are negative, on those boxes that jostle with threats to explode in expression. This is because we tend to have the most trouble with these. That's also why anger gets the headline here. We've all been intimate with the little red guy. But the same process of attention applies with the positive emotions, the long lost friends that we tend to hold with iron grips. Although the typical goal is different from the negative emotions, (we want to keep the positive ones out of the box), the process for avoiding being trapped by their seductive powers is the same. We do it through attention, by realizing that there is a wind, by being aware of whether or not we're in it and by gaining the perspective that it is just a wind, one aspect of experience. The catching process, the position of outside looking in, the release; all remains the same for the positive emotions.

Being Aware of Our Thoughts and Emotions
— *So That We Can Learn From Them*

No, I haven't forgotten about the dangling question regarding the woman in the example. She just could not seem to regain balance and perspective without great effort, could she? Despite the small stuff nature of the incident. Breaking in line is not catastrophic. That's laughable. And despite multiple catchings and attempts to regain perspective through multiple reminders, she just couldn't release and glide out of the wind. The emotion and fantasies and thoughts were simply too powerful for her. Why? Well, that is the question that she begins to consider at the end of the scenario. And what she bumps up against is a potential theme. She realizes upon reflection that there may be a trend when it comes to allowing others to take advantage of her. Maybe she has been walked on a lot in her life. Maybe she has had enough. That could be a possible reason why she was overactive. The theme was sore and sensitive, ready to pop at the slightest stimulation. The woman breaking in line provided the stimulation.

And the venom from the theme and the other times that she had experienced something similar; the entire sore subject got pricked. Now we know why the multiple catchings were necessary and why the many attempts to gain back the values and perspectives failed so miserably. It was the power of the theme. Too overwhelming for awhile.

But it was the attention to the thoughts and emotions that lead her to contemplate the theme. Said another way, the theme seeped out through the heavy emotional reaction and, because she was paying *attention*, she was able to see where the reaction was pointing. If we're paying attention, our thoughts and emotions will point us in the direction of growth and evolution. Our learning about ourselves, when we are Aligned with Soul and when we are not, can begin here. They will point to the patterns and reactionary triggers. They will reflect our perceptions. They will show us our themes. It's true that we pay attention to our thoughts and emotions so that they won't get too wild on us, so that we can direct our course and not be victims of the winds. But our attention to them will also enable us to evolve. And *that* means we will more often be responding from the Soul.

What we can learn from our thoughts and emotions; well, the list is virtually endless and completely unique to the individual. But to give you some ideas... You could learn that you're so grumpy in the morning because you always wake up thinking about the list of "to do's" and how you will not have time and how you shouldn't be the only one to do these "to do's." You'll figure that out if you're paying attention to your thoughts and then, of course, you can intervene. Your Soul probably has a whole different perspective on the "to do's." You could learn that repetitive noises, like a steady drum beat or a beeping alarm, pluck your last nerve and send you quickly into a small fury. You would want to know this, wouldn't you? Then you could think about how to free yourself. Aligning yourself with your Soul, you'd probably perceive those noises in a whole different way. You could learn that being late makes you sweat, no matter how often you manage to put it back into the small stuff department. When you're late, you're agitated, flushed and disjointed. Paying attention to this trend will enable you to do something about it. And what would the Soul say about this? Through your overreaction to someone breaking in line, you could learn that you hold some buried fury about being taken advantage of. The fury stays buried because you allow this same sort of thing to happen frequently, too frequently. You might never have caught this if you hadn't been paying attention to the thoughts and emotions. You could learn that a cynical, suspicious perception is how you tend to view the actions of others. Paying attention to your thoughts would point this out. All the while your emotions would be displaying the resulting negativity and unhappiness of such a viewpoint. Of course, you'll have to be watching to catch it. Thoughts and emotions are powerful vehicles to the start of our evolution, to the start of our Aligning ourselves with the Sacred within us, but we must be paying attention.

This section, paying attention to our thoughts and emotions so that we can learn from them, doesn't get much space here. That's because of the individual nature of the discoveries that you'll make when you start to pay vivid attention to thoughts and emotions. You are unique and your discoveries will be unique. There is no way to predict them. But please don't underestimate the amount of growth and evolution or the power of this attention. It is enormous. Thoughts and emotions will mirror our perceptions, our patterns of reaction, our themes. If we're paying attention, we can be aware of them all and make our choices and direct our course. Paying attention is the beginning. You'll have to take it from there.

Being Aware of Our Thoughts and Emotions
— So that We Can Fully Experience Them

All this work and so little play. Are you feeling dull? Well, here is a reason for paying attention to thoughts and emotions that might be less strenuous, not quite so taxing on the neurons. We pay full attention to the thoughts and emotions so that we can fully experience them. Finally, you say, some levity. So far, the focus about these internal experiences has been on how to avoid becoming victims of them and how to learn from them. There was a whole chapter about the winds, wasn't there? And we'll be getting to the themes soon. All this watching and learning and changing and evolving. But what about just *having* thoughts and emotions? What about simply experiencing them? Good point. Thoughts and emotions are not intimate parts of our experience, put in place only so that we can learn from them. They add the richness and creme to experience. They can nourish us. Some folks might say that they *are* the experience. But let's not get into a philosophical debate. If we were to delete thoughts and emotions from our experience, we would become those mechanized robots that move through and scan with their senses. They take in data, but make no interpretations, have no related thoughts about it, experience no swells or waves of emotion. How boring. Thoughts and emotions fill in the details, make experiences richer, and add dimension to our world. So we pay attention to grasp the fullness of these aspects of our experience.

Here's something else to consider. Freedom. The freedom that comes with not being the victim of the winds. The freedom to experience fully. For, when we are aware of where we are in our thoughts and emotions, when we take the position of outside looking in, our Souls are the ones in that director's seat. Our Souls are the ones behind the curtain, not the winds and not that quacky guy from Kansas. Knowing this and being comfortable with this knowledge allows us the freedom of choice. We can allow ourselves to be fully immersed in an emotion, without the worry of falling prey to it.

Now we can feel that disappointment fully about being stood up on a date and not have to worry that it will turn into depression, because we will be watching our thoughts and will stop them before they fuel that exaggeration. Before, we might have felt a twinge of disappointment as we sat alone at the dinner table, watching the candle flicker back and forth from the invisible wind of passing waiters. Waiters going to other tables. And the moment that the disappointment pinched, we would have brushed it off, dismissing it quickly. We've felt that before. We know what it can turn into. Fear of that state of depressive mind jumps up to motivate us to keep that disappointment at bay. *We'll have none of that now,* we mentally say. But with practice and a confidence of knowing who is behind the curtain in the director's chair, we can go ahead and feel that disappointment. Now, we know that we can catch ourselves at any point in a downslide. We don't have to tackle the disappointment box and struggle with the lid. We can feel the disappointment fully and then let it go. The negative emotion doesn't linger so much that way. We can go ahead and order our meal and move ourselves into a mindset of a quiet evening alone without the distant funk of a lingering disappointment or the threat of sliding into depression. It's kind of ironic, isn't it? Taking the position of outside looking in removes us, in a way, from the immediate experience and moves us into Alignment with the Soul. Catching ourselves has the effect of pulling us back away from the experience. Yet these are the skills that can give us the freedom to fully feel.

What this means is that we can play with the carefree attitude of a puppy. We can romp in and out of the winds as we wish, knowing that, at anytime, we can easily maneuver out of them. With some practice, we can gain the confidence and the frivolity of our power. Go ahead. Glide into the heady jolt of lusty ecstasy. With an ability to step out and catch yourself whenever you want, there's no need to be anxious about doing something too irrational, dangerous or stupid. You'll catch yourself long before you get to that point, so now you are freer to sink fully into the experience. And when you're sitting at that the opera that your date dragged you to, wondering what the hell they're singing about and wishing you had paid more attention in French class, you can choose to spin off on some trip in your mind. Go ahead, find yourself an entertaining fantasy. It's your choice to float away on that wind of thought, because, now you know that you can come back again whenever you want. When we're not panting from the effort of combating the winds, they can be so much more fun to play in. Being aware of where we are in relation to our thoughts and emotions gives us freedom, choice and spontaneity. Now, who's gonna turn that down?

Being Aware of Events

Being aware of events means that we are paying attention to what is happening around us so that we can fully experience these chunks of our lives and so that we can grow and evolve from messages that hover in front of us, so that we can Align ourselves to the Sacred within us. The reasons are probably becoming like a mantra by now. (I hope so.) Paying attention to what is happening around us might sound a bit foolish. We're not, after all, sleepwalking through our lives. We know what's going on. Well, most of the time. At least when we're not caught in some wind. Still, despite the awareness of the winds, it might seem as silly to consider being aware of events as it seemed when we thought about awareness of our bodies. You know what? In a way, it is the same thing. The same thing? Being aware of our bodies and being aware of events around us is the same thing? *Now*, you might be thinking, *the ideas are getting strange here*. But think about this for a minute. If we are paying attention to what our senses are taking in, then we are necessarily paying vivid attention to the events around us. And we get to experience these events through five or six different instruments, the instruments of our senses. If we are paying attention to the *details* of what we are seeing, then we are simultaneously aware of *what* we're seeing. If you are looking at the creamy color of a soft protrusion from a tree, then you are simultaneously aware that you are looking at a dogwood petal. When we're paying attention with our senses, we already have an appreciation for the fullness of the experience of the events. That is, we have already immersed ourselves in the events of our lives through the instruments of our senses. The nourishing aspect of this way is taken care of. Paying attention with our senses simultaneously makes us completely present and aware of the events around us. That was difficult to say.

But, being aware of events through the instruments of our senses does not necessarily mean that we are aware of the *messages* for our growth and evolution that those events hold. We may not be aware of how these events point to learning about how we can better Align ourselves to Soul. We may be absolutely paying attention to the details of our experience, be completely immersed in the power of the Sacredness of the present and still be oblivious to the messages that are silently screaming for attention. And, if we want to improve in our flying ability, if we want to evolve, then we'd better be listening and watching for these. After all, the events of our lives will highlight messages about our perceptions, our reactionary triggers, our themes. Just like the thoughts and emotions. They hold monumental potential for growth. So, too, the events of our lives hold that same potential. Here we are again. Meaning and growth are everywhere. We want to be able to get the messages inherent in our lives so that we can actively pursue our evolution to the point where we are always acting from Soul, to the point where we are completely restored.

At least for the events of our lives that don't involve other people, like walking in the woods or the local mall by ourselves, getting the messages for growth can be relatively easy. So long as we're paying…well, you know. But even to get these more straightforward messages, we must be paying attention with the *anticipation*, even the expectation that the messages will indeed be there. This goes back to the basic flying position or perception of knowing and anticipating the messages. When we hold this position, allowing the perception to shadow what we take in with our senses, then we can easily get those messages that may, at first, appear to be subtly hanging around the events of our lives. With attention and anticipation, the messages no longer seem subtle. They seem suddenly louder, more obvious.

For over a month now, you've been toying with the idea of making some major changes in the place where you work. The changes that keep popping up in your mind in the form of radical ideas, though, just seem too risky to try. Yet you're sure that the changes will make an enormous difference, a positive difference. Still, you might lose your job. You've been going back and forth, miserably stuck in that waffling place. Now, you're walking through the mall toward the food court where you will have lunch. While you're strolling along, you find yourself trying to weigh it all out again, mulling and attempting a new logical approach. Frustrated, you wish you could simply decide. You round a corner and notice a new exercise store, so you wander toward it. They probably have those thick warm socks you like so much. As you get closer, you look up to see a sign swaying slightly from the air of the vent above it. Boldly and silently, the sign shrieks, "Make the Commitment." You know that the sign is probably referring to getting started with an exercise program, but you also entertain the idea that it might mean something about that decision that you can't seem to make. *Hum...well maybe,* you think.

Later, during lunch, you are half-aware of the TV playing above your head in the corner. While you're wishing that restaurants didn't have TVs in them, you glance up to see some guy on a talk show. He is talking about his girlfriend. He has asked her to move in with him, but she hasn't made up her mind.

You're only half listening when you hear the guy on TV say, "She keeps wanting to talk about it, process it out, think about it logically. On and on and on. Sometimes I just want to yell, 'Will you please just make the commitment?'"

Upon hearing the same words that were on the sign, your listening mind slides to a halt. *Okay,* you think, *once might be construed as a Rorschach projection and twice might be considered simply a coincidence, but it's enough for me.* Message received. You decide to commit to the changes at work. Then your guide your mind back to the lunch you are having.

With this example, you might be tempted, particularly if you're more logically minded, to wonder about whether the message was actually there, and whether someone should base such a large decision on a coincidental event. If you do all that wondering, though, you're likely to miss the point. The point is that attention and anticipation are often enough to discern the messages that settle into those events that do not involve other people.

But we don't live in a vacuum. We don't live a solitary existence. Well, not most of the time. Most of the time, we're surrounded by other people. Which is a good thing. Because, it is through the interactions with others that we can often learn the most about ourselves. Interactions are some of the most fertile, rich events of our lives. And they run deep with the potential for growth and evolution. Indeed, interactions can contain comprehensive reflections of ourselves, reflections that will show us when we are Aligned with our Souls and when we are not.

You'll know exactly where the end of that value of tolerance for other people's beliefs is, when you come face to face with a KKK member. He has decided to take this opportunity to enlighten you about your "liberal" racial views. Suddenly, when confronted with the epitome of racial intolerance, you find yourself quietly slipping into intolerance yourself, only now you're intolerant of intolerance.

"Whew," you sigh as confusion seeps forward, "I've got some thinking to do."

Without the interaction, though, you might never have extended your thinking about your belief. The interaction provided the fertility for growth. Then you can wonder, *Okay, what would the Soul say about this?*

And you will certainly and clearly become aware of where the end of your patience is, when you have children. They'll show you, through the interactions. And, while you're listening to yourself talk to a co-worker about how best to approach that business deal, you might hear your own perception of suspicion. You always assume that the other guy is not trustworthy. You never noticed that before, probably wouldn't have picked it up either, if it weren't for you paying attention to the opinion you offered during that interaction with the co-worker. Interactions hold the potential for massive growth and evolution.

The problem is that interactions are messy. There are, after all, other folks involved. And those other folks are full of their own thoughts, emotions, perceptions, reactions, and themes. So when we come together and start interacting, well, things get sticky. The other person is loaded with past experiences, perceptions and filters, biases and desires, intentions and blind spots. And we've got all that too. This can make the interaction and our potential for learning from it, a whole jumbled, gooey, confusing mess.

"Well," we begin, consternation screwing up our faces, "where exactly does my stuff end and the other guy's begin? I mean, well, did the interaction happen that way because of who I am or because of who he is or… was it, maybe because of who we are together?"

Good questions, even if they are stumbling.

Your friend is a computer expert. He lives and breathes computers most all day long. So when you run into him in the parking lot of your office building, you naturally bring up the fact that you've been having some trouble lately with your computer. You suspect that it is a computer virus and tell him so. When he hears the word virus, he looks briefly toward the sky and a smile begins to tweak his lips. Was that an eye roll? Is that smugness creeping over his face? The irritation box starts to rumble on the floor of your subconscious. When he tosses out a comment about how the problem is more likely due to how you are operating the program, you notice that the irritation box has its lid completely off and has bumped into the anger box, which is starting to rumble. As he continues in his casual explanation of the problem with your computer, you cannot even focus on his words because your mind is filled with thoughts. *He thinks I'm paranoid about viruses. That I'm making the problem bigger than it actually is. He doesn't think I know what I'm talking about.* The thoughts continue their buzz as the guy continues his explanation. You're looking toward your car, escape the only agenda now.

Here are two people coming to this interaction full of their own themes, reactions, and perceptions. And we return to our questions. How do we know where one person's "stuff" stops and the other begins? What is ours and what is theirs? The woman in the example makes an interpretation of the computer expert's behavior. She decides that he is being smug and has a know-it-all type of attitude. Maybe. Maybe the computer expert does indeed need to show off his vast knowledge of computers and looks down on others who know less. He might need to show off in this area because he feels so inept in other areas of his life. Like the social area. If this is the case, then the interaction reflects much of the "stuff" of the expert. But perhaps she completely misinterpreted the expert's behavior. His look toward the sky could have been contemplation instead of an eye roll and the smile could be gentleness instead of smugness. If this is the case, then, what we have is an interaction in which the expert is relatively clear and she is left holding the bag of "stuff." In other words, the interaction would be reflecting nothing at all about the computer expert and everything about her. Maybe *she's* insecure when it comes to the computer. Or maybe she is sensitive to criticism and thus tends to perceive criticism where there is none. Whatever the form the biases, perceptions, triggers, and themes take, (a.k.a. "stuff"), it is just not often clear whose is whose. Interactions can be messy that way.

What we need within the fertile world of interactions, then, is clarity. We need to be able to sort out the mess, see with crystal sight what "stuff" is ours and what is theirs. And, not only do we need to be able to separate out whose is whose, we also will need a purer vision of our "stuff." It all goes back to the idea of evolution. We need clarity in order to understand and learn about ourselves and our living. Once we have a clearer understanding, then we can choose whether we will continue with our same perceptions, triggers, reactions and themes or whether we will change. We learn when we are Aligning ourselves with our Souls and when we are Aligning ourselves with some pseudo-director. It begins with attention, which expands into clarity, which, in turn, leads to understanding and learning, then a choice about change. There. We have jumped from the small picture aspects of this way back to the big picture aspects. It always helps to step back and see it from another perspective.

Gaining Clarity by Shifting Positions of Observation

As a matter of fact, seeing from another perspective is exactly how we can gain some clarity about the events of our lives, particularly those messy interactions. We can begin to sort out interactions, begin to purify our view by shifting positions of observation. Seeing an event and/or an interaction from several different positions widens our view, expands our attention and can give us some clarity. And shifting positions of observation will mean that we are at least not Aligning ourselves with some pseudo-director and may even mean that we are beginning to Align ourselves with the Soul. Indeed, the Soul is the great observer. To shift out of our usual position and adopt a more objective position means that we are coming closer to that Alignment. Becoming objective means that we are beginning to see from Soul.

To think about shifting positions of observation, imagine looking at a cloud. You could position yourself directly above a thunderhead cloud and what you would see is light puffs of cottony softness. But you wouldn't have any sense of the depth of this cloud. To understand just how deep it goes, you would have to fly to a position beside it, where you could see the top and the bottom at the same time. From that position, you would still be able to see its puffy white top, and you could also see its heavy gray bottom. But even from this position, you wouldn't have much of an idea of its power. To understand its power, you would need to move your position to below the thunderhead. Here, you would be blown by the wind and pelted with the drops that seemed to be thrown from a vast darkness that hangs overhead.

The cloud never changed. Only our position did. Yet after flexibly flying all around the cloud, after taking it in from several points of view, we have a clearer understanding of the dimensions of this cloud. We know about its softness, its depth, its power. We are not limited to one point of view. Thus, in our flexibility, the clarity of our understanding grows as dimensions are added to our perspective. By shifting our positions of observation, we have enhanced the field of our attention, expanded it, so that we can see all the dimensions of, in this case, the cloud.

We may not be that concerned about understanding and gaining multi-dimensional views of clouds, (although they *are* uniquely beautiful.) But we are interested in gaining more clarity and understanding about the events in our lives so that we can evolve and eventually become Aligned with our Souls. And if we can manage to perceive the events, particularly those messy interactions from several points of view, then we are likely to get some of that clarity and progress in our evolution. We already know about a couple of points of view. There's the one that we grew up with, the position of inside looking out.

"I'm in here, looking out at all of you and those things out there."

This is the old familiar assumed position that we happily plopped ourselves into as babies. And we already know about another position that we can shift to. The position of outside looking in. We did this when we were catching our thoughts and emotions. We know about these two positions already.

But, as you might have guessed, there's more. We still haven't finished flying all around that cloud yet. For now, we can also attempt to position ourselves to view the entire situation. This is when we pull back and view the entire event as if we are some objective observer. That's one position. And we can fly around to another position as well. We can view those messy interactions from the inside—of someone else. Here, we step into the perspective of the other person and attempt to see the world through their eyes, through their filters, through their "stuff." Les voila. Now we have a total of three positions that we can take, three different viewpoints to help us gain the clarity that is so desperately needed, particularly with the interactive events of our lives. We're going to step up closer for a more detailed view of these new positions, but there is another skill to consider first, one that must necessarily come before we can do any of this flexible shifting or lovely flying around the events. And that is: Letting go of our old familiar position of inside looking out.

Letting Go of Our Usual Position

Before we can do any shifting at all, we must give up our position. What this means is that we let go of our emotion, of our fueling thoughts, of our opinions about the whole event and willingly take on another position. We don't like doing this. It leaves us feeling unsettled and sort of floating. The ego balks and pouts in its childish way when we even think of giving up our usual position. Fear and insecurity slither forward in our experience. Or worse. After we shift around, we may find out that we were, gosh…wrong. We'd much rather dig ourselves into our positions like a crab who backs into its hole, all the while holding its pinchers in a ready position. Ready for defense and attack, if necessary. Letting go of our position makes us, well, vulnerable and exposed. We have to put those pinchers down and walk forward. We have to step out. We've talked about stepping out before, when we let go of our position and took up the position of outside looking in. But that was different. We were just looking back into ourselves at our own thoughts and emotions. We always had the assurance that it was only us and, at least some of the time, we can trust ourselves. Now, though, there is another person involved, the one that we are interacting with. Add this factor in, and it is so much easier to withdraw into our hole, pinchers extended and ready. There seem to be so many good reasons to hold our position.

The minute we even begin to consider stepping out of our usual position, these reasons, either overtly or covertly bubble up to inhibit that move. This is the time, then, to remind ourselves about why we're doing all of this in the first place. This is the time to underscore the value of evolution. The idea is to learn about ourselves, to focus on flying so that we can allow our Souls to Soar into our living. We can remember that we are moving toward a complete Alignment with our Souls, toward restoration.

But, maybe these ivory tower values seem too pristine at the moment that you are considering the safety of that backing-up-toward-the-hole maneuver. It can be difficult when you're in the middle of some energy-sucking event to stretch your neck up and lay claim to the values. As you glance back toward that safe crab hole, you think about how awfully good it looks back there. Familiar, safe, no risks involved. Thinking of future growth might not be enough to make you leave the safety of that hole. You may need something less hazy, something a bit more concrete. Then, it is time to remind ourselves of the past successes and the experience of the freedom of growth. Even remembering small freedoms can serve to inoculate us somewhat from the evasive tendencies of the crab in us. Like when you really *weren't* bothered by the verbal battle that your two children were having over the toy, the same verbal battle that occurs every single time over any toy that both happen to want. In fact, not only were you not bothered by it, but you actually smiled and glided quickly over to coach them through a solution. There was no struggle against the old thoughts that used to come up, thoughts like, *Oh, here we go again,* and *How many times are they going to have this argument?* There was no struggle because the old thoughts *weren't even there.* They had been replaced with, *Looks like they need some more practice,* and *Wow, I'm not even bothered by this.* Gosh, were you energized after you realized the freedom. We can remember these moments of freedom when we hesitate to let go of our position. They will energize us, inoculate us, and infuse us with courage.

The skills of shifting our positions of observation, moving around the events of our lives as we did with the cloud, will give us clarity about our "stuff" and will help us to figure out where ours is and where the other person's is. But the shifting is not the difficult part of the process. The most trying aspect is the stepping out of our position, the letting go of our emotions, our thoughts and opinions about the whole event. If we can pull ourselves away from the crab-like reasons that tug at our psyches, then shifting to another position will be as easy as flying around that cloud in our minds.

You and your best friend have worked at the same company for five years now. Though you work in different departments, you talk quite frequently over lunch about the dynamics and progress in your jobs, as well as the other aspects of your lives. So you were not surprised when she started talking about her job over lunch. She was excited. You could tell. She could hardly stop fidgeting in her chair. The fidgeting stopped, though, when she announced that she had received a promotion. As she began to explain all about how it had happened, her enthusiasm was contagious and soon, the two of you were buzzing off each other like schoolgirls. She would be getting a new office, a real office. For the first time. Together, after lunch, you went to see the empty room. The furniture would be delivered on Friday so that she could move in on Monday. As you left her to return to your desk, you were full of happiness for your friend. You wanted to think of something that you could do for her, some sort of celebration. Then you had an idea. You could buy a few decorative items to surprise her with on Monday. Plants, perhaps or pictures. If you could get the key, then you could set it up over the weekend. It would be perfect. Then maybe a cake with some sparkling cider in champagne glasses. Would balloons be too much? You could get a few, then, if it seemed overdone, you could just pop them. Actually, that might be fun. Wow, this is gonna be great.

When the furniture is delivered on Friday, you and your friend spend your lunch hour trying out different arrangements. You revel in the shared excitement and the secret excitement that you will be decorating over the weekend. Your boss got the key for you, no problem. On Saturday, you practically skip through the stores, happily mulling over different types of plants. You found the perfect peace lily for that empty corner of the office and for the desk, you purchase some ivy. A brass planter would look lovely, too, against the wood of the desk, so you buy that. Pictures are next. They have to already be framed because you don't have much time. On Sunday, as you decorate the office, you can imagine the face of your friend as she takes it all in. Surprise, joy and warmth will be in that expression tomorrow. You just know it.

Monday comes. You go to work early so that you can meet your friend at her new office. You catch her in the parking lot. Great! Just what you wanted. Like a bouncing child, you lead her in, making her close her eyes. She gives you the key to open the door to her office, but you don't need it. You've already opened the door.

"Surprise!" you yell, then you wait. She opens her eyes and her jaw drops open.

"But how did you...," she starts to say, then glances down at your hand, the hand that is holding the key.

She looks from your key to hers and back again. You quickly explain how you got it. But she doesn't seem to be listening. She just seems to be stunned as she moves her vision from one item to another, soaking it all in. You wait quietly now and watch her face. Any moment now, you are going to see that expression. As soon as the surprise of it all starts to fade, the joy and warmth will come up. Any second now. Soon. She's still scanning and her face is blank.

"Oh...wow...you've...you've decorated my office." Her voice trails off as she wanders over to touch the ivy sitting on the desk.

Was that hesitation, you heard? Disapproval? Disappointment? *Nah, no way*, you think. *She's probably blown away by all of this, that's all.* You think she might be ready for some details now, so you start to tell her about how you found the various items. But she is not looking at you. With a glazed expression, she is still stroking the ivy in slow absent movements. When you finish your rapid explanations, you wait another minute.

The silence seems loud, so you fill in and finally ask her, "So what do you think?"

"It's...nice." Now it's your turn to be stunned and quiet.

She quietly adds that she would like some time alone to unpack her supplies, so you leave with an awkward, "Well, then, um…see you later."

Before you even make it back to your department, you're fuming. The anger and disappointment have followed you all the way, fueled by the dancing thoughts of injustice. When you reach your desk and sit down, you catch yourself. The pause allows you to consider that maybe you don't have a clear understanding. Maybe there is more to all of this. But before you can even contemplate shifting to another position of observation, your thoughts jump back up again. An internal conversation begins.

I worked my butt off all weekend long to find the plants and pictures that would fit in perfectly. I had to scheme and plan to get the key, to make the delivery on time. I had to expend so much energy to think it all through. All that work, all that effort, all that money and the only thing she can say is, "it's nice"? How could she be so ungrateful? She didn't even say 'thank you.' No thanks at all.

No, she didn't react like I expected. I need to stop and step away from this. Think of it from another angle. There's probably some learning to do here.

Learning to do? Not on my part, there isn't. She's the one that needs to do some learning. She needs to learn how to be polite. She could've at least acted as if she was excited. Out of a sense of politeness. Well, she should've at least said, 'thanks.' What's the matter with her anyway?

This is not helping. I need to step away and get some clarity. Condemnations are only fueling. It's time to let go.

Plowing through your morning work has the effect of distancing yourself from the whole event, so you reflect a bit. Lunchtime, though, rekindles the feelings because you don't see your friend anywhere. She is probably avoiding you. *If she's having a problem about all of this, she could at least talk to me about it. I don't see what the problem is anyway. I did something nice for her.*

Several days go by like this, with your friend avoiding you and the thoughts and emotions rekindling and building. You start to think that maybe you have lost a friend over this whole silly situation. This idea motivates you to find some time to reflect. You review the scene and see it now without the taint of your own feelings and thoughts. Instead you see it from an observer's point of view, from the situational position. There you are, obviously excited, waiting for a reaction from your friend, expectations about that reaction stuffed into your back pocket. She is there, looking back and forth between the key in your hand and the one in hers. *Why would that be so disturbing?* you wonder. She is quiet and reserved, holding in her reaction. Even from this observer's position, there are no other possible interpretations of her behavior. She didn't like it. She was sullen. You felt the rejection and disapproval. *But why didn't she like it?*

Naturally, you decide to shift to her perspective, to the position of inside—of someone else. This will be telling, you are sure. You imagine getting a promotion and how proud you would be. The thoughts of a real office for the first time would be so exciting, so delicious. You love to share all those feelings with your best friend. You're looking forward to Monday when you move in. Then your best friend says she has a surprise and walks you to her office. You're squirming with anticipation. When you open your eyes, you discover that she has a key to your office. Your best friend has a key to your brand new office. How did she do that? What right did she have? You imagine looking around the office which is completely decorated. You had been looking forward to making those purchases yourself. She has picked out everything for you. When did she do it? How dare she assume that it would be okay? Whose office is this anyway?

You stop yourself from this mental shifting of positions. There's no need to go on. Now you know. You got so caught up in the excitement that you missed the main point. It's her first real office. *Hers.* Not yours *and* hers. From her point of view, you have invaded her space. And by decorating it without consulting her, you have taken away the very thing that made the office such a treasure. You took away her independence, her newfound power to make her own decisions about her own office. Now you know. But you had to let go of your position to gain this clarity and understanding. You plan to talk to her about all of this later, check it out with her, apologize and mend the situation. For yourself, you plan to be particularly careful when it comes to those positive blasts. You have discovered that you can easily get swept away. Also, you notice that you managed to make this situation about you, when it wasn't. Maybe this points to a basic perception, a way of approaching situations. You think that maybe you should keep an eye out for this. See if you filter most of your experience through these glasses. Hum…there was some learning to do after all.

The example points to how difficult it can be to let go of that old familiar position of inside looking out. She spent several days with the negative emotions and thoughts before she could finally do it. It's hard to let go, especially with all that internal fuel rekindling the position every couple of hours. Plus she was emotionally, physically and financially invested in that position. She *had* spent time, energy and money on the decorations. And she was invested emotionally through her excitement and expectation about how her friend would react. The refueling coupled with the investment made it particularly difficult to let go of her position. It was only the thought that she might lose her friend that motivated her enough to let go. Then the shifts came fairly easily.

With this example, you get a taste of the other two positions: the situational view and the inside — of someone else view. We'll do more with these in a minute, but first, I want to point out something else. Notice that, at the end, she has discovered that she is susceptible to being carried away by positive blasts of emotions. The experience has left her wary and watchful about this. She also observes a potential underlying perception, a method of viewing the world that might be typical for her. The event held within it seeds for growth and evolution related to reactions and perceptions, in this case. Once she was able to let go of her old position, the shifts had the effect of expanding her attention and clarifying these areas. She was able to step our of her usual position and see the situation from a more objective point of view. She was seeing from Soul.

One more thing. She is now ready to approach her friend with an understanding, an understanding that comes from her Soul. And when love steps into a situation, resolution and growth are not far behind.

Seeing From the Situational View

By now, you already have a sense about what it means to view events, to attempt to gain some clarity about those messy interactions, from the situational position. We step out of our position and attempt to see the whole event as if we were some objective observer perched above the entire thing. Now let's not quibble about whether we can ever be truly objective or not. It's a no-brainer. We can't. But in taking the situational view, we are attempting to gain some objectivity, to gain the clarity that would result from that. It is the clarity that comes from perceiving from Soul. This semi-objectivity allows us to begin to figure out what is happening in the event. Interactions are messy and we sometimes walk away with a hazy feeling, not even certain what happened. Taking the situational position can be a starting point in figuring out the event. Leaving our biases, feelings and thoughts from our ordinary position behind, we take on a more objective perch.

From our semi-objective perch, then, we could see aspects of the situation that we might otherwise miss. The Soul can see so much more than we can. Like whether or not there are any echoes hanging around from the events that occurred just before this one. You remember the echoes, those lingering feelings that can be carried into the next situation like a strong aftertaste. Perceiving a current event through the filters of that aftertaste is necessarily going to affect our perception. If you decide to eat a spoonful of mint ice cream right before you swivel in your chair to pop a bite of sushi saturated with soy sauce, then the flavor of the sushi is going to be affected. Not a particularly good combination. If someone gives you a mouth-watering compliment, you are very likely to all but wisp into the next interaction, and in tow will be the lingering mellow radiance that was prompted by that compliment. And, while we don't mind allowing positivity to free float from one event to another, we still have the problem of being the victim of these reverberating feelings. Positive or negative. Viewing an event from our situational perch will give us the power of making the choice between allowing the lingering to continue or not. This skill particularly comes in handy when we want to rid ourselves of some of the negative residual feelings.

You're getting dressed to leave to visit a friend and your spouse picks that moment to bring up a heavy subject, one that typically leaves you both reeling: money. Within five minutes, you're dressed and out the door, but predictably you are reeling and resentful. You've been looking forward to seeing your friend, since you haven't seen him in over six months. *Why now?* you wonder. Why did your spouse pick that particular moment to bring all this up? The feelings seem to continue, fueled by the usual thoughts, but then you realize what is happening. You step back and see from the situational view. There's the interaction between you and your spouse. That is one event. And there is the upcoming event of going out with your friend. With the feelings holding on, you understand that they could echo into the next situation. You make the decision, though, that you will let them go for now. At the same time, you acknowledge that the subject, while tender and sore, needs to be addressed. With the promise to yourself to do this, you are able to let go of the feelings. Now you are clear and can be with your friend. Shifting to the situational position allows us to see that the echoes are happening. It allows us to begin to Align with our Souls, then we are free to make the choice about whether or not we will allow them to sink into the next event.

Our situational perch will do something else for us. From there we can start to sort out facts from interpretations. In any event, there are the facts of what actually occurred and how we interpreted them, or sometimes, misinterpreted them, as the case may be. But here is where the shifting comes in handy. Because, if we can sort out fact from fiction, then there will not be so many misinterpretations to stumble over. There will not be so many times that we'll end up slinking away from some snowball that we created in our minds. In the chapter about the winds, you met up with a woman who couldn't get away from her desk long enough to get her usual morning cup of tea. Some gentleman in the department delivered the tea to her desk. Then it started. The interpretations began bouncing around her cranium rather quickly and within ten minutes, she was in a full-blown relationship with the guy. The snowball effect. Let's say that this is exactly what happens, that is, she goes ahead with her lengthy fantasy. But before she actually begins to act on it, she catches herself. She recognizes the whirlwinds of the fantasy and the waves of lusty emotion that lap up. But she wants to be clear about where the facts are and where the fiction starts. So she moves to the situational position. The facts are clear. The guy brought her tea. It is something that he's never done before. This is true, but that doesn't open the door enough to warrant a full-blown fantasy. Now the event is clearer. The woman can decide what to do. She has already begun to think about this guy in a romantic way. From this more objective position, does she want to pursue this? If she does decide to pursue this guy now, it would be based on her new way of thinking about him and not on some fantasy spurred by some sparse facts.

But there is still more that the situational view can do for us. We're still perched above the situation, observing in a relatively objective manner, all that is occurring. And from here, it is certainly easier to see the underlying messages that dance under and through interactions. In many interactions between folks, there seem to be layers of conversation. There's the surface layer. This is what is actually being said. And there can be other layers as well, the subtext or the underlying message. As a caveat, clear communication has only one layer, since the underlying message and the one that is actually communicated are the same. We can aspire to this. On the other end of the continuum are interactions that are intentionally multi-layered to obscure and confuse. Business interactions are notorious for this. No aspirations here please. We can be sure that we have entered the confusion of layered interactions when we walk away feeling fuzzy brained. What just happened, we ask ourselves? From our situational perch, we can begin to sort it out.

You notice that it is raining, so you grab two umbrellas as you are leaving the house for school. As you let your daughter out at the bus stop, you snatch up the first piece of umbrella you can feel because the bus has just pulled up. Your oldest bounds up the steps of the bus umbrella in hand. She never opened it. *Well,* you think, *maybe she will use it when she gets off the bus at school.* As you get back into the car to take your son to kindergarten, he bluntly states that you gave her the wrong umbrella. His was the pink one, hers the green one. You check and the green one is indeed the umbrella that is left. For a few minutes of the drive, you point out how both umbrellas will serve their purpose.

"The green one will keep you just as dry as the pink one," you say.

He says he wants the pink one and that he wants you to stop the bus to get it. Astonished by this request over the color of an umbrella, you abruptly tell him that you will not stop a bus to get an umbrella. The finality of this statement pushes him over the edge and he starts to cry. You start thinking about acceptance and how he might be less miserable if he could learn this, so you tell him that he can choose to cry or he can accept that he will be using the green umbrella today.

After several seconds, he stops crying and you think that maybe what you said hit home. His face in the mirror tells you that he is still miserable about this as he looks passively out the window.

Still driving, you try to balance yourself so that you can reflect. You take a deep breath and try to watch your anger. It fluctuates in intensity as you bounce between becoming immersed in it and observing it. Your thoughts push you toward immersion. *Like it really matters. Like I'm really going to stop a bus to get...* Then you catch your thoughts and try to watch them too. After a few minutes, you have released the emotion and accompanying thoughts enough to begin to reflect. What were the ideas being conveyed beneath the surface of the exchange? If you translated the conversation into underlying messages, what would it look like? He tells you that the color of the umbrella was important to him. Your message to him is that he is wrong, that the function of the umbrella is important, not the color. To think that the color is important is ridiculous. You bet that he felt hurt in hearing this silent insult. In talking about which umbrella is his, it occurs to you that he might also be saying that he values his sense of ownership. You can understand this, since you have always emphasized sharing and he might be reacting against this emphasis. Maybe he needs some things that are just his own. Then he suggests stopping the bus to get the umbrella. He is attempting to think of a solution. Your message to him was that his solution is ridiculous. Again another silent insult, a criticism that probably cut into him. You bet he felt that one too. *How often do I silently criticize?* You'll think more on that potential trend later. *What about now?* You're about ten minutes away from the school and you want some resolution before he goes in. You don't want him to carry the negative energy or insults of this exchange with him. *What else?* You prod yourself. You review the interaction again. You said something about how he needed to accept the situation. Now you're amazed at yourself. You have managed to spin a positive value into a negative message. Without going down the judgmental thought stream too far, you pinpoint the underlying idea here. It's something like "it's just too bad," and "it's stupid to cry about it when you can't do anything about it." You were essentially telling him that his crying was wrong. *Wow,* you think, *no wonder he was crying.*

The mom in this example probably would think it was just plain mean to overtly tell her child that he was ridiculous, that his ideas were stupid, that his opinion doesn't count. It was unacceptable to her to allow herself to say all of this directly, so she did it indirectly. Her words made up the surface layer and she backed up these jabbing words with the crafty tools of logic and values. Our minds are amazingly agile, aren't they? The real messages, though, the potent ones that the child reacted to, were buried underneath the surface of the interaction. They can indeed be potent, these dancing, subverted messages. That's exactly why we need to be able to know what they are.

To do this, Mom had to first let go of her own position though, didn't she? This necessarily had to occur before she could jump into the situational view. And letting go wasn't easy. We can see the struggle. When she was able to let go, though, she was able to pick out the underlying messages. She has moved out of the winds by taking the situational view. She has taken a more objective view, stepped out of the situation. She is seeing from Soul. The effect is a clearing that opens the way for the Soul to act. I don't like scenarios without some resolution, so let's go back to this example and see what she does. They are still driving. Both are still in their own mental worlds.

With a clearer understanding of the underlying messages in the situation and, having let go of your anger, you claim the intention of resolving, and of learning. You decide to try to tell him of your reflections about all of this in a way that he can understand. You say that if the color of the umbrella is important to him, then the color is important and you didn't mean to say that it was silly or ridiculous. You talk about respecting ownership and what he could do next time to ensure that he got his umbrella. You say that crying to express how you feel is okay. You explain that you simply didn't want him to dwell on it, because doing that would make him unhappy and you don't like it when he feels bad. Saying all of this has the effect of undoing some of those silent insults, since you are essentially acknowledging the worthiness of his feelings and thoughts. When you arrive at school, he takes the green umbrella, not with a sense of beaten sacrifice, not begrudgingly, but with a sense of confidence. There are no words said as he smiles at you. On the drive home, you begin to consider the trend of silent insults and criticisms. (It's obvious who's in charge now, isn't it?)

There. Resolution. Which leads gently into the next point. Up to now, there has been a quiet implication that shifting to the situational position was something that we do *after* an event has occurred. Certainly, we can do this and we will still gain clarity and understanding from the shift. Even though the event is finished and we have moved on, there is clarity and understanding which can lead to growth and evolution. This is exactly what happened in the example with the co-worker who decorated the new office of her friend. She did her reflecting long after the event or interaction had ended. And we saw how much learning occurred. But notice in this example with the mother and child just how powerful it is to be able to see from the situational view *while* the interaction is going on. If we can manage to let go of our position while the interaction is still occurring and see from the situational point of view at that moment, then we can acknowledge the echoes, check out the interpretations that we made and bring to the surface the underlying messages. And, with all this information, we will certainly be able to see whose "stuff" is whose. *And*, given all of *that*, we are much more likely to get to the thing that started this paragraph. Resolution.

Now, admittedly, that was all said a bit quickly, so let's slow it down. Being able to shift to a situational point of view *during* the interaction, means that we can begin to our growth right then and there. We can begin, right then and there, to Align ourselves with our Souls and then subsequently to act from that Sacred place. The mom in the above example shows us how powerful it can be to get clarity about the underlying messages straight away. Taking the situational position *during* an exchange can also be powerful with echoing. You arrive home from work in a foul mood because of the last nasty interaction of the day. When your spouse asks if you had time to drop off that jacket at the cleaners, you snap viciously back. You catch yourself and step back, then you realize that there was a negative echo. It all happens in a few seconds. Now you are free to tell your spouse why you were so short and apologize, if that's what you want to do. This has the effect of clearing the air immediately and not allowing that echo to continue right on through the evening. Resolution can be immediate like this.

And with those interpretations, a shift to a situational position will allow us to check them out straight away as well. The woman who got that tea delivery could, when she found a free minute, go up to the guy and ask about the meaning behind his kind gesture.

Sure, she's not going to say, "Um, by the way, did that tea delivery mean that you are interested in me romantically?"

Depending on her style, of course, she's probably not going to blast him with a rocket. But she could initiate a casual conversation that could give them both the opportunity to express a more overt interest in each other. In matters of the heart, we often prefer a more subtle approach, although it is not always the best way. Still, in whatever form we choose to do it, seeing the event from a situational perch means that we can check out those interpretations and thereby gain a more immediate clarity.

Back to the umbrella example and the mother who sends several underlying messages to the child. By shifting to the situational position, Mom certainly was able to pick up these messages and repair and resolve the event *right then*. Once she was able to move out of the winds, her Soul was there to guide her and she acted from there. And she saw a potential theme, a possible pattern of covertly criticizing her children. Certainly, this will need further exploration, as she suggested at the end of the example. So, what the shift did for her was to allow her to have a clearer understanding about whose "stuff" was whose. From the semi-objective perch of seeing the situation as a whole, the "stuff" starts to filter out. The silt tends to settle towards it rightful owners and we can therefore, begin to see where it belongs more clearly. Mom now has the chance to extend her learning and explore this potential theme. As for the child's "stuff"? Well, as with many children, power and control are central. This child is trying to assert himself and be in charge of his life. He wants to be taken seriously and to make his own decisions. As he should. With short reflection, then, it becomes clear that the real bag of "stuff" lies with the mom in this case. Now we know whose is whose.

What this means, then, is that we can focus on the work that we need to do, on our own "stuff." For, once we can sort out whose is whose, we'll know what we need to work on. We'll know what gets in the way of allowing Soul to direct our lives. The rest of it, the "stuff" that settles into the other guy's corner; well, we can just leave it there, not get caught up in it, and let the other guy deal with it when he is ready. That smug computer expert who exuded an air of arrogance, who postured and gave out what he probably considered to be precious advice; his need for self-importance and admiration from others has completely to do with him and nothing to do with the woman who listened to that advice. He's not really commenting about her with his smugness. He is commenting about himself. A shift to the situational position will reveal this readily enough. Then, she can simply allow the silt to settle back where it belongs. There's no need to get caught up in it. Shifting to the situational view during or after the interaction means that we have managed to let go of our own position and perch ourselves in a more objective place, a place that is beginning to be Aligned with our Souls. From this higher ground, we can see so much more. Echoes, interpretations, those underlying messages; all seem a bit more evident from our newly found perch. With our enhanced attention and clarity, then, we can choose how we are going to be and what we will learn. We can choose to act from Soul. From this perch also, we get a clearer sense of whose "stuff" belongs to who, which means that we will more certainly know what we need to work on about ourselves. Expanded attention. Clarity and understanding. We learn so much better when we're equipped with these. And we are free, free to act from Soul, which not only leads to understanding. It leads to peace and love.

Seeing From the Inside of Someone Else

Do you remember when you were little and in the middle of some battle over some toy, a miniature boat, maybe? The other guy had it. You got tired of "asking nicely" and snatched the thing from him.

His wailing brought your dad over who probably said something like, "Now, how would you feel if he did that to you?"

If your dad didn't actually wait for a reply, you likely thought something like, *What do I care? I got the boat.* If you actually had to answer, then you had to think. Before you considered it, though, your thoughts went something like, *Geez, I hate it when he asks me these kinds of questions.* Your dad was trying to get you to see the situation from the other guy's point of view. Moving into the position of inside — of someone else, we are doing exactly what Dad would have us do. We attempt to view the event through the filters and biases, opinions and tendencies, through the eyes of someone else. Dad would be pleased. We are finally taking his request seriously. Now we can truly begin to answer the questions. How *would* you feel if he did that to you? What would it be like to be in that situation? To have those personality traits and experience those events?

Now, I know that we have already talked about the necessity of letting go of our own position before attempting to shift into another. We won't dig though all of those points again, *but*, (you knew that "but" was coming, didn't you?), nowhere is it more difficult to let go than when we're attempting to slide into the perception of someone else. Think of how it would be to attempt to perceive from your best friend's point of view. You've got to take into account how he compartmentalizes events, how specific he is in his thinking. You'll necessarily have to leave behind your breezy intuitive approach. That doesn't match the experimental, must-check-all-avenues-before-making-a-decision approach of your friend. If you're going to see through his eyes, you must attempt to adopt these approaches and characteristics. These are, after all, the filters and biases that all events come through for him. When we can truly imagine seeing from the inside — of someone else, we start to realize just how agile and flexible we will need to be. It's gonna be hard.

This type of shift is even more difficult when the interaction has been negative. We saw this with the woman who decorated her friend's office. She was unable to let go of her own position for several days, so entrenched she was with those swirling thoughts and emotions.

And that's with our *friends*. Imagine attempting to see through the eyes of someone who has been antagonistic toward you for the last, say, ten years. Every time the person's face comes up in your mind, it is automatic for those negative thoughts and associations to spring forth. It would be plenty difficult, wouldn't it, to leave those thoughts behind, *really* leave them behind and step into his perspective?

But by far, making this shift is the most difficult with children. At least for some of us. We look at these short versions of humanity with amusement sometimes, sometimes with disdain and disgust, but we rarely seem to be able to imagine what it would be like to perceive from their little heads. Maybe it's because we don't take them seriously. Maybe *that's* because we're always focused on the fact that they're not as developed as we are. But for whatever reason, we have trouble making this shift with our kids. Now you may not have children, but at some point in your life, you are likely to come into contact with them. (I hope so. They are some of the best teachers around.) Okay, I'll get off the soapbox now, and move on to an example.

It is field day at school and the weather person is calling for an unusually hot day for the spring. You're thinking of wearing shorts, although you haven't yet worn shorts this year. You're not sure that you will feel comfortable and you're not so sure that shorts are appropriate for school. Your doubt and self-consciousness leads you to seek the advice of another family member. She tells you that you definitely should wear shorts, that it is supposed to be ninety degrees today. You go to the drawer and slowly pull out the ones that you wore last year and you're wondering if they will be long enough. You pull them up, do the snap and glance down to see how high above the knees they actually go. Before you can make up your own mind, she is already talking about how great they look, how much cooler you will be. The reassurances are not enough and after she leaves the room, you put on the old long pants that you're used to. You're feeling a bit fearful as you walk into the kitchen to get the cereal bowl because you're wondering if she will say anything. Fear is confirmed. The minute she comes in, she looks at the pants and it begins.

"You know, it's gonna be *ninety degrees* today. That's the hottest day we've had this year and you're going to be outside all day long. And you'll be running and sweating. And those pants are dark too. They're just going to absorb the sun and make you even hotter. You can change into the shorts after you eat breakfast."

Now the pressure is really on, but you don't change after breakfast. Instead, you try to hide out in your room so she won't see you until the last minute. That way, there won't be enough time to change. This is what you try to do, but it doesn't work. She finds you and insists that you put on the shorts. You refuse. She gets mad and tells you that you will put on the shorts or you can't have any toys later. You feel so tense and angry. It starts to seep out from the edges. You cry. She tells you to stop crying, that shorts are nothing to cry over. Then she tells you to put them on. Feeling horrible and small, you sob as you put on the shorts. With all the venom that you feel, you throw the pants against the wall and stomp out of the room, slamming the door behind you.

You have probably figured out whose head we were in. Looks different from down there, doesn't it? And aren't you, too, feeling just the slightest bit of venom toward the mom after reading this? She seems unreasonable, controlling and demanding, not to mention disrespectful. She's not someone we would want to be around for long periods of time. But the child in this situation doesn't have a choice, either about being around his mom or about what pants he wears. Without a doubt, the mom in the above situation has good intentions. All she wants is for her child not to be hot. The problem is that she can't step out of that position. She is not seeing from the other person's perspective, in this case, the child. From her limited perspective, she reacts with limited responses. The consequences? Well, the child won't be so hot, but he will feel awkward, dominated, self-conscious and out-of-control. Now let's see what happens when the parent here is able to make the shift and see from the perspective of the child. Since we're going to stay in the mind of the child, these shifts will be implied. But the results of them will be obvious.

It's field day at school and you're thinking of wearing shorts because it's supposed to be really hot. But you haven't worn shorts yet and you're feeling self-conscious, so you ask Mom what she thinks. She says that you should definitely wear shorts because it is going to be ninety degrees. As you put them on, you want to make sure that they are long enough and when you look down to check, she says that they look great and you'll be much cooler. After she leaves, you change back into the long pants. As you're walking into the kitchen, you're afraid of her reaction. She looks at your pants and you think, *Oh, no, here it comes.* Then she squats in front of you and the conversation begins.

"You put the long pants back on."

"Yeah," you say and stare at the grains of wood in the floor.

"You don't really want to wear the shorts today, do you?" She doesn't seem furious.

"Nah." You see a dark spot on the floor and focus on that.

As she takes your hand, she says, "What is it about the shorts that you don't like?"

You look up and say, "Well they're not long enough." Meanwhile, you're thinking that maybe she won't be so mad after all.

"Um…Well, if you wear the long pants, you're going to be hot and if you wear the shorts, you're not going to feel comfortable." She pauses and looks away like she's thinking, then she asks, "What do you suppose is the worst that will happen if you wear the long pants?"

"I'll be hot."

"That's right. So what's more important for you today?"

"I want to wear these pants, Mom."

"Okay."

The child is going to be hot. There is no doubt about it. But he is able to make the decision himself. He is able to make this decision because Mom has stepped out of her position and put herself into his. From the shorter point of view, the heat doesn't matter. He doesn't care how hot he will be. What he cares about is how he will feel about himself. When Mom sees from his perspective, she sees what the issue is. Now she can weigh it out. Will the heat be dangerous if he wears long pants? No. So she lets him make the decision based on what is important to him. He'll be hot, but he'll also be positive and self-confident. Mom is able to let go of her own position, Align herself a little more to her Soul and act from there.

Children and our not-so-close adult friends. We seem to have to most trouble seeing from their points of view. (You might now remember why we had that long example.) But if we can manage to make the shift and see from the inside — of someone else, we will have tapped into a rather vast amount of information. What we will see from this new seat, is ourselves. Gosh, that could be an insightful perspective, if we take into account all the filters and biases of the other person. Imagine trying to see *yourself* from the perspective of that guy who has been antagonistic towards you for ten years. Whoa, you say, let's not go that far. Yes. Let's. Because you are likely to see aspects of yourself that you might not have seen before. That is, you might gain some clarity about your own perceptions, reactionary tendencies and themes when you see yourself through someone else's eyes. Especially someone else who doesn't seem to like you.

And, seeing from the inside — of someone else will not only give us that fresh view of ourselves, but will also give us a rather close up, more intimate view of the other person's perspective. Standing inside their shoes and looking out, we'll be better able to imagine what it's like to live in there. Dad would be so proud. We can answer all his questions from our new position and we won't even have to think too long. From this point of view, we probably will be able to understand why this person holds the opinions he holds, has the perceptions he has, reacts the way that he always seems to react. Now we can know. Now we can understand. Now we can choose how we will act.

With this intimate knowledge and understanding then, the Soul leads us into the lovely arenas of resolution and compassion. Step up one at a time please. Ah, resolution is first. We've had some encounters with him before, when we were shifting to the situational perspective. And resolution will even be more willing to come out of hiding when we shift to the position of inside — of someone else. Doesn't this just make intuitive sense? Most of the time, when we're wrapped up in some disagreement, it's because we can't see the other person's point of view. We adopt our crabby stance and ready our pinchers, all the while we're backing toward our hole and our hold on our opinion. But once we can let go of our position and truly see from the other person's perspective, resolution is only going to be a creative step away. With both viewpoints in mind, we can quickly and often easily use our creativity to find that compromise that seemed so impossible before, for love and creativity adore dancing together.

Now, compassion, it's your turn. This sweet, dear, quiet, old friend is really *powerful*. Compassion can cut through the thickest of rampages and rocketing winds. Better even than the bright nose of that Christmas reindeer, Rudolph. For, compassion not only has the light of the intimate knowledge of the other's perspective behind it, compassion has the warm glow of love pulsing there too. Quite a powerful combination, these can be. Our Christmas shopper who was in line, actually used imagined scenarios to help herself ease out of some hefty emotional blasts, emotional blasts that were powered by a potential theme. These are definitely difficult to dodge. But she imagined some possible reasons why the woman would want to or need to break in line. At this point, she didn't know the woman's situation, so she couldn't really slip into her perspective. But she could imagine some likely reasons, reasons that would tug at the compassion within herself. In other words, she was imagining what this woman's perspective could be. Doing this worked for her. These imaginings helped her pull out of those winds and into the currents of warming love. When the shopper found out later the real reason that the woman needed to be on time, namely, to mail her son a present, she was utterly filled with compassion. It's those histories again. They don't show on the outside. (No, they don't. So let's just assume them, okay?)

You work in the main building of a large office complex. Your building is larger than the rest, which spread out from it like tentacles of an octopus. Although the offices are all connected by the mission of the company, it is rare that you see or interact with the people in the tentacle offices. There are lunch date exceptions, of course. You have gotten to know a few people from the D wing and have rather been enjoying the development of these new relationships. The three guys from D wing are comical, intelligent and can be serious too. They laugh at the jokes you tell, which is something because not everyone does. And, even though your mom tells you that you talk too fast, that you should slow down, these guys don't seem to mind. You've worked at this company for a number of years, made quite a few lateral type moves and therefore know how to do several jobs. In fact, you've had the jobs that two of the three guys now have. So, every once in a while, you like to pass on advice about how they could do the job better. After all, you had it yourself and worked in that department for five years. And they certainly seem receptive to your advice. That woman on the sixth floor — you had her job last year and she almost blew a fuse when you tried to pass on some helpful suggestions. You're not sure what her problem was. These guys, though, they seem more receptive. One of them had been talking just the other day about the gorgeous date that he had last Friday. Well, that happened to be the day that you had a date with the cover girl from Sear's catalogue. She was the swimsuit model. They seemed to relish hearing about your date, so you told them your whole strategy for working up to the Vogue cover.

It's lunchtime and all of you are sitting around a picnic table. A cool breeze of autumn filters through the nearby trees. As the food disappears, conversation picks up. You like to start the conversation. Usually, you're the first one finished with the food anyway. Your mom says that you eat too fast. You tell the new jokes that you heard from the office manager this morning. They'll like these, you think. After a few minutes, you remember that Halloween is coming. You particularly like Halloween jokes. You've got probably twenty of those memorized because you can use them every year. Most of the time, people don't remember the answer, even if they heard the joke last year. So you decide to try a few on the guys.

"Hey, did you hear the one about the ghosts?" You notice that the guys are looking around at each other. They're probably scanning their minds. Nobody says anything, so you go on.

"Why do ghosts go to ball games?" There is a pause. They're silently trying out some clever responses most likely, you think. The silence continues so you pop the punch line.

"So they can boo the referees." You guffaw and look around the table. One of the other guys decides to comment.

"Wow, that was a good one. One of your best. I'll bet that'll make some women laugh."

The other guys start to chuckle a bit. Was that sarcastic? You check out his face to be sure, but you're not sure, even when you stare a second longer. His face seems to be mixed with attempted genuineness and ridicule. You flick a glance at the others for verification. They have mixed expressions too. You're growing uncomfortable. You twitch a little and want to leave. Then one of the guys asks you to tell them again about your date with that cover girl. The guy sitting at the end of the table bursts out laughing at this moment and you whip your head around to stare.

"Sorry, I was just thinking about the ghost joke," he quickly says, but there is ridicule on that face.

Now you're sure of it. Your mind takes on a tunnel focus. There is one agenda — escape. You imitate the barely disguised masks on their faces with one of your own, make your excuses and leave.

The anger and hurt float in and out of awareness for a week. They're hard to get past along with the reviews of all the other conversations with these guys and the realization that subdued rejection and ridicule were constantly there. You mentally whack the side of your brain. Why did you never see it before? Those guys are just like the children in the neighborhood who used to relentlessly tease you when you were five years old. When the emotions start to lose some intensity, you decide to do some thinking. You never have liked rejection, but then, nobody does. Completely natural, you think. There's more to this. To help, you decide to make an observational shift that will require a sustained strength. You decide to try to see yourself through the eyes of one of the guys, one of your co-workers.

From his point of view, you review some of the conversations. You see yourself relying heavily on jokes. Now that you think about it, you do tend to tell several jokes a day. From this guy's point of view, it's stale. And how would it feel to have someone telling you about how to do your job better? You would probably think that you already do your job well enough, that you don't need help and that the advice is just a way of questioning your competence. Perceived through the eyes of the co-worker, then, the advice might sound like the advisor is trying to display strengths and knowledge, to maybe illicit some admiration. Do you really sound like a know-it-all? Are you trying to dredge up some respect and admiration, using your knowledge about company jobs as a tool? And, from the co-workers point of view, the stories about the cover girl sound like you're trying to compete, like you're trying to prove that you are at least as good as they are, maybe even better. Also, maybe the co-worker is astonished that you seem to be missing the minor behaviors of himself and the others that are clearly pointing to ridicule. From his perspective, he may be stunned that you don't get it.

Seeing yourself from the co-worker's perspective gives a new dimension to your understanding and leaves you thinking of a couple of potential themes that will need further exploration. The jokes and the blindness to the hints of ridicule point to a need to fit in, to be part of the group. While belonging is probably a common need, you consider that perhaps you are a bit too desperate. You contemplate another theme related to self-security, maybe self-esteem. If you are frequently trying to build yourself up and receive affirmations from others, then perhaps you are not as secure in yourself as you had previously thought. These two potential themes certainly need some exploration, you decide. To see what other themes might be lurking about, you reenter the co-worker's perspective. You try to see yourself ridiculing someone like you, someone who constantly tells jokes and pathetically tries to prove himself. You see yourself bantering with the other two ridiculers about the disgusting joke teller.

Then, suddenly, it occurs to you: These guys are struggling to belong too. They want to be accepted and admired, too. That's why the little group exists. That's why they play off each other and look to each other for support in their banter. You know now that you are the subject of their ridicule, but you realize too that the ridicule is a sort of pallid attempt at pulling the group together, of belonging. You are the tool that feeds their own theme. It comes as a bracing jolt, though, that your own themes and theirs are not that different. The foulness towards them that you had been feeling before, fades quickly with this realization. With this understanding, the seed of compassion is planted. Still, you're not exactly ready to think of these guys with radiant tenderness. You are, after all, stinging from the ridicule and the embarrassment and the themes. But the seed has been planted. Maybe they aren't just mean bullies. Maybe they're not just the grown up versions of the five-year-olds in your childhood. Maybe they are just as desperate as you seem to be. With these last thoughts, you turn to the plan and work of clearing.

This is a full example. It is full of shifts and perceptions, histories and feelings. It is full of juicy points. To start, our main guy, the joke teller, probably has a long history of this type of behavior. His themes have been calling the shots for a long time. Since he was a child. And, most likely, he's been in similar situations, where he is telling jokes and someone starts to covertly ridicule him. Think about how many times in his life this same event must have happened. Hundreds? Yet, this time, he could clearly see the ridicule. This time, he got it. Here is an example of readiness. The guy was ready to see the ridicule. He was ready to face it and look behind it. Before, he probably would have remained blind and thus protected. He wrote off the woman who didn't listen well to his advice about how to do her job. Presumably, he's done this kind of writing off before, like when the joke telling didn't go over well. Here, though, he sees the ridicule clearly.

Actually, he first suspects the ridicule, then he opens himself up and shifts to a situational position. From there, he can clearly see it. Of course, the ridicule prompts an emotional shrinking, embarrassment, anger, probably the same emotions that he felt as a five-year-old. With himself open, vulnerable and in pain, he runs like hell. We would too. Between the shift and his readiness to face all of this, he bumps directly into some themes.

Instead of continuing to run, though, he decides to further his understanding and clarity, (which is another testament to his readiness). He makes a most difficult shift to the inside—of someone else, the someone else in this case being the person who ridiculed him. Now, try to imagine just how difficult it would be for this guy to make this shift. Here are these dangling, painful emotions backed by a theme that is at least twenty years old. He's been made fun of, ridiculed, verbally hammered for at least twenty years and he's just come to realize it. He could likely go back in his memory and review other conversations in which he was being ridiculed, but didn't realize it at the time. Those reviews are going to bring up massive embarrassment and shrinking. Yet, in order to make the shift to the rediculing guy's point of view, the joke teller has to let all of this go. Amazingly, he does manage to do it.

Shifting to the inside—of someone else has a grand impact. It clarifies and highlights several potential themes and plants the seed of compassion. When we stop to consider just how powerful this position is, we can see a quiet, lasting strength that penetrates deeply. The shift has given him clearer views of his themes which is the best place to launch the clearing process. You've got to know what you're dealing with. The compassion will help cool the heat and pain of the intense feelings that typically go with themes. If he can remember and bring compassion to center stage when needed, then he's probably not going to be so intensely hateful toward his antagonizers. After all, they have their themes too, he can remind himself. And compassion will help him be gentler with *himself* as he grows and evolves.

With this last potent position of inside—of someone else, we now have several positions from which we can view our life events and all of them serve to help us become more objective, to help us see from Soul. They are: outside looking in, the situational view, and inside—of someone else. From each of these positions, we gain a unique view, a view that tends to highlight aspects of the event that we might have otherwise missed. We can fly all around that thunder-head cloud now and expand our perception to a full three dimensions. We can have a fluid clarity about its softness, it's depth and it's power. And with all that clarity and understanding from the interactive events in our lives, we can take those first unique steps toward Aligning ourselves with the Sacred within us, with our Souls. From there, freedom is just around the corner.

* * * *

Admittedly, this section holds quite a bit of information to absorb. But if we take a step back for a moment, the big picture perspective might just reveal how truly simple this information is. All of the above, the switch to the manual mode so that we can be in the present, the whole catching process, the shifting of positions, are only ways or methods that we can use to enhance our attention. And, if we have finally made that choice to live in the way of Jonathan, then attention becomes central to the "how" in our efforts to adopt that conscious path toward Aligning ourselves with the Sacred within us, toward a complete restoration. It really only comes down to attention. So you see, Ikkyu was right all along. He just kept it simple and eloquent. Attention. Attention. Attention. (Maybe I should've left it at that as well. It's just that…well, there's always this tendency, this need to try to *explain* things.)

Meditation

Now, from here, we need to consider a gift from the East, one that is also simple, eloquent and has just as profound an effect on this way of living as attention. Meditation. If you have never had any exposure to meditation before, you might be having some strong reactions about now as the word seeps into awareness. The free associations that are tied to clichéd preconceptions might be oozing up. *Oh no*, you think, *not meditation. Not that. Does this mean that we're going to start tripping into the world of gurus, shaved heads, and contorted body positions? Undulating robes, golden idols and all that?* Just the mention of this word, meditation, might start a flow of slight anxiety, causing some of us to twitch a little.

219

If you are among the twitchers, you can relax. The reason that you can relax is because meditation is a completely malleable concept and practice. It becomes what you make of it. So, simply because you choose to meditate doesn't mean that you are suddenly going to be inspired to shave off those treasured locks of hair. Nor are you likely to suddenly grab up some crystals to carry around with you. On the other hand, you might. It depends completely upon you and what you choose to do with your meditation experience. Meditation can be as innocuous as relaxing on a bench by the side of a lake. Or it can be as mysterious as undergoing a life-altering experience where the ego is shed and you become one with your surroundings. (You still won't have to shave your head, even if you do have the latter experience, though.) So relax. Meditation is what you make it.

Here, in the way of Jonathan, meditation is indispensable and serves many purposes. First and foremost, meditation is a way of Aligning yourself with your Soul. Period. This is the primary reason for meditating. And meditating provides an arena where we can practice *all* of the skills we will need to hone our attention. We can practice catching our thoughts and emotions, decreasing our reactionary tendencies, and shifting observational positions. We can even work on our themes. From this vantage point, meditation becomes a sort of exercise program for practicing the Alignment to the Sacred, a way of practicing for life. Let's consider first, how meditation eloquently allows us to practice all that you have read about so far and then I will tell you about how it allows you to touch your Soul. We begin exploring this way of practicing by focusing on the process of meditation itself. I begin with a story.

When I was a child and took piano lessons, my teacher was constantly on me about keeping my fingers on the piano keys. I would sincerely try, but was unable to keep that pinky from drifting upwards when I was concentrating on hitting the right note. I couldn't seem to do both at the same time. She would admonish. Then I would feel guilty and think, *Geez, woman, can't you see that I am trying and that there is too much to think about here?* And the pinky or the thumb would go up and I would be swallowed by admonishments again. She never did tell me *how* I was supposed to keep those fingers down. I quit piano.

Later, in my thirties, I decided to try again. I was fortunate to begin my lessons with a teacher who was not only an amazing pianist, but also a proficient flyer. Again, I was told that I needed to keep my fingers on the keys, only this time, it was a gentle suggestion, followed by a completely logical reason. My fingers would be ready to play the notes when the time came and my playing would be more fluid. *Oh, so* that's *why*, I thought. (I think he might have added some other reasons, but I was so stunned that there *was* a reason that I didn't hear the others.) Then my teacher did a strange thing. He actually told me *how* to practice doing this. I was excited about learning until I heard the method. I was to play the scales, (which is one of the most *boring* things one can play in piano,) very slowly and watch my fingers while I was playing them. When one of my fingers would start to rise off of the keyboard, I would stop and simply put it back down again. Then I would continue playing the scale until another finger lifted and the process was repeated. A couple of notes, up, down. A few more, up, down. It was painfully meticulous, excruciatingly boring and…it worked. With much practice, my fingers stayed down and they were ready when the time came. Through various other equally painstaking methods, my piano playing improved. Soon I was able to forget about the technique of playing, (keeping my fingers down, etc.,) and I could focus on letting the light of me flow out through the music. From a musical perspective, the experience is somewhat like Soaring. To be sure, my musical Soaring moments were irregular because I had more practicing to do. But I had a taste and I still play the piano.

Practicing paying attention during meditation is a bit like keeping those fingers on the piano keys. We settle down in a comfortable sitting position, in a quiet place and have our attention be focused on one thing. The object of the focus of attention could be many things, but most often, we use the breath. It's simple and common to everyone. Everyone breathes. Now, when we're sitting quietly and not moving, invariably, just like those wandering fingers that lift stealthily off those keys, our minds are going to start to roam. *This is boring*, the mind says, *just sitting here like this. Let's go do a fantasy or something.* And off it wanders. You know what we do? We put our fingers back down on the keys. Quite simply, we bring our attention back to the focus, our breath. Simple, meticulous and methodical, it works. And we do it over and over and over again.

This is how it can play out. You're thinking about your breathing, about how the air feels cool going into your nostrils...*Is that the dryer I hear? Um...I thought those clothes would've finished drying by now. I wonder what time it is?* Breathe in and out, in and out, cool air in the nostrils, in and out. *My knee hurts.* In and out. *Why am I sitting here anyway? I've got so much to do. I know it's only ten minutes, but it feels like an hour. Does this stuff really work? Oops, I'm thinking again.* In and out. Cool air in the nostrils. Feel my breathing. In and out.

Now, if you're beginning to get that eerie sense of deja vu, you shouldn't be surprised. For, the process here is almost exactly like the catching process that was described when we were talking about reining in thoughts and emotions. When we bring our wandering attention back to our focus, we are acting like our first grade teachers prodding our attention back to the lesson at hand. In other words, while we are meditating, we are attempting to maintain, for as long as possible, the position of outside looking in. From there, we can catch ourselves when our thoughts start to wander or those emotions come up. The mind starts to slide into a fantasy or review a situation from the past and, eventually, we catch it. Then we bring our attention back to our breath again. Or an emotion swells up, usually because of some triggering thought, and we can watch the full life of that emotion then redirect our attention to the breath again. This is how we practice being aware of our thoughts and emotions in meditation. It's not that much different than how we do it in life. But, like physical exercise is for our bodies, our meditation "exercise" for our minds and Souls is more intense. Meditation provides a concentrated dose of practicing our awareness.

Being aware of thoughts and emotions is not the only aspect of attention that we practice during meditation. We are also practicing being aware of our bodies and our immediate surroundings. In other words, we are practicing being in the Sacredness of the present. You do notice the slight twitch in the muscle just above the knee. You do become aware of the gentle rustle of leaves outside the window, a sound that seems to be so much louder than before. While you are meditating, you become keenly aware of your body and it surroundings. You can become immersed in the present. This is good practice for life.

And here's where the eloquence of meditation makes another

appearance. For, at the same time that we are catching all those thoughts and emotions, at the same time that we become aware of our bodies and the small noises around us, we are practicing non-reaction. After all, the only thing that we are doing is just sitting there. Meanwhile, though, thoughts are pushing through the cranium at sometimes a breakneck speed, accompanied by some frothy emotions. What do we do? Just sit. Just watch. We do nothing.

And the body itself is a great vehicle for helping us practice decreasing our tendency toward reaction. This is because the body always seems to be full of sensations, sometimes tiny sensations that we might not have been aware of before. When we sit down to meditate, we're going to start noticing all those tiny physical nuances. And we won't do a thing about them but watch. Now, when it comes to physical sensations during meditation, itches, by far, can be the most maddening. An itch comes up on your thigh. It starts out small then grows, until it is screaming for a scratch relief. You think about where your hands are on your lap. *That itch is so close,* you think. *Maybe I could just reach it with my pinky.* With this thought, your muscles start to comply, but then you catch yourself. No reaction. There will be itches and pains, urges to sneeze and scratch, and just plain move. But we sit there just the same. Great practice, the body gives us in not reacting.

Now, the meditation that has been described above is a method of practicing paying attention, a way of increasing our *awareness* of the present and decreasing our tendency to react. Of course, this is so that we can immerse ourselves in the poetry of life and so that we can pick up the messages that surround us and point us in the direction of evolution. But meditation can also be a forum for the more *active* aspects of Aligning ourselves with our Souls. Meditation can be a time when we practice shifting positions of observation, for example. We could choose some event from our day and review it, viewing it from all of the positions. The woman who decorated her friend's office could have done that shifting work during a meditation session, when her mind was less cluttered with the debris of the day. And it's not just shifting we can do during meditation. We could do some visualization too, as a method of helping us work through a theme or an issue. In fact, meditation can be used in so many different ways that it seems that the possibilities for our growing from it, are only limited by our imagination.

A word of warning here, though. This type of active engagement of the mind during meditation could easily go far too far. This is because a bored mind, a mind that is not used to the quiet of meditation can be incredibly seductive in trying to find any possible way to insert some mental activity. When you experience brief moments of stillness of the mind, it can be unsettling at first. We're not used to it. So the mind is going to try all types of machinations to get us to do something, anything besides non-thinking. You remember when you were in grade school and you got a substitute teacher for a day? Wow, the class tried all kinds of new behaviors that day. You probably did a few things that you wouldn't have done ordinarily, like keeping your straw from lunch and trying out a spitball. Well, when you sit down to meditate, it can be like that substitute teacher walked in. The mind goes berserk. And, like that class, the mind is going to try every trick it can to sway you from paying attention to your breath. One of the most seductive of these tricks is to convince you that you *are* doing what you're supposed to be doing.

You're giving a speech in two weeks and you're feeling more than a little uptight about it. In fact, you're downright anxious. And you know that trying to see everyone in the audience in their underwear is not going to work to put you at ease. So you decide to do some visualization during meditation. First, you do the meditation as you usually do and bring back that wandering mind every few seconds. Then, in this more relaxed state, you decide to picture yourself standing up on stage in front of the audience. You can see all the details of the stage and the podium. You visualize yourself confidant and calm. As you start your speech, you notice the woman in the front row is wearing a short skirt, an *extremely* short skirt, so that you actually do think that you might see… Then you look at the woman who is sitting next to that short skirt. All she's got on is a fancy bra. At this point, you catch yourself and think, *this is not a visualization.* The mind, who is having a grand old time being entertained instead of still, rushes to its defense and counters with, *oh, yes it is. You're visualizing being at ease during your speech. If seeing people in their underwear will do it for you, then it counts as a visualization.*

Please. I'm not convinced, are you? You can see how easily and how seductive the mind can be in moving toward activity. This is particularly true when we allow it to have some leeway, when we actively engage our minds in meditation so that we can extend our learning by shifting or visualizations or whatever. While this is a legitimate and useful way of learning, we will need to keep a suspicious eye out and watch for the winds that claim to be learning devices. They're so clever, those winds. In fact, we'll probably want to spend most of our meditation time doing the type that was initially described, where we attempt to maintain the focus of our attention on the breath. We sit quietly and bring that wandering mind back to the focus.

Practicing our attention skills, being aware of our bodies, our thoughts and emotions and even practicing non-reaction all fall in to the category of the functional. Meditation can provide a concentrated period of practice for the skills, skills that can later be used in the larger arena of life. If we can bring ourselves back to the center of our Soul during meditation, then we are more likely to be able to do this when we're going about the rest of the day. This reason alone is enough to begin a daily meditation regime.

But there are other reasons to consider as well. One of these is balancing. Meditation can balance the ordinary rush of activity with stillness and non-doing. Most of the day, we are doing and running and accomplishing something. The work, the errands, the getting ready, the meals. On and on and on. Our bodies and minds are almost constantly occupied. And even when our bodies slow down, even when there is a lull, our minds are continually roving. Reading the paper, listening to music, and (if I must include it), watching TV, are times when we slow down physically, but our minds continue. We may think of this as down time, as leisure time, yet the mental part of us never really seems to get a break, even during leisure. And not even during sleep, because the mind roams around in the world of dreams. With enough of this type of living, we begin to feel disjointed, awkward, like those living Picassos. Part of us here and part of us there. We need some *real* down time. Meditation is a time when we can give that mental part of ourselves, the whole thinking and even feeling part of ourselves a true break. Mediation helps to balance all of that running and doing and the onslaught of accompanying thoughts and feelings. For a short period of time during the day, we can actually take a real break. We can realign ourselves into a better balance and allow ourselves to sink into whatever amount of time we experience the stillness of meditation.

Admittedly, much of our time during meditation will be consumed with that seemingly constant catching that we do. We keep the fingers on the keys. Oops, there the mind goes again. And again. And again. We seem to spend our time just bringing it back. But then something happens. The fingers stay down without so many reminders. For a second, maybe during an inhalation, there is a hesitation in the thoughts and all is still. Maybe it only lasted a second, but for that second, there was nothing going on at all. A pause. A bit of practice and the pauses will expand. Seconds will turn into minutes. Then, instead of noticing all of the *activity* of our minds, we will begin to pay attention to its *stillness*.

When we listen to a piece of music, we tend to concentrate on the notes that we hear, their speed, their rise and fall that give us the drama of melody. We hardly ever notice the space around the notes.

You never hear someone say, "Wow, did you hear that rest? That luscious pause?"

No, we never hear a comment like that. Yet, it is that luscious pause that makes us hang with heavy lust, waiting for the next chord, the chord that gives us resolution. The rest, that pause at the end of a hymn between "A" and "men" is powerful. Can you imagine just ending the hymn on "A"? You would be left falling forward trying to get the pianist to get to the "men" part. "Amen" just goes together and the space between them is what dramatizes the whole thing. What we come to realize is that the pauses define the music as much as the notes do. Without them, the music that we hear would not exist. Without the pauses, the music would just be a dull, steady drone or a raucous cacophony of endless noise. We've gotta have the pauses in music.

And we've gotta have pauses in life. Through meditation, we can experience, perhaps for the first time, the natural pauses. When we get to a point where we can actually focus on the pauses, on the spaces between the notes, we may be surprised to find not only stillness, but tranquility. Tranquility is a soft beauty. Timid at first. But if we listen long enough to the tranquility of those pauses, we may begin to sense a volume and fullness that we were missing before. Funny how such nothingness can be so full.

Here is something else ethereal about meditation. The nothingness that is so full. Once we get to that stillness, once we can sink into that tranquility, we might begin to recognize where we are. For, right next to tranquility sits the source of our wisdom, the divine within us, the Soul. In this space, there is no raucous cacophony of thoughts and emotions reverberating off of the cranium; there is no need or desire that lurks in the shadows; there is no push and pull, worry or any importance assigned to the pains that we feel. Here in this place, there is tranquility, quiet wisdom, love and compassion. There is a quiet certainty that everything is truly alright. This is a beautiful place. Meditation is a way of getting there.

Welcome to your Soul.

Beautiful, isn't it?

There you have it. The reasons why meditation is such an integral part of this way.

One quick caveat. If you do nothing else with the ideas in this book, meditate. It is the most important addition you can make to your life. The rest will follow from there.

Getting Started with Meditation

While this is not a manual on meditation, you may feel like you want to get started right away. Therefore, I am including some scant start-up suggestions, particularly for those of you who may not have ever meditated before. The guidelines below are only intended as a starting place. Without a doubt, you'll need to do further reading.

First, find five to ten minutes in your schedule when you will not be disturbed, either by the children, the telephone or your spouse. This might already seem like a challenge, but motivation will lead you to find these golden minutes, even if you have to get up earlier or go to bed later. Once you have found the time, try to insure a relatively quiet environment by turning off the phone, radio, etc. Find a comfortable chair and sit with your back as straight as the chair allows. Or you may choose to sit cross-legged on a cushion on the floor, always with a straight back. I do not recommend lying down because it is too easy to fall asleep. Keep your hands in a comfortable position in your lap.

When you are settled into your position, allow your attention to turn to your breath. Focus on the feeling of the breath as it enters and goes out of your nose. Do not try to control your breath. Just follow its rhythm and watch as an observer. Your thoughts may wander and emotions emerge. Attempt to become aware of the thoughts or emotions, to catch them, watch them, let them go and then return to the breath. This process is familiar to you. What you may find is that you go on long excursions of thought before you catch yourself not paying attention to your breath. This is normal. Please avoid judging yourself or your thoughts when they do arise. These judgments interfere with the process and are none other than thoughts themselves. And you may end up on a self-deprecating mind roll. Let's not go there. Simply continue the process of redirecting back to your breath.

If focusing on the breath is not enough to keep your mind from sprouting off in another direction, there are several other simple techniques that are helpful. I will list two here and leave you to research others if these two do not fit you well. One technique is breath counting. With this technique you count each breath *on the exhalation*. On the inhalation, you do nothing. It would look something like this. Breathe in, out — one; breathe in, out — two and so on until you reach the count of ten. When you get to ten, start over at one again. If you lose count, start again with the count of one. The activity of counting keeps the mind occupied enough, but prevents being consumed by the activity. You're not likely to be swept away in a train of thoughts about counting, not as likely, at least, as if you were thinking of how you were going to speak in front of several hundred people tomorrow. And, if you pay attention to the stillness of the inhalations when you are not counting, you are that much closer to Aligning yourself with your Soul.

Another technique for avoiding mind rolls is noting or categorizing what we are thinking. When a wandering thought comes in, you note it with a name and then let it go. The noting or categorizing gently forces us to realize that a thought is just a thought and therefore has no more weight than what it is. Here is how this technique might be experienced. You have just begun meditating and have taken those first few breaths with a relatively quiet mind. Then it starts. *Got to go get that grass seed this afternoon. I wonder what time that store closes.* Thoughts. *My nose itches.* Face. *Wonder if Catlin's poison ivy cleared up.* Thought. *I should be able to stop thinking for a few seconds.* Judgment. *There I go making a judgment about my thoughts.* Judgment. *Okay, Okay...* Thought. *My knee hurts.* Body.

Noting or categorizing is comical to read about and sometimes it is comical to experience, but the training is just like learning to keep those fingers down. And it forces us to take the observer position, the position of the Soul.

Life

And so the journey begins. The day unfolds before us with the opening of an eyelid and at that moment we choose how we will live. In fact, every moment holds this choice. Life is always there in front of us, this vivacious, perpetually changing thing. It dances and plays, pokes and prods, shoves and hits, and whistles around and through us. Life is the way. The moments and the situations, which are really just a series of moments, will provide all sorts of occasions for us to Align ourselves with the Sacred that is within us and around us. We can be nourished and evolve. We can immerse ourselves in a golden space of the Sacred and allow that click to occur and we can listen for the sometimes not so loud messages about our perceptions, reactionary tendencies and themes. Then we can take the next step toward Alignment and eventually toward restoration.

Watering that plant in July. Click. Pure poetry. Someone breaks in line in front of you while you're Christmas shopping. Pop. There are those reactions. And later you realize that a theme surfaced. Immersing ourselves in the Sacredness of the present and gathering the messages for growth. Meditation is the concentrated way of practicing Aligning ourselves with our Souls, one that we methodically insert into the day. Life, those roving, flamboyant circumstances that seem to randomly show up, is the fluid way of practicing. Not so predictable. Definitely interesting.

When we think of life this way, then every single second is so precious, so meaningful, and so filled with purpose. Those pauses that were perhaps introduced to us during meditation, the pauses that signal the tranquility of Soul, surround us in the moments of our lives as well. It's the attention that will pull them up front into awareness and show us the full color. With some practice, then, we come to realize that the spaces in between our highlighted activities are just as full as the activities themselves. What this means is that when you drive to the beach for your vacation, your vacation begins, not when you arrive at that hotel, but the moment that you get into the car. (Or the moment that you stopped working the day before.) Walking toward the ice cream counter becomes just as significant an event as plunging your tongue into that creamy coldness. A lazy unplanned Saturday morning is as good as going to the circus or concert, if we can absorb with relish the spontaneous tidbits that life tosses our way. The run to the grocery for the bread and the milk is no longer a pain. After all, when people are around, interesting encounters, engaging, connecting encounters are always a possibility. Well, as long as we're open to them. The pauses in our lives are just as full as the activities which means that *every single moment* is full.

This entire chapter has been about paying attention, being more aware of our bodies, our thoughts and emotions and the events of our lives. And, paying attention, by itself will bring out the nourishing color of the moments. All by itself, the act of paying attention will show the glossiness and depth of the pauses and spaces in our lives. Just paying attention will oftentimes be enough to immerse ourselves in the Sacredness of the present.

Yet paying attention is only the beginning of growth and evolution. Most often, attention will show us the questions. Attention will point to the reactionary tendencies, the deleterious perceptions, the themes that pervade our psyches. And when we see our "stuff" with some clarity, we will have arrived at the crossroads of choice. Here we decide whether we will allow the Soul to Soar into our lives. Paying attention brings us awareness and clarity then we get to choose.

Now, suppose you decide to venture forth and make some changes. Of course, you're going to hear some rising protests from Fear of change, Fear of the unknown and Fear of pain. You can expect their voices to get louder as you go ahead and commit yourself to practicing Aligning yourself to your Soul, to growing and evolving. But let's say you pass by them for the moment and press forward. What now? Attention has served to bring to consciousness some areas of change. But what do you do with all of that?

Well, in most cases, you will need to figure out, for yourself, exactly what to do. It is your path, your *unique* path and no one else is going to be able to plot out strategies, make up techniques and then carry them through. Only you can do this. It is because of your uniqueness that makes it so. Consider for a moment the uniqueness of any individual. Each person is planted with a unique genetic wiring and has unique experiences, all in the background of a unique culture. Then, we must consider that life's situations and circumstances are unique as well. With all of this uniqueness floating around, it's no wonder that we have to figure out our own path.

Figuring out our own path may seem onerous at first. So much responsibility. *Gosh, this is a lot of work,* we think. And there's no recipe or guide to tell us what to do. Yeah, we know we'll have to do the practice part, but can't somebody at least tell us how to go about it? Well, sure, we could find someone to tell us what to do. Advice givers are common. But maybe their solutions don't quite fit our style. Or maybe they were missing a piece that makes their solutions ineffective. In either of these cases, their advice fails to suit our uniqueness and we will still be the ones to do the figuring. Yet, what if we could find someone, some wise advice giver who was able to tailor an absolutely perfect plan for our unique situation? Well, that would be wonderful! Then the only work we would have to do is carry that plan through. And the next time we had some more changes to make, we could just find the same wise advice giver for the perfect plan. The problem with this is that we never become wise ourselves this way. We would always be reliant on that wise advice giver. Relying on that advice giver is like when your mother constantly buttoned your shirt for you. How were you supposed to learn to button your own shirt, if she was always working that button through that hole in a quick mass of flying fingers? You must do it for yourself. Same thing here. We must find our own unique way through the aspects of our growth and evolution.

At the risk of sounding contradictory, though, sometimes we may need some help. We may need to bounce some ideas off of someone else. Family, friends and counselors are all out there, surrounding us like a gentle web of support, as we, in turn, support them. So, when it comes to the sticky areas of deeply imbedded perceptions and themes, we may need to seek out someone to help us further our clarity and understanding. Fine. But, at some point in this process, we must necessarily take responsibility and be the one to do the figuring. While it is true that we are never alone, we will never escape our uniqueness no matter how much we talk.

Our path is our own to do. This is the point. We are here in the process of Aligning ourselves to the Sacred that is within us and around us, being nourished and evolving. And in that evolution, we have our own unique tasks ahead of us. Attention will give us the nourishment of color and move us toward clarity about our "stuff." Then we make the choice. With our web of mutual support backing us, we seek out, try out and sometimes, creatively make up strategies and techniques that move us in the direction of Alignment with our Souls. Meditation provides a concentrated, deliberate method of practice. Life provides an unpredictable, fluid method of practice. And we relentlessly continue to focus on flying, until we find that more and more, the Soul is directing, love and all of its companions are showing up in ourselves and in our lives. We are Soaring in Life.

Recommended Readings:

Arico, Carl J. *A Taste of Silence: Centering Prayer and the Contemplative Journey*. Continuum Publishing, 1999.

Davich, Victor N. *The Best Guide to Meditation*. Renaissance Books, 1998.
   This book definitely lives up to its name. It is the BEST guide, particularly for the beginner. Seasoned meditators might want to try some of the methods presented as meditation from most every approach is explained and/or represented. The depth of coverage is necessarily limited due to the breath of this book. Resources are given for those desiring more in-depth material. There are also two chapters on mindfulness or living in the present which are excellent.

Gawain, Shakti. *Creative visualization and Meditation exercises to enrich your life*. New World Library, 1991.
   A good guide to basic muscle relaxing meditation and visualizations during meditation.

Hanh, Thich Nhat. *The Miracle of Mindfulness: A Manual of Meditation*. Beacon Press, 1975.
   This book encompasses not only methods of breathing for meditation, but also addresses what it means to live in the moment.

Moody, Harry R. and Carroll, David L. *The Five Stages of the Soul*. Doubleday, 1997.

CLEARING FLYING PATTERNS THAT KEEP YOU FROM SOARING

A Review of the Common Process of Transcending a Deeply Rooted Issue

Let us continue the practice,
        Even when the path becomes hazy.
Let us continue the practice
        Even when we do the same stupid behaviors
        Over and over and over again.
I can show you a bit about how to transcend those patterns.
        I can show you a method,
        But that's all I can show you.
The repetitions are uniquely yours
        And so are the answers.
Are you willing to tackle some of the toughest challenges
        On your own?

Transcending Themes

All along we've been referring to themes, saying that we'll get into that sticky mess later. Well, finally, now is later. We are finally going to explore the area of themes. At this point, you might have a general idea about what themes are and how they can take over the director's seat, but the idea might be vague and somewhat fuzzy. So what we need now is a bit of clarity. You might be expecting a definition here, one that would succinctly draw clear, solid lines around the concept of a theme, one that everyone could point to and say, "oh, so that's what a theme is." It's not going to happen. Themes are broad and nebulous by nature. To attempt a concise definition would mean that we would be consumed by tedium for several pages. A full example works so much better. And this chapter is mostly example. However, to begin to lift some of haziness that surrounds the concept of themes, let's start with a description. You'll fill in the rest later.

Themes settle at the base of our subconscious and hover there, ready to affect how we think, how we feel and how we behave. They leak forward into our behavior in the most furtive sort of way. At least, it feels sneaky to us because most of the time, we're not even aware of their existence. They hold a commanding presence. A situation comes up that stirs the theme from its temporary remission and it stealthily starts commanding our behavior and thoughts and feelings. Usually, themes are old. They wear the gray hair and skin folds of something that's been around for awhile. Perhaps they formed when we were children, as a result of our predispositions and supporting experiences. Like maybe we were pre-wired to be more anxious than the average Joe, so the criticisms of our parents were soaked inward and inflated that anxiety. Now, in the face of even the slightest criticism, we shrink backward and are transformed into that whimpering child. In fact, any situation that holds any similarity to the original one will produce the reaction prompted by the theme. We react in the usual way, thus forming those repetitive patterns. Maybe the themes formed early in life or perhaps these ripe themes were formed during our last lifetime and lingered into this round. It's a matter of belief, I suppose, when they began, but we know they've been here for awhile. The gray hair gives them away.

The gray hair gives them away when we can manage to *perceive* them. Most of the time though, we don't even notice these old themes. We are blind to them, mostly because they have been with us for so long. After awhile, we start to think that they are who we are. When this happens, of course, we are not Aligned with our Souls. Far from it. We have Aligned with the theme.

"I'm just an anxious person, that's all."

Well, maybe. Maybe it is one of those furtive themes, one of those old guys who thinks he is side-locked to you like a Siamese twin.

No matter what you do, you can't seem to shake him off: "Will...you...let...GO...PLEASE!"

He doesn't move, so you start to think that maybe he belongs there, that maybe he's a part of who you are. So your blindness then is complete. He is you.

But somehow, you get the sense that, at least sometimes, you are not the one behind the curtain and start to feel queasy with this sense of knowing. And what we ordinary do when we intuit that the Siamese twin is in charge, is to either deny its existence or push it away.

"*I* am the one behind the curtain," we yell.

This is the ego talking. Maybe we're attempting to convince ourselves of this with the volume of that voice or maybe we're trying to scare away any wacky Kansas professor who might have slipped in without our noticing. Either way, we are denying, pushing and yelling. Of course, the voice doesn't work, no matter how loud it is. And the next time a situation eases into our lives and disturbs that sleeping theme, we feel, think and react in the same way. We have bumped into our old friend, repetition again.

We tell ourselves that the Siamese twin doesn't exist in our vehement attempts to deny it. We attempt to convince ourselves that we are indeed the ones in charge, despite our volatile behavior and repetitive actions. If someone asks about our out-of-the-ordinary behavior, we'll find some way to write it off.

"Oh, *that*...that was just a...a fluke. It's never happened before...well, not *exactly* that way and well... it will *never* happen again."

Of course, it will. What happens when we deny or attempt to push the theme away is that it can actually end up fueling the power behind it. It's a bit like the emotional boxes when we tried so hard to keep those lids on. The more we pushed, the more powerful they demanded expression. It takes an enormous amount of energy to constantly monitor and keep themes at bay. Sweating energy, it takes. Themes are always there, threatening to overtake us. And, like those boxes, trying to push the themes out of existence simply doesn't work. They come right back around to smack us in our lives again. No, ignoring and pushing aren't effective.

Imagine a person who is a bit insecure about themselves. In fact, he is so insecure that whatever circumstances he finds himself in, largely determine how he feels about himself from moment to moment. If someone tosses a positive comment, then he swoons with pride. A few minutes later, a negative evaluation darts in his direction and he shrivels. Back and forth his self-esteem swings, going in whichever direction the wind is blowing. He is a victim of a theme. Now, denying and pushing this theme away, he might try to always position himself to receive positive evaluations. He would attempt to surround himself with affirming situations or people and avoid experiences that would likely lead to being criticized or evaluated negatively. But notice the amount of energy that he would have to expend to maintain that protected world. He'd have to be thinking about it *all* the time. *Do the people at this party like me? Will they say affirming things?* Such constant monitoring would be exhausting. And—it doesn't work. For, no matter how hard he tries to insure that he surrounds himself with the needed experiences to bolster his mental self-image, he will inevitably fail to foresee an unpredicted criticism. Then the shriveling will occur. Back and forth he goes, victim to this ride. Denying and pushing *actually* ends up giving the theme more power.

So, then, what are we supposed to do with these old, hidden, sly ghosts? Well, we can choose to transcend them. I like this word, "transcend." It implies a non-fighting, non-pushing method for surpassing themes. We don't push or combat. We don't deny. We undercut the power the theme has over us by facing it squarely and working through it. Then, as we blow on past that theme, we can glance backward toward that feeble thing that used to hover so dramatically and threateningly above our heads and casually wink at it. Yep, wink. Why not? That thing is just a shriveled, old shadow in the face of our transcendence. So, having transcended his theme, our insecure gentleman could hear affirming comments and he would not inflate. He could listen to the criticisms and not melt. His feelings about himself would hold a steadier hum of solidity. And there would be no need to monitor his surroundings in order to protect himself. His freedom would expand. Certainly, then, he could afford a casual wink.

Transcendence sounds good, doesn't it? But just how do we go about doing this? Well, to some extent, each of us will have to find our own unique way through each unique theme. We've already talked about the idea of uniqueness and how finding our own path is central to growing. No, this is not a cop out. It is absolutely true. Yet, fortunately, the *process* of transcendence, the general work of transcending a theme is probably similar for us all. So at least we can talk about this process.

The process of transcendence begins in a very familiar place. Attention. Attention will pick up potential themes from our interactions and experiences. If we're paying attention, we will get a hint of a theme, a quick flash before our eyes. Then, of course, we'll need to go back and do a double take. A long double take. We'll need to look directly at this furtive ghost and get a clearer picture. A few observational shifts could help in gaining some clarity. Flying around the ghost will give us a broader, perhaps three-dimensional perspective. Ah, now that ghost doesn't look so translucent anymore. Now the theme is taking on some definite lines. With this clearer view, then, we might want to do some exploring, some digging around to find the roots of this thing. When did all of this start? How far back do we have to go? The digging will bring up more pieces and more dirt. This theme looks like it goes deep. They usually do. All of this exploration reveals an even more profound clarity of the theme and some intellectual understanding may occur. Finally, the whole thing gets uprooted and we can see it. Wow, it is big. With this full view, then, we sometimes experience a sort of internal transcendence. There is an emotional understanding, maybe even a psychological release. But we're not done. The internal transcendence needs to infiltrate our actions in order to be complete. So we translate our internal transcendence to the practice of it in our behavior. This is when we giggle with the exhilaration of freedom.

Here's what it looks like:

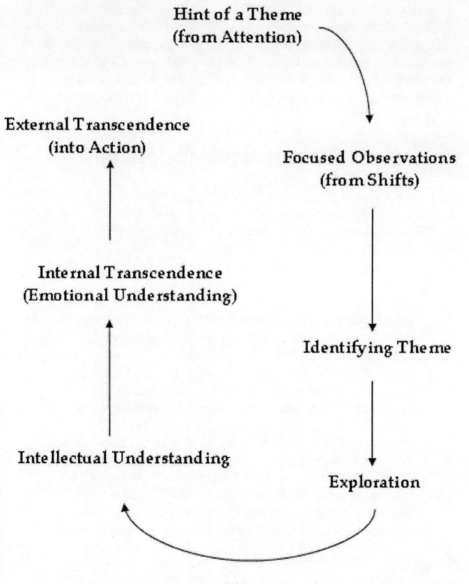

Hint of a Theme (from Attention)

External Transcendence (into Action)

Focused Observations (from Shifts)

Internal Transcendence (Emotional Understanding)

Identifying Theme

Intellectual Understanding

Exploration

Now, admittedly, we went through that process of transcendence quickly. And, at this moment the whole thing might seem abstract and removed. It also might seem slightly too pristine for the muddiness of real life. Theories are often like that, aren't they? A little dry, leaving you feeling like you could use a slug of water. With the cursory review of this process of transcendence, then, we will leave the parched arena of the abstract and step back into the lovely murkiness of real life, the "real" life of a fictional character, Susan. We will follow the entire process of transcendence of a theme with Susan, dodging in and out of her life and in and out of explanations. What we are likely to find is that the murkiness of real life does indeed muddy up the clean lines of the abstract. That is, the process is not quite as linear or circular as it might first appear. This is as we expected. This is as it should be.

A Cycle of Transcendence for "Susan"

The story begins:

Susan stands up from her cross-legged position on the floor, where she has been playing make believe car games with her two children, Kendra and Adam. The tops of their heads in sight, she contemplates with a loving regard how straight Adam's part in his hair is compared to Kendra's. Even after brushing, Kendra's hair never seems to lay well. Susan thinks about Adam entering first grade this year. And Kendra will be in kindergarten full-time next year, which means that she will be working more at the agency. With an angst filled sigh, she leaves her children in the den and goes to the kitchen to begin preparing dinner. Her mind takes up the subject while she is taking food out of the refrigerator. The agency. Has it really been six years since she worked there full-time? Thoughts of the agency always bring up an image of Kay. Kay is more of a best friend than a business partner. Susan smiles to herself while she pulls up the eggplant from the bottom drawer. Kay always does that to her. Makes her smile. Kay had been so good to her the day that Susan had announced her first pregnancy. The agency had only been up and running for two years at that time, a business in its infancy. And, although it was doing well, both women had understood that continual effort was needed to keep that success. But flexible Kay had bounded toward Susan that day with a bubbly smile, a hug, and a plan about how she could take up the slack at the agency for awhile.

"Besides," Kay had added, "you could use some work on your nurturing, maternal side."

Susan had laughed, but she knew it was true. What she didn't know, then, is just how much she would grow as a result of that decision to cut back her hours. Now she laughs for a different reason. She'd had no idea what she was in for. Well, maybe now that the children will be in school full time next year, she can begin to make up for some of those years that Kay overworked. With all of the food on the counter in front of her, Susan decides to focus on her immediate experience and give her thoughts a rest.

From the kitchen, she can hear the muffled voices of her children. The words are smothered by the distance, so that she can only hear the tones and melodies of their individual voices. *Adam's voice is already more bass than Kendra's*, she thinks. The pop of the knife hitting the cutting board as she clips the eggplant into half-moons, blends with the song of the voices, much like a metronome. She feels a smile creep to her lips. With her awareness on the voices, Susan is more quickly alerted to the change in tone that she hears from the den. Although she quiets her chopping, she remains where she is, knowing that an argument is forming between the children and hoping that they can work it out for themselves. After all, they have spent a lot of time practicing how to find solutions. The voice volume increases and the words now become clear. It is a classic argument over who will have a specific Hot Wheels car.

The black sports model is always popular. Susan decides to peek around the corner to make sure that the argument doesn't turn physical.

Adam leans toward Kendra and with his face a few inches from hers yells, "It's my turn! Now give it to me!"

Kendra can't take the proximity of the lashing, and, putting the black car under her knee, she reaches up with both hands to release the built up emotion in a wash of tears. Adam, meanwhile, seizes the opportunity, snatches the car out from under her knee and runs to his room. Susan hears the door slam shut and also the renewed wailing of Kendra who yells something unintelligible at the closed door. Susan feels the heat rising inside her. She is angry, but not at Adam. She is angry at Kendra. She sinks to the floor in front of Kendra and holds her rigidly at arm's length. After a heavy pause, she launches into a long tirade about how Kendra just can't allow other people to take advantage of her, how she needs to stand up for herself and that crying doesn't help. These last words seem to have had the opposite effect that Susan wanted because Kendra is crying harder than ever now. Stunned, Susan stands up and walks back into the kitchen, looking back at her daughter with a hollow disgust.

Susan goes back to chopping the eggplant, but this time, she is oblivious to the popping of knife against wood and of the half-moon shapes. This time her thoughts take a different direction. *She can't even take the smallest confrontation. And of course he's gonna take the car, if she just lays it down like that. What did she expect? That he would give in? Maybe she thought that he would give in when he saw her crying. Maybe she wanted him to feel sorry for her. Well that won't work. I guess she'll find that out the hard way.* Then Susan catches herself. She sees the thoughts and realizes that they are just fueling her anger. The moment of realization, the thoughts stop and the anger starts to lose some of its heat. Now, intentionally, Susan calms her mind and body. The pop of the knife and the half-moon shapes reenter her awareness. When this happens, she allows herself to slip back into her mind. The situation calls for reflection. She's not sure why her reaction was so strong and plans to contemplate that further a bit later, when there is more time. At the moment, though, she is certain of one thing. She crashed and the situation needs to be addressed — now.

She walks back into the den. Kendra is still sitting there, rocking her body and pushing a piece of dirt back and forth on the carpet in rhythm to her rocking. Susan's heart immediately swells with sadness at the withdrawal of her daughter, the withdrawal that she sealed with her own crash. This time, Susan is aware of her own sinking feelings of guilt at the idea that she may have hurt her daughter, but she doesn't allow these feelings to overwhelm her. She stays focused on what she has come to do. Slowly this time, Susan glides to the space on the floor right next to her daughter. With a single soft caress from Susan, Kendra starts crying again. Susan thinks that the crying is probably a good sign, since it may mean that Kendra is coming back out. When Kendra is calmer, Susan talks gently.

"I didn't mean to say that it was all your fault or that you can't let your feelings out by crying. Of course you can cry when you feel bad. And I'm sure that it felt pretty bad when Adam jerked that car out from under you." Susan pauses, then positions herself in front of Kendra to finish.

"I am so sorry that I said what I did. I didn't mean to hurt you. I think I kinda got swept away in being angry and then let it out on you. You remember when we talked about that before?"

Kendra quietly says, "Yeah."

"Well, anyway, I'm sorry."

"Okay, Mom."

With another full hug, Susan suggests that they call Adam out so that a better solution can be found. Kendra agrees and Susan does exactly that, still not knowing why she crashed or what was behind it all. That reflection will come later.

This is a common scene. In fact it is so common that it may, at first, appear to be clichéd. Here is Mom cooking dinner and the children are playing in the other room. They start arguing over a toy. Like so many households in so many states, this type of situation occurs every day. But that is the point exactly. For, notice how very rich this hackneyed example is. There is layer upon layer of crispy life to practice flying with. This common, ordinary slice of life is teaming with potential. And we watch as Susan practices.

Even at the beginning of this scene, with the initial focus on the details of the parts in her children's hair, we know Susan is fully immersed in the Sacredness of the present. That is, she is fully there until some free associations and feelings of angst transport her backwards. The lure of the past pulls at her and she replays the scene when she tells Kay about her first pregnancy. Now, between the lines, there is her value of growth coming forward. At the time of that transition, Susan contemplated how she would grow from the changes that would be coming, especially how it would affect her atrophied "nurturing" side. And we watch as Susan catches herself in this review of the past and refocuses herself on dinner. With the conscious decision to refocus, she sinks into the silkiness of the present, a present full of the moon shapes of eggplant and rhythms of sounds in the air. And it *is* beautiful, peaceful and Sacred. We can almost hear the click when the smile creeps onto her face. She is paying attention.

Then, we watch her humming attention detect the crackle of the argument between her children. At this point, Susan does something interesting. Nothing. She doesn't think, *Damn, I can't even do dinner for five minutes without them getting into a fight!* She doesn't slam the knife down, resenting their interruption and neediness. She doesn't angrily spin into the den, barking about why they fight so much. She does nothing. There is no reactionary temptation. This is what we don't see. What we do see, yet again, is the value of growth and evolution. She wants to allow them the chance to work it out. Automatically, she is perceiving the situation as holding growth potential for her children. Now maybe she had to practice this, maybe it just came naturally to her, but the reactionary tendency is replaced by the value of growth. She even quickly reviews in her mind the times that they have practiced this very situation together.

But then something happens. She slips off course. Something about the argument has pricked her anger and she slides right into that reddish current. Up until this point, she is watching and waiting. Up until this point, she is emotionally removed from the interaction between the two children. It is as if she had been watching from a situational view. But the reddish current catches her. With Susan's preachy tirade, Kendra gets the blast of rotten vinegar. Yep. Kendra does cry harder.

Eventually, though, Susan does manage to catch herself. She takes the position of outside looking in and sees the swirling of the thoughts and emotions that are just fueling each other. Then with deep intention, she calms down. She knows at this point that the slide into that reddish current was too swift, too easily made. She knows that this fact most likely means that somehow the situation tapped into — something, but there is no time for long analytical reflections. Susan has the sense that she is not the one behind the curtain, that something else is in control of her reactions. This is the theme beginning to emerge. It is an old, automatic pattern that comes up furtively to overpower her when she is least suspecting it. Her attention and her sense that she is onto something is the first movement in the direction of recognition. At this point, though, the theme remains hazy. But she doesn't need to have a clear, full picture to know what to do next. There's the rotten vinegar of anger all over Kendra. Love and gentleness will help to clean it up. It starts with an acknowledgment and a hint of Susan's shifting into Kendra's point of view. Then there's an apology and a statement about being carried away by an emotion. This is a good beginning.

Once the whole scene is over and some of that rotten vinegar has been cleaned up, we might just be tempted to forget about the heavy dose of anger and what that could mean. We might just be tempted to write it off as an anomaly. We'll promise ourselves that it will never happen again. After all, the argument is solved, isn't it? And there is that dinner to prepare. Then after that is homework and baths. The potential of a theme could seamlessly pass right out of our thoughts and attention. But then, those insidious repetitions start to occur. We get that sense of deja vu. We *have* been there. We *have* done that. The repetitions are like the lovely naggings of our lives to finally transcend a theme that we have been procrastinating about.

Being in the nourishing present, catching the swirling effects of thoughts and emotions, dancing with the reddish current, crashes like golden cockroaches, emerging themes to learn about. Yes. This is a clichéd, hackneyed cross section of life. Just a mom cooking dinner and the kids arguing over a toy in the next room. Full, isn't it? Crispy with opportunities for practice Aligning ourselves with the Soul and the Sacredness of everyday life.

Now, let's see what happens to Susan's developing awareness of that theme.

Later, with a guaranteed few minutes to herself, Susan replays the situation in her mind to look for any clues that might clarify any potential theme. She realizes that her anger was quite strong. Too strong really. The situation didn't warrant it. And there was the disgust too. She had been disgusted at Kendra. She remembers thinking that maybe Kendra was just letting herself be the victim. Like this was a role that Kendra plays. Like she wanted attention for it. The helplessness was revolting. And there was her stunning non-reaction to Adam's behavior. She can't remember any connected feelings, but the thoughts that she had about Adam all pointed to justification. As if there was nothing wrong with what he did. Her strong feelings toward Kendra…they are probably the key. Disgust, revulsion, anger at her allowing herself to be victimized, helpless, weak.

Susan paws at the recent past, attempting to unearth any related reaction. As she sifts through her recent memories, she scans for her reactions towards victims or people who showed weakness. There was the client at the office last Wednesday who was sort of wishy-washy about the kind of campaign he wanted for his product. He almost whined when she and Kay had finally pressured him to make a decision. She had felt irritated then. Maybe that was disgust? Or maybe it was just because she was in such a rush. She's not sure. No other situations come to mind at the moment. And this one doesn't give her much information. Still unclear, she decides to let it rest for now and promises herself to be on the lookout for events and reactions that might contribute to an understanding of this thing, whatever it is. She is certain that these clarifying events will now occur with greater frequency.

Very little time passes before confirmation of her certainty comes. Susan is in her car the next morning, listening to the old rock of a mix station. She is moving with the natural slowness of the merge lane. The progress is slow, but steady. Steady, that is, until the guy in front of her tries to take his turn. He looks over his left shoulder at the continuous stream of rush hour cars, and, with furrowed eyebrows of anxiety, he makes several false starts. Finally, he comes to a full stop. Honks from the cars behind Susan penetrate the air. Impatience makes the line of cars inch forward even though there is nowhere to go until the guy makes his final move. In the rear view mirror, Susan can see the woman directly behind her losing it. She is flailing one arm out of the window and stamping the horn rhythmically with the other, all the while yelling obscenities. *It's odd to see someone opening their mouth that wide, with their neck muscles pulsing, when you can't hear anything,* thinks Susan. Then the angry woman suddenly jerks her car around to use the shoulder to enter the freeway. It is at this moment that the guy makes his final move into the stream of traffic and the two cars collide. Susan pulls onto the shoulder herself to offer assistance.

As she approaches the wreck, she takes in the scene. The angry woman is still flailing her arms, only this time, she is out of her car and standing over the man who sits in his car, hunched over and staring at the pavement. His face is stone. Hers is dancing with the tension of muscles that anger can bring. Judgments are popping out of her mouth at a machine gun rate. As Susan gets closer, she can see that the only response from the man to the barrage of verbal attack is a nondescript flinching around his eyes.

Observing this tiny behavior around his eyes sets off a sudden flood of anger in Susan towards him. Instantly she recognizes the emotion. The intensity of it would be difficult to deny. She turns around and walks back to her car to make a call to report the accident. This is the only way she can help now. As she finishes the call, she watches the guy who is still maintaining his stoic victim position. Disgust eases up her throat like bile.

Later on that same day, Susan and Kay are casually talking over the Chinese lunch that is their Monday favorite. Kay begins to tell her about the recent turmoil in the life of one of their mutual friends, Amelia.

"Amelia called over the weekend."

"Amelia?" Susan answers with a hazy voice that indicates her bland interest. Amelia has been one of those casual friends that she found both likeable and irritating at the same time. "Gosh, we haven't heard from her in…"

"About three months, right? Well, there is a reason for that. That tyrant husband of hers was starting to restrict the friends she sees. He's been telling her who she can and can't talk to. This last crap on top of the list of other demands that we've been hearing about for the last six months. You know, dinner at 6, not at 6:01 or it's late, blah, blah, blah." Kay never did like Amelia's husband, Robert.

"So we're not on the list of friends that she can talk to?" Susan asks.

"Apparently not. We're not the sort of friends Robert wants her to have. Too ambitious, not meek enough. A bit wild, I suppose, without the guiding hand of a man." Kay is smiling mischievously.

"But she called you, so the restrictions must not be so bad."

"That's just the point, the restrictions have gotten so bad that she really is going to do it this time."

"Leave him?" Susan is incredulous. Amelia has been threatening to do something for a long time.

Kay automatically reads Susan's expression. "I wasn't convinced either until she told me that she had moved out and had talked to a lawyer."

Susan soaks this information in. Amelia has actually taken control of her life. *Perhaps I was a bit too quick to write her off,* Susan thinks. Both Susan and Kay agree that their mutual friend will likely need support from them through this transition.

On the drive home, Susan mentally reviews the car accident of the morning, knowing that the event has likely tapped into the theme that had emerged during the dispute between Kendra and Adam. There was the same flood of heady anger and the sour taste of disgust for the victim in the situation. The intensity was so powerful! A bit nerve racking, really. And once again, there was a clear lack of feelings toward the woman. Just like the void of feelings with Adam. Always a sort of harsh rush of feelings toward the victim and nothing for the aggressor. And then there was that situation that Kay was telling her about with Amelia. Susan had felt her own attitude toward Amelia changing when she learned that Amelia had moved out. Finally Amelia had stood up for herself. She was no longer letting Robert victimize her. Amelia's defiance had opened the door for Susan's respect and a developing friendship in the future. Susan no longer felt so rejecting toward Amelia now that she was beginning to step out of the victim role.

With these new situations occurring in a synchronistic way, Susan begins to realize the form of the obvious theme. Without a doubt, there is something to be cleared, something that keeps coming up through her overripe emotions in situations related to victims. She seems to have some empathy for the aggressor or maybe it's apathy. She's not sure. There is consistently anger and disgust toward the victim, a sort of distaste for weakness. The shape of the theme is a bit clearer, but Susan wonders where this might have come from. Recognizing that she needs to do some deeper exploration, she decides to do some digging around in the past for some answers after the children are in bed.

That evening, there is dinner as usual, some playful moments with Adam and Kendra, followed by the bedtime routine complete with the soft kisses on their foreheads. Kendra wants an extra kiss on the tip of her nose so Susan absorbs the elfish expression on Kendra's face while she plants that kiss. Now, Susan thinks, now I have some time to dig around about that victim theme, and she walks into the silent den toward the couch. But that novel that she checked out from the library over a week ago catches her eye. It's been a week and she hasn't even had time to start the book. It will be due back soon. *The digging around doesn't have to be done at this second. It could be done later or any night after the children are in bed for that matter.* With these thoughts convincing her, Susan decides to read just a few pages. In less than thirty minutes, she is too tired to think or read. So she wanders to her bedroom where she sinks into the coolness of sheets. Days go by. Then weeks, but Susan never seems to find time to do that digging. After several weeks, the doubts start to sway into her thinking. Maybe she had been making too much of those situations. Maybe she had been reading interpretations into them, creating a theme when there really wasn't one. She has done that before, after all. Perhaps this was just one of those times. Soon, the theme fades from the bright foreground of conscious thought into the murkiness of the subconscious.

Through this slice of Susan's life, the theme starts to take on a more solid appearance, but only after some early reflection and confirming situations occur. We start this part of the story with Susan going through reviews of the crash that she had with Kendra. She had a sense that someone else was behind the curtain. Now she wants to know who. The crash with Kendra is all she has to go on, at this point. So she reviews the situation mentally to look for clues. Shifting to the situational view and the outside looking in help, but she still seems uncertain about what exactly happened. She still doesn't see a clear form of the theme. So she combs her mind for recent events, looking for reactions that might be similar. She is like the scientist who has an inkling of a hypothesis, a sort of nagging idea that pushes to find more evidence. And evidence is what she is searching for. If she had been able to find any suitable situations, she could have then reviewed them much in the same manner that she did with the first situation. Were her reactions the same? Were her feelings consistent? Unfortunately Susan can think of only one event at work, having to do with an indecisive client, and she is not certain that the situation is similar enough to use. Here, she decides to wait and be watchful of other events and reactions that might point to the theme. No, she still doesn't have a clear understanding of this theme. Even after her reflections, reviews and observational shifts. But her reflections and heightened attention have served to open the door to eventual understanding. For now, her attention is keenly open and sensitive to this area.

Lo and behold, the very next day, there are two events that prick and thus point to the theme. Now I realize that I can make the two-dimensional paper Susan and her life do most anything I want them to. And yes, these situations are convenient to showing some points. But, coincidences and synchronicities happen without ink and paper. That is, if you are working on some theme or perception in your life, you are quite likely to run up against similar circumstances that can point you in the direction of growth and evolution, so that you can eventually transcend the theme and allow Soul to direct your life. Perhaps the needed events won't occur the very next day, but they will occur. Here, we are bumping up against one of those basic flying positions: that the moments of life are precious because they hold the questions and the answers that we need to Align ourselves to the Sacred within us, to our Souls.

Through these two events then, the car accident and the conversation about Amelia, Susan gets a clearer picture of the theme. That ghostly character has started to take on some definition. For this to happen, though, Susan had to be paying attention. These two events were only part of a full day of living for her. Other events and situations filled in the rest of her day, but only these two tapped into the theme. She had to be paying attention to get all that. Admittedly, one is not likely to gloss over such a dramatic situation as a car accident. The details of that kind of drama do tend to stick in one's mind. But Susan had to be paying attention to her own reaction and she had to pick up the fact that the event did indeed rouse that theme. And her attention truly had to be keen to see how that conversation about Amelia related to her theme. Susan wasn't even much interested in hearing about Amelia. But she was able to observe how her feelings toward Amelia changed and to reflect about what this change meant. She had to be paying attention to do that.

So, now Susan has a clearer idea that there is a theme behind the curtain and what the form of that theme is. And she knows that it can sweep her away in the right circumstances. The intensity of her emotions and her crash with Kendra testifies to the power of this theme. Her attention has brought her this far. She arrives now at the crossroads of choice. She can choose to take on the work of clearing and transcending this theme or she can allow this particular Siamese twin to stay firmly attached. Her decision to do some exploration tells us that she is moving toward making the choice of transcendence. But then what does she do? She reads a novel! What is going on here?

Susan has stumbled on a barrier that we are all intimately familiar with, a barrier that can prevent our growth and evolution, a barrier that can actually lead us toward stagnation. Fear. Here is Fear with a big "F." Remember this guy? Now, it might not seem like Susan is Fearful about tackling this theme. After all, she is only reading a novel for one evening. There is no overt feeling of Fear. But that one evening turns into days and weeks. And thoughts about the theme turn into doubts about its existence. Somebody doesn't want to dig around and explore this thing. This passive type of resistance is none other than Fear lurking behind a mask of bus-i-ness and activity. Fear can even make friends with logic and insert doubts into our thoughts. Fear can take many forms and put on many faces. Procrastination is a potential face it wears. And there is overworking, filling in the space of life with inane talk, passively accepting life's circumstances. All kinds of forms Fear can take. We see Susan's Fear surfacing in her own unique way, through procrastination and doubts. And this type of running *will actually work* to avoid any anticipated pain that she might have to go through in taking on the theme. At least for awhile. That is, until life decides to smack her with another event that will prick that theme. Life just won't leave us alone about our themes. They keep coming back at us.

The trend in the weather the past few days has been toward warmth as springtime fulfills its promise of return. As Susan flings open the back door, she inhales the scent of the earth. The spring always reminds her that the earth does indeed have a smell. Susan wants to join her children who are now sprinting toward the birch tree at the back of the yard. Adam has made the climbing of this particular tree a sort of springtime ritual. On the first warm day, the day when the sun actually can soak through the clothes to warm the body, Adam climbs this tree. Kendra has never done it before. Even though she had the physical capability, Susan hadn't allowed her to climb the tree. She had thought Kendra was too young. But not this year. And Susan watches Kendra following Adam now as, giggling, they scurry for that wide trunk. Susan thinks that maybe she will climb the tree herself this year, right along with the kids.

With agile monkey movements, Adam jumps to the first branch and swings upward. Practice has taught him the best hand and foot holds, so he appears to climb without much thought. His focus is on the whoops of glee and laughter as he pauses occasionally to blare out one of these whoops to Kendra. Kendra can hardly contain her body. She is so excited. Feet moving and twitching under the tree, she tilts her head back to catch the full visual of her bother's ascent. And Adam comes down as easily as he got up. Susan and Kendra clap furiously to his dramatized bows, then Susan tells them that she might just do it this year. With this quiet announcement, the children are jumping up and yelling words of encouragement. It doesn't take much urging before Susan is gracefully pulling herself up to the second branch. She doesn't go as high as Adam did, but she knows that the children are impressed when she lands with a thud on the ground in front of them. Her climbing has given them an excuse for more clapping and whooping.

Now it's Kendra's turn. The ruckus ebbs a bit and Kendra becomes quiet as she stares at the first branch.

The excitement seems to have collapsed into studied seriousness as she places her hands on that branch. Eyes wide, Kendra looks up at the other branches to be scaled and repositions her hands. She manages to hoist herself up a little before losing her grip and sliding down to the ground. On the way down, she has scratched her arm on the bark. A glance at the tiny pencil line of blood on her arm and the tears flow. Susan steps closer and tells Kendra that the cut is not that bad.

"It's hardly bleeding, see?"

Then she tells her to stop the crying and simply try again. After a small sniffle, Kendra looks up at her mother with an unblinking coolness and gets up. Adam is absolutely quiet and watching. Kendra stares a moment at the tree again, then, moving slowly, she approaches it. Susan can only see the back of Kendra, but the coolness remains. And Susan becomes aware at that instant of her own anger and disgust at Kendra's behavior. She thinks that Kendra will probably try and fail again—on purpose. It is the disgust that reminds Susan of the theme and the thinking that she had done about it, was it weeks ago? She never did do that digging and so here it is again, coming back up. With this realization, she knows immediately that she is in a risky situation. She knows that emotions could overwhelm her, which could lead to a crash. So Susan decides to pay attention to her feelings with a vengeance to insure that she does not become an emotion. She also decides to watch her actions closely. *I've got to really be on point now. Every moment,* she thinks. All of this reflection occurs in the few seconds of Kendra's walking toward the tree for that second try.

This time, instead of tentatively placing her hands, Kendra grabs the branch and pulls with her muscles and her frustration. The frustration must have given her too much extra strength because she flips right over the branch and lands with a thud on her bottom. The swiftness of the fall has stunned her, so there is a pause before she starts crying again. This time the crying is harder than before and Susan's repulsion is more intense than before. The display of weakness has tapped into the depth of her disgust. Susan watches the crescendo of her own emotion before she moves toward Kendra. She must act— now. With that thought, Susan has the experience of another emotion—fear. What if she does something that makes it worse? That hurts her daughter? That victimizes her for the second time? Or what if she does something that plays into the theme that is starting to emerge in Kendra?

There is not much time for reflection. Susan decides to take the safe route. She decides to force herself to behave in a way that is opposite to her internal reaction, to the behaviors that would naturally follow the emotions of the theme. She wants to yell at Kendra, tell her to get off her butt. Instead she walks over to her daughter and consoles her with a hug and a gentle understanding remark.

"It's kind of hard, isn't it? The tree seems so high and you want to climb it so much." Susan waits for a moment while Kendra's crying slows down a bit. Kendra turns her head slowly and looks out of the corner of her eye for Adam. He is squatting on the other side of the tree, poking a stick at something on the ground. In a voice just above a whisper, Kendra says,

"Adam climbed it. You climbed it. I want to climb it too. Why is it so easy for everyone else? I hate that stupid tree anyway."

What Susan hears in this is weakness, a "poor me" attitude, and sour grapes. Her disgust is renewed. Again, she wants to tell Kendra to just stop all of this crap and climb the damn tree! Again, she forces herself to act differently.

"Kendra, you're feeling so bad about this. I know it's hard. Listen, we could just try again another day. Or you could just decide that you don't want to climb it…or, I suppose you could try again, if you want. You decide what you want to do."

"Mommy, will you just put me on that first branch?"

Susan's thoughts of disgust rush forward with this request. *She doesn't even want to try! She just wants to be there without the effort. Why can't she just let me help her climb?* Susan watches these thoughts and knows that they are connected to the disgust. With a forced smile, she agrees to put Kendra on the branch. Kendra is now beaming her delight at being up so high, despite the tears that still streak her face. Susan wants to suggest that she try to climb higher, but stifles this thought before it slides down to her voice. When Kendra asks to be put down, Susan sweeps her playfully from the branch and swings her down to the ground. The tears are forgotten.

Nope. Life just won't leave us alone about our themes. We can procrastinate or "forget" about them. But not for long. Because another situation will occur that stirs that theme and we'll find ourselves reacting in that old familiar way. It almost happened to Susan again, didn't it? She almost fell into her old reactions. Her "consoling" comment to Kendra was, "It's hardly bleeding, see?" There are a lot of underlying messages here, aren't there? Messages directly related to the theme. Messages like, "Don't take it so seriously," and "It's not worth crying over," and "It's not worth quitting over." And Kendra probably hears them all. Susan's comment was about Kendra's arm, but was laden with less than consoling messages about Kendra's pride and ego. Her disgust for Kendra's behavior is what comes through.

And it is through Susan's attention to this feeling of disgust that she realizes the presence of the theme. At this point, she knows that the situation is extremely risky. In fact, this particular situation seems to dig at the heart of the theme, rousing it and pulling it forward. The theme writhes with disgust and thoughts pop up to feed it, almost before she is aware of them. Added to all of this is the fact that Kendra is her daughter, a little person who she wants to teach to be mentally tall and independent. Susan certainly doesn't want her own daughter to be a victim. The risk is indeed great.

And Susan is faced with a choice. To stay in the situation or to withdraw. A true dilemma. One thing she can't do is a quick transcendence. She can't just excuse herself, run off to the house, rush through exploration and transcendence, then run back down to join her children. That's absurd. It won't happen. She could decide that the risk is too great, that she won't be able to control her thoughts or behaviors in the face of such a strong theme and withdraw into the house. She could make some excuse about why she can't stay outside. And leaving this risky situation would guarantee that no crashes would occur, that nobody would get burned. After all, she has already injected Kendra with some negative messages. Withdrawing from the situation is safe and allows time for addressing the theme later. The downside to withdrawing is that she would be running from the theme, thereby giving it more power in her mind. Running also inflates the Fear. If she's running and cannot control herself, then this monster theme must be pretty potent.

Susan decides to stick it out. What this means is that she is going into battle, a head-on battle with a potent, experienced opponent. This guy's been around awhile. The theme knows all of the effective buttons to push. The risk here is that losing will inflate the theme and the Fear. Crashing will most likely scorch everything around Susan and we know who will suffer from this fiery spray — Kendra. Of course, it does work the other way. If Susan manages to not respond to all of that button pushing, to not behave in a way that the theme dictates, she will have undercut some of its power over her. This is helpful. The decision is not easy and must be weighed out by each of us. Yes, you will face a predicament like this one day.

With Susan's decision to stay in the situation, she has committed herself to a constant internal struggle. The theme forcefully pulls her to react in one way as the old disgust and fueling thoughts froth up into consciousness. And she decides to behave in an opposite way. Here, in this scenario, behaving opposite to the dictations of the theme is a good idea. This may not be true, of course, for all themes, but it makes sense for this unique situation and this unique person. So Susan engages in the struggle with a plan to behave opposite to the theme. Susan is not Aligned with her Soul here, but what she is doing is refusing to be Aligned with the theme. There is a battle coming.

In a head-on battle with an experienced opponent, you're gonna need some weapons, right? Susan has two weapons. She has attention and she has her plan. Her attention will serve to catch feelings and thoughts that the theme constantly send up from the depths of her psyche. That's the theme pushing the buttons, prodding her to react as she always has. He is relentless about this button pushing, so she will have to be just as relentless with her attention. She will need to constantly monitor and watch for any signs. She can do this best by staying, as much as possible, in the position of outside looking in. Guarding this position, then, she can put her plan into place. It is as if Susan is perched outside herself and watching with the intensity of squinted eyes for any behaviors that might be pushed forward by the theme. She must stop and examine each of these behaviors. "Sorry, guys, all behaviors must be pre-approved before they are allowed expression." With the paper and ink Susan, her attention and plan work and the battle is won.

But we won't start celebrating. Not just yet. For notice what we have here. We have an exhausted Susan, a depleted of energy Susan, a struggling, chained Susan. This is why battling against themes regularly is not good. This is why transcendence is so much better. During the battle, she was doing that worn out imitation of Picasso again. Feeling one way and behaving in another. And the folks on the receiving end of this act probably aren't going to be thoroughly convinced that the act is real. Kendra probably sensed that Susan wasn't being completely genuine with her. And, of course, these type of Picasso imitations absolutely delete any potential spontaneity. Susan couldn't be spontaneous in her behavior and enjoy the tree climbing. She had to pre-approve behaviors because she couldn't trust herself. Also, the battle has left Susan drained of energy which means that the next activity will likely be perceived with a dullness that echoes from the battle. How likely will she be able to immerse herself into the rainbow colors of the next series of moments after engaging such a worthy opponent? Not likely. Nope. Doing battle with a theme may be the choice to make in a pinch, but regular warring is out of the question. Besides, regular warring doesn't work because we lose too often and crash.

On the more positive side—what this whole event has done for Susan is to bring the theme back up into her awareness once more. The battle has served to amplify the need to address this old guy. The message from this life situation about getting to the work of transcendence is loud and clear.

The children are in bed and this night, Susan keeps the promise to herself to reflect. It was tough holding herself back like she did today. Kendra's failed attempts to climb that tree tapped the heavy emotions of the theme. It had been a good thing that she recognized that disgust before it got out of hand, though. Susan congratulates herself on staying in the situation and not crashing. She reviews the events in her mind for a minute then she thinks back to several weeks ago. The theme had been so in the front of her mind at that time. She admits to herself that she had not realized just how much she didn't want to address it. She admits that maybe she was a little afraid at what she might find once she went digging in the past. And she marvels at how easily she deceived herself into procrastinating and causing the delay. Simply amazing how the thing had just dissipated from her thoughts like that. But the situation today certainly underscored the need to work on this theme. She knows that it will keep coming up until it is addressed. It had been difficult, extremely difficult to force her behavior this afternoon. She didn't like feeling one way on the inside and behaving another way on the outside. Holding up this incongruence required way too much energy. Besides, it was transparent to the children. She doesn't want to be modeling tension and incongruence to her children. And she reminds herself that any pain that she faces will probably be less than the effort of the struggle to force her own behavior. She tries to think of the pain as the precursor to the inevitable growth that will follow transcendence. And the taste of joy and freedom once the theme is cleared.

With these reflections and repositioning of perceptions, Susan starts digging around in the past. She combs her mind to fasten onto any memories that might be related to weakness or victimization. Knowing that early family experiences are usually rich with the beginnings of themes, she focuses on these memories first. Her parents. Did her parents victimize her in any way? The obvious mistreatment can be ruled out, she thinks. There was never physical abuse. She doesn't even remember getting spanked. What about criticism from her parents? She doesn't recall being put down particularly, although her father could sometimes become sarcastic. And there wasn't much yelling in her house because her parents were big on "talking things out." There doesn't seem to be much juicy evidence for this theme in Susan's relationship with her parents. So where did this start? Could it be some dynamic between her parents? Susan considers how her parents related to each other when she was young. The scanning of memory turns up nothing, so she decides to be watchful for any events that could give her some insight into her past. She plans to be particularly attentive over the next few days.

Several days later, she is in the car on the way to pick up her children from school. As usual, she is listening to that mix radio station and hears a song about a father who walked out on his son. Suddenly, a vague heavy sadness settles in on Susan and tears flow at the stoplight. The tears feel good, like there is a release happening. She stays with her feeling until it starts to fade. Then she thinks. The song is tapping into something about her father. She is certain of this, but she doesn't know what. The obvious doesn't fit. He never left her. She arrives at her children's school still baffled about how it all fits together, but lighter because of the release. Knowing that she will eventually figure it out, she lets the ideas go and focuses on her children.

On the way home, they stop at the grocery store to pick up that ever-necessary gallon of milk and they soon find themselves in a long line. Apparently others had a similar idea, stopping into the store to grab a necessary item or two. Susan uses the opportunity to find out what happened with her children at school today. She particularly wants to know how Kendra did on her math test and how Adam handled that disagreement with his best friend. She squats down so that she can be at face level with them. Kendra tells them some of the details about the problems on the test, then she says that she might've aced it. Susan is just about to verbally applaud when her attention is drawn toward the couple in the line in front of them. From her squatting position, she looks up at them. Kendra and Adam are watching the couple also because their conversation has just turned louder and a little nasty.

"You saw it coming and you still didn't do anything about it!"

The man is straining to contain his voice to one that is appropriate for the public. He continues saying something, but Susan is unaware, as she is propelled backwards in her memory. Dad said this exact thing to Mom one time...or maybe it was more than one time. But there was one time when Susan remembers looking up at them when her father said this to her mother. His voice had been calm, but Susan's remembers feeling the heady awkwardness of the tension. She can see the interaction happening clearly on the screen of her mind. Except for that one phrase, the words are muddled, but the expressions and the underlying tone of the conversation are quite clear. Dad is berating Mom about letting someone victimize her. Mom is looking very much the victim as Dad's disgust is oozing all over her. The look on her face is pained. She just stands there and takes this verbal pounding. Susan has no clue what the exchange had been about either in her memory or with the people in line at the grocery store. Clearly, though, this incident points to the evidence in her past that she had been looking for.

Susan becomes aware of the poking on her shoulder.

It's Kendra who whispers, "It's not polite to stare, Mom."

The reminder brings Susan back to the present. Although she is excited by having stumbled onto this and wants to explore further right away, she focuses on putting the gallons of milk on the rolling belt. The jugs ride toward the cashier. Now she relishes the idea of the reflecting that she will do later.

Susan didn't particularly relish the idea of reflecting before, but she kept her promise to herself anyway. This section starts out with some reflections, but not about the theme, per se. Susan begins by considering her procrastination and the Fear that was probably behind all of that "forgetting." With these thoughts comes a sort of realignment of her perceptions. She reminds herself of some of those basic flying positions. And, with the internal battle still fresh in her mind, she considers all the reasons why she doesn't want to engage that opponent head-on again. What this sort of reflecting does, is to inoculate her from some of the Fear that might be dangling and to motivate her to push forward into the murky digging of the past.

And the murky digging begins. She filters through some old family memories looking for the seeds and roots of the theme. What might have happened in her past that would make her so sensitive, so easily disgusted to people in the victim role? This initial attempt at exploration turns up, well...nothing. Considering the likely candidates, namely her relationship with and between her parents, gets her nowhere. Now, we know that later, it turns out that there was indeed a dynamic between her parents that could've caused the sensitivity. So why doesn't this initial reflection show it? It could be that there is some part of her that is blocking access to these juicy, revealing memories. That would be the Fear part. This can happen. Fear can block us right out of our memories. Or, more simply, it could be that she just wasn't able to remember anything at the time. For whatever reason, sometimes exploration turns up no leads. Then, barring other creative digging mechanisms, we might have to wait.

So Susan waits and watches the events of her life with a more intense attention. Once again, she is listening for any clues that would lead her to an understanding about this theme. A song on the radio stirs up something in her, although she is not sure what. Not knowing doesn't really bother Susan though, does it? She just rides with the feelings and enjoys the emotional release. There's no obsessing here about what is behind these feelings. There's no anxiety about the mystery. There is only acceptance and gratitude. We can't always know the why's or how's of every event that occurs on the floor of our subconscious. Susan is completely at ease with this mystery.

Then the grocery store interaction solidly triggers a memory in Susan. Maybe her memory is jolted because she is squatting and looking up at the couple, much like she would have looked up at her parents from the short position of a child. Or maybe it was because the words that the man used were exactly the same as her father's. Whatever the reason, the event has triggered a memory that might reveal some of the roots of her theme.

The intentional thinking type of exploration turned up nothing for Susan to go on, but the events of her life triggered a mysterious release and a helpful memory. Now she is ready for some deep digging.

The children are in bed and the precious hour of reflection is hers. She had to retrieve her mind from wandering several times during the evening. Her thoughts kept turning to the reflections about this theme. The scene of memory between her parents came up over and over again. Susan would refocus herself on the present, not wanting to fall into a problematic split attention mode. But now the hour of reflection had finally arrived. She is alone. She replays the scene again with full attention to see if she missed anything. No. The scene remains as it had come up in memory at the grocery store. She had never thought of her mother as a victim before. Nor had she considered her father as critical. She decides to think back to how they related to each other again, but this time she does it with these new glasses on. A few flashes of memory from their daily lives and a whole new light comes on in her mind. Mom was often in the victim role. There were times when Mom would point out how she had been taken advantage of. And even though Mom had clearly been responsible for allowing this to happen, maybe even asking for it by putting herself in that position, she would try to get sympathy for the injustice. But it was the injustice that Mom had invited, that she had initiated herself. She wanted sympathy or attention or emotional energy. Dad's response to Mom's histrionic displays were the dripping disgust and critical soliloquies. The reason that they never seemed particularly harsh is that he never raised his voice. *Maybe that is why I missed it before*, Susan thinks. The negative undercurrent was too

265

subtle to clearly identify from her perspective as a child.

What was clear through Susan's perspective as a child, was that Dad was rejecting Mom. Even with tiny eyes, even with the subdued voice, Susan as a child understood that Dad rejected Mom whenever she acted weak. And Susan never wanted to have to endure the pain of that kind of rejection by her father, so she never acted weak. Even when she felt weak and wanted to seek support from somebody, she would blast right through the situation with persistence and determination. She had wanted her father to be proud. She had wanted his respect. And he did grow to respect her. And she had grown to be disgusted by her mother's behavior. Eventually, she had started to reject her mother as well, whenever any weakness was ever shown.

Now Susan understood more about the song on the radio. She didn't have a father who had left her, but she did have a father whose rejection was always threatening in the background. There had always been the shy tension of that rejection hovering behind behaviors. Susan suddenly realizes that she has somehow incorporated that rejection. Now she, Susan is rejecting and repulsed by any sign of weakness. She has never allowed herself even to feel deficient or to show weakness in any way. She has always fought when someone tried to take advantage of her. Susan knows now that she has been rejecting a piece of herself all along. The weak self. The self that feels small sometimes. The feelings and accompanying thoughts of frailties and flaws had, at first, been unacceptable because of the feared rejection of her father. Now they were unacceptable to her. She feels repulsion and disgust for a piece of herself.

And there is Kendra. Now Susan understands that she has essentially been playing out the dynamic of her parent's relationship in the relationship with Kendra. She herself has taken up her father's role as the one who rejects and berates the victim. Now she uses that calm voice, (or not so calm, sometimes), to criticize Kendra whenever she shows any weakness at all. Then Susan considers something else. Unlike Susan's mother, Kendra doesn't really put herself in a position to be taken advantage of. She doesn't really try to be the victim so that she can later solicit sympathy. When Susan thinks back to the argument between the children over that Hot Wheels car, she can see now the innocence in Kendra's putting the car down by her knee. Kendra was overwhelmed with emotion. Sure, Adam did take advantage of the unguarded car, but Kendra hadn't wanted him to do that. She had probably been genuinely hurt by his sneakiness. Her crying and yelling was a testimony to her anger. And the tree. She was the smallest and physically weakest of the three. She simply couldn't do it. When Susan's replays the situation, what she sees is Kendra's determination pitted against her physical weakness. She did want to climb that tree, not pretend as though she couldn't. Susan realizes now that her own perception of Kendra's behavior was clouded by the theme. Susan had been reacting to Kendra as if Kendra's behavior was like her own Mom's, but that wasn't the case at all. She just perceived Kendra's reactions as the same. She hadn't been seeing clearly. *Gosh, how intricate and complicated these themes are*, she thinks, *like a spider's web. Or the Internet. One thing leads to another.*

Over the next few days, Susan contemplates ideas for transcending the theme. She considers just how embedded the theme is, and decides on a full-scale plan. There is the emotional work to do, that deep transcendence that dances in the subconscious. Some type of exercise during meditation might be helpful for this, a visualization perhaps. As for practice in everyday life, Susan thinks that some re-ordering of thinking might be called for. She doesn't think that she will have to work terribly hard at catching situations that provoke the theme. Staying on the lookout for any feelings of disgust and knowing what situations would tend to dovetail with the theme are ways that she has already practiced with. So the catching probably won't be too difficult. Then she will have to retrain her thoughts. First, she plans to question one of her automatic perceptions. That is, is the victim in this situation actually inviting further abuse so that others will pay attention and feed into it? Are they really flaunting their weakness? Most of the time, Susan suspects that the answer will be "no." In that case, her understanding will be as automatic as the perception had been. The compassion will flow naturally at that point.

But what if the perception is true? What if the person is flaunting their weakness, intentionally putting themselves in a position of victim so that they can solicit the comfort of others? How is she suppose to weather her disgust then? Susan ponders this for a moment. It would really be difficult for her to see someone deliberately put themselves in a position to be mistreated and not be saturated with disgust and repulsion for that person. Now what? Susan thinks for awhile, then realizes the obvious answer, the one that seems to come up for most every issue. Compassion. In situations where the person is deliberately being the martyr, she can consider how they are caught up in their own theme, and, in this way, that person is really no different than she. They are caught up in the same theme, but on the other end. Considering how she and the victim are both caught will erase the judgmental thoughts and the repulsion and inflate her compassion. The actions are likely to follow the compassionate perception.

Okay, so there's the plan for the events and experiences that come up daily. Now Susan realizes that she will necessarily need a plan to change the undercurrents of this theme in her subconscious. She doesn't want to be struggling against herself as she did with Kendra climbing the tree. She doesn't want her actions and thoughts to be doing battle with the tides of the subconscious. It's too much of a struggle and besides, the tides would eventually win. So she considers how to go about the emotional transcendence. Some type of visualization during her meditation might help her learn to accept that rejected piece of her. But she worries. She knows that meditation can tap into the depths of her mind. What if, after a week or so, all this makes her actually behave like a victim? What if she actually becomes weak? Maybe she should reconsider this idea. Then, with a sudden internal eye roll, Susan recognizes the old familiar friend—fear. A gentle laugh and a quick thought about how silently it had crept in, though, and the fear easily dissipates. These very thoughts are coming from the theme itself, she realizes. Here is the distaste for weakness, the rejection of any piece of her that even begins a feeble thought. She is frightened of becoming weak herself. *Well, of course,* she thinks, *that is what the theme is all about!* Then Susan thinks of something else. Before she was aware of the theme, she had thought of herself as strong. Stronger than most, since she didn't cave into weakness. Now she realizes that the perception was completely faulty. In cutting a piece of her away, she had been undermining her strength. She had been embracing a brawniness that was no more than posturing, really. But, in transcending the theme, in accepting that piece of her, she will be increasing her actual strength. Ironically, she will be stronger because of her acceptance of her weakness. The irony of this taps into her humor and she starts to snicker a bit.

That evening, Susan decides to try the visualization. She starts meditating and waits for her body to relax and her mind to slow in its jumping around. Her mind tries to leap ahead to the intended subject matter, the visualization. It always is in search of entertainment and distraction from the silence and spaces of meditation. Susan remains firm, though, in bringing that roaming, playful thought machine back to her focus. She will decide when it's time. With her mind finally staying mostly on focus, then, Susan makes her move. She draws a vivid mental image of the home where she grew up. The gray aluminum siding and the maroon shutters loom up on her internal screen. Red impatiens run along the edge of the front porch. They almost match the shutters. Susan feels the wind push her hair toward her face and a few strands catch on the wetness of her lips. She frees the hair, then reaches for the gold doorknob and turns it with a click. She goes straight up the old stairs and anticipates the creak in the floorboard by the vent on the fifth stair. The wood makes the predicted noise as her weight presses it. There is the familiar smell of candle perfume in the air that her mother created with the scented candles. As she makes her way down the hall to her old room, she can hear the smallness of muffled crying which gradually gets louder with her approach. It is the cry of a child, a cry that is not hurried or sudden. The child has been crying for awhile. Susan knocks on her own bedroom door then turns the knob and slowly opens the door. There, on her bed, lying on her pastel blue comforter is the little girl who is crying, head buried in her hands as if she had flung herself haphazardly onto the bed. The child seems completely absorbed by the raw feelings of hurt. The noise of the door, however, has startled the child and she looks up. Susan sees her own face. Now the room and its details seem to disappear as Susan and the child absorb each other for a brief second. Then Susan, allowing love and compassion to fill her heart, moves to the child. She sits with the child and holds her comfortingly, rocking rhythmically back and forth. And the peace swells in both of them. At this point, Susan allows the scene to fade from her mind. She continues to meditate without images and then slowly brings herself out of meditation. She feels peaceful herself, almost relieved.

As the days go by, Susan continues to meditate with visualizations. She allows them to change. As she is eventually completely comfortable with the child, she adds in her father who is accepting of both Susan as the adult and Susan as the child. She makes these changes gradually, allowing her level of fear to guide her. If she experiences no anxiety at all during the visualization for a few sessions, then she moves on, to incorporate a version that is more demanding. Too much anxiety that slides into fear is a sign that she moving too fast and so she takes out a demanding element in the visualization. This continues for some months. In the meantime, she is practicing in the way that she had planned when situations and events come up that tap into her theme.

Whew! It's enough to make you want to sit down in that Laz-y-boy chair and rest the neurons for awhile. Most themes are, by nature, dense and complicated like this, which is why this long example is necessary. They've been around for quite some time, long enough to spread out on the floor of that subconscious and play around with quite a few of those boxes. They like to play with perceptions too, as you can see. Yet, as dense and as complicated as they are, they are not beyond understanding. At this point, Susan likely has a full understanding of her theme. She knows about the seeds that her parents unwittingly planted and about how the theme grew. She can even see how it lays in her mind now. That is, she has a clear perception of what this theme is. Gone is the ghostly appearance and the furtive darting here and there. Susan has identified it and pulled it out into the spotlight. And she knows how the theme plays out in her life currently, how it skews her own perceptions and behavior, and how it affects Kendra.

With the paper and ink Susan, all of this understanding and insight occurred overnight. One triggered memory from the grocery store interaction, and boom! Spontaneous, comprehensive under-standing. Sure, sometimes, understanding does happen this way. We can have that sort of "Ah-Ha!" experience and have the whole thing illuminated in one evening. But more often, pieces emerge, one or a few at a time and we have to work these pieces into some coherent, understandable whole. Instead of the "Ah-Ha!" we get a smaller "hummmm..." It works. It just usually takes a bit longer, that's all.

But, after awhile, the pieces of the theme fit into place and we get a full intellectual understanding of the theme. The understanding will then naturally point us in the direction of transcendence. We may have to be creative about *how* exactly to go about doing it, but more often than not, with that understanding under our belts, we will know *what* needs to be done.

Susan recognized that there was a piece of her that she was rejecting and that transcendence would necessarily involve accepting

271

and incorporating this piece of her. The *what* was clear. The understanding did this for her. Then she thinks of a *how*. She chooses visualization during meditation to tackle this aspect of her theme. This means that she is a regular mediator and that she is comfortable with visualization. The *how* that she chooses fits her. Another person with another theme would choose another method for tackling the internal aspect of the theme.

And the specific visualization matches her unique theme. She will be attempting to accept the "weak" part of herself and picks herself as a child to symbolize this weakness. This fits nicely, doesn't it? And going back to her old house where she grew up is a fitting way to collect a piece of herself that she left behind. She even opens a door, which is a fitting symbol for the passage that she is to make. Furthermore, the adult Susan gets to practice consoling a child that is the victim of something, which is like role playing the behavior that she will want to engage in herself with her own children. Not to get too heavily back into Susan's theme. You've probably had enough of the density. The point is that her simple, but thickly loaded visualization was created by her for her unique theme. The work of transcendence is individual and is ours alone to do.

Now, with a full intellectual understanding and the work of emotional transcendence well underway, it would be very tempting at this point to let it go at that. The intellectual understanding alone is going to bring some psychic relief. Already the theme is rendered weaker through knowledge. After all, the theme is no longer that dramatic, mysterious ghost that makes furtive appearances. Now the lines around the theme are completely clear. When we know who we're dealing with, we're no longer so impressed. *Gosh*, we think, *you're not so big or powerful as we thought.* Themes may be complicated, but once we take the mystery out of them, they are not nearly so powerful. And with the work of internal/emotional transcendence moving along, maybe we're done.

Well, maybe we *are* done. Maybe, that is, if our behavior falls neatly in line with that internal transcendence. Sometimes, when we work through the themes at their roots, on that floor with the boxes and all, the behavior naturally and effortlessly changes. What this would mean in Susan's case is that she would no longer feel repulsed by or have judgmental thoughts about victims, nor would she have any urge whatsoever to berate them. Sometimes, the behaviors do fall right into line.

Sometimes they don't. In fact, most of the time, more work is going to be needed. This is because themes, by nature, are long-standing patterns. We've been doing the same thing in all those similar situations for a long time. A very long time. What this means then, is that our behavioral habits tend to linger long after our intellectual understanding is complete and even sometimes after our emotional transcendence is complete. We may need some retraining in order to step out of these automatic ways of being. In Susan's case, she thinks that she will have no trouble recognizing the events that might prick her theme. She has already had some practice with this and plans to use that familiar emotion of disgust as her attention alarm. Once she detects disgust, she will be on the alert for any of the old follow-up emotions or perceptions. Thus, her primary focus will be on changing her perception. She wants to delete that automatic judgment that she tends to make and she has an alternative perception ready to substitute. Here the focus is on changing the way that she thinks. She is assuming that the behaviors will flow naturally from there. Perhaps later, she will find that she needs to focus on the actions themselves, but for now, her plan is intact.

Spring is here again. Already Adam and Kendra have climbed the ritual tree and the days are growing longer. The warmer weather means more playtime outdoors. The children are outside, but Susan is seated at the dining room table doing something she doesn't like to do. Susan is paying bills. She is usually not in the best of moods after this activity and is prone to becoming easily irritated. She realizes that there is probably something to this general negativity of paying bills, but doesn't want to think about that now. She just wants to get them done. From the window she can see Kendra, Adam and some neighborhood children playing soccer. The last time she looked up from writing checks was between the mortgage and the electric bills, and she had watched all the children playing happily. She had heard muffled whoops of glee through the closed window. Now, with the car payment in front of her, she hears another dull, muted sound, the sound of Kendra crying which she recognizes with the immediacy of a mother. Looking out the window only verifies what she already knew. Kendra is on the ground crying. Susan automatically goes out the door to her daughter. She sits next to Kendra and rubs her back, knowing that Kendra probably doesn't want to be hugged boldly in front of the neighborhood boys.

Susan waits for her daughter to calm down a bit before asking, "What happened?" Through tears, Kendra's words bubble up. She can never get the ball. And they don't want to pass it to her.

Susan says, "You're frustrated because you try and try, but it's hard to keep up." She pause, then adds simply, "Well, what do you want to do now? Would you like to just take a little break? Or do you want me to help you figure out a way to try to join in again?"

Kendra's crying stops and she looks directly at her mother. She decides to take that break and walks with Susan back towards the house. Kendra yells back over her shoulder that she is only going to get some water and will be back in a minute. Inside, Susan tells Kendra that she must finish paying the car payment and then they can be together. Kendra does get that glass of water and sits quietly at the table, waiting for her mother to finish writing the check. As Susan gathers the papers and stuffs them into a drawer, she looks up at her daughter.

"Well, now, you're almost finished with that water. What do you want to do?"

"Oh, Mom," Kendra says with a sigh, "I want to go back out to the game, but I'm just so tired of it. I never get the ball. They don't want to pass it to me."

"You like to play, but you get so frustrated 'cause it seems like you never really get to play."

"Yeah, that's right. I run around and around. All I'm doing is running. I never can get the ball. I'm really trying!" At this, she looks down at a dried grain of rice left over from last night's dinner. She starts to push it back and forth between her feet then adds more quietly, "Maybe they're just better than I am."

"Maybe." Susan responds just as quietly as Kendra. The grain of rice is forgotten as Kendra's face pops up to search her mother's eyes. Susan continues.

"Listen, Kendra. You've got to remember that you're playing with Adam's friends who are two and three years older than you are. They've been playing longer than you and are bigger than you. If they are better than you, it has nothing to do with how good you are." Susan pauses for a moment then continues. "Maybe when you're playing sometimes, you don't feel so good about yourself. Maybe you're thinking some pretty negative things like, 'I'll never get this right,' and 'I just can't do this.'"

Kendra's slow nod is serious. Susan goes on.

"Well, it's not exactly fair to compare yourself to kids who are older and bigger than you, now, is it?"

"I suppose not."

"If I were to go out and try to shoot some basketball with Shaq O'Neil and Michael Jordan, they'd beat the pants off me! I'm sure I'd never get the ball in the hoop. Gosh, I'd probably never even get to touch the ball! They've been playing a lot longer and…well, I know I'm tall, but I'm not that tall!" To this Kendra laughs.

"I'll tell you one more thing." Susan looks around playfully pretending to be concerned that someone might be listening to this very important secret that she is about to impart. She leans close to Kendra and says, "It doesn't matter how well you play basketball or soccer. You're still a fantastic, unique, wondrous, magnificent…"

Susan continues with the adjectives and crescendos with her voice. As she ends the sentence with the word, "person," she tickles Kendra who wriggles and laughs in delight. After the laughter ebbs, Susan asks her daughter again whether she wants to join the game or not. With a moment's reflection, Kendra says that she will stay inside just for today and suggests that they play backgammon. Susan smiles in anticipation of some one-on-one time with her daughter. She smiles, too, because she realizes that this is exactly the type of situation that would normally have pricked her theme. But it didn't.

No, it didn't. But it could have, should have really. It was the perfect situation to prod Susan's theme. Here was Kendra crying about not being able to do something. Those circumstances had usually lead to swelling feelings of repulsion and disgust, judgmental thoughts and a general rejection of the person. But this didn't happen. Susan's work paid off. In fact, the circumstances were even more risky in this scene because Susan is preoccupied with an activity that she deplores, that tends to leave her irritable. Early on in the scene, she was simply reacting to Kendra's crying in an automatic way because half of her mind was left with that car payment on the dining room table. The irritation with her bills left her less aware of the present, less likely to catch any oozing up of disgust. But that was okay because there wasn't any disgust to catch. Anger, repulsion, judgments and rejections are no longer leading Susan's dance. Susan is leading. Here is the freedom that comes on the heels of transcendence. Now she can afford that wink backwards at a deflated impotent theme. In fact, when she looks back, the theme seems to have mostly dissipated. She can hardly make it out. No longer are there buttons being pushed. No longer are her perceptions being skewed. Susan has accepted and incorporated the "weak" part of herself. She no longer rejects either herself nor others who are showing signs of weakness. Through her work of transcendence, she has freed herself from all of that button pushing and behavioral dictations of the theme. In this situation that would have normally prodded a furtive appearance, Susan is accepting, supportive and spontaneous. Without a doubt, Kendra can feel the love and acceptance behind Susan's words. And Kendra probably senses that her mother is being completely genuine with her. There are no bad Picasso imitations here. Susan is completely free to be spontaneous because she can trust herself. There are no battles, no tiny internal wars going on. Susan is clear. Susan has Aligned with her Soul.

This last scenario moves us ahead in Susan's life by one year. What we see is the freedom of transcendence. I wanted to give you a taste of this freedom because there is a purity to it, a kick-your-feet-up-in-the-air—I-don't-care-what-I-look-like sort of freedom. You ought to have a glimpse of that, so that you'll be able to anticipate it. The freedom of transcendence is enchanting. But jumping ahead like that made us miss something—her work, her practice. She did countless visualizations. These experiences were probably like a process in itself. And, most likely, she had to practice not making those automatic judgmental, rejecting thoughts when she found herself in a theme-pricking situation. She might have had to change her plan along the way too, substituting ideas and actions, honing a unique method that worked for her. We didn't see all of this practicing. But it was there. So, anticipate the freedom, but anticipate the practice too, okay?

What often happens is that we get little tidbits, finger fulls of freedom during all of that practicing. Initially, the theme continues to try pushing those same buttons and we feel the struggle of not following its dictations. Certainly, this struggle is not as tough as one of those head-on battles would be, because those head-on battles occur prior to our understanding. Prior to our understanding, we're still dealing with that furtive darting ghost. We don't know what it is. Can't even follow its movements. With our understanding intact, we *know* who we're dealing with and just how we're going to handle his best moves. This doesn't mean, though, that we won't still feel the pinch of a struggle. It's just that the struggle won't be as painful as before and we'll be better equipped. So we continue to practice. Each situation that comes up, we attempt to undercut the power of the theme, respond in a way that we have planned. Sometimes we'll follow our plan. Sometimes we won't. (That's why it's called *practicing*.) When we don't follow our plan, when that old theme gets the best of us and we fall prey again, we step back and maybe change our plan a bit. When we do succeed, the power behind the theme weakens and we get that little tidbit of freedom. Bit by bit, situation by situation, we gradually practice our way to transcendence. A knowing smile might creep to the lips at this point. We may not be ready to wink yet, but we can sure see it coming.

Now we have joined this paper and ink person, Susan, through a complete cycle of transcendence from the beginning hints of a theme to the joy of the freedom from that theme. The process of transcendence is not quite so neat when we overlay life onto it. There are no cute lines and circles, no lawyer-type definitions being casually tossed around. There is just life and the practice of being in the Sacredness of the present, of evolving to the point that we are Aligned with our Souls and can act from Soul. Susan dodges in and out of exploring and digging around in the roots of that theme. She falls on her face, she battles and she glides effortlessly past a risky situation. There is awareness and moving, Fear and pausing, the back and forth pull of success and failure. The process is not neat or clear or pain-free. But transcendence is freedom. And freedom *is* truly enchanting. Without the barrier of the theme, the Soul Soars right into our lives. And then we can return to the joy and Sacredness of the moment. With one less theme agitating the currents of the subconscious, the moment is even more peaceful than before.

"ARE WE SOARING YET?"
The Effects of This Way of Living

You want to know what Soaring in Life means?
I can tell you.
It means lightness.
It means joy.
It means spontaneity, meaning and laughter.
It means freedom.
It means transformation.
It means compassion, peace, harmlessness and…love.
It means setting your Soul free.

"So...*Are* We Soaring Yet?"

Here is a good question. It kind of reminds you of the question that you always get when you're taking a vacation car trip with children. You know that car trip question is coming. Probably sooner than later. Then that half smile comes to your lips and you nod ever so slightly with recognition when you hear the inevitable coming from the back seat.

"Are we there yet?"

Keep your sense of humor and you can have a playful conversation with this trigger question. After all, this question has a few hidden assumptions that could be pried open for play.

"Are we where yet?" you respond. You glance toward the backseat using the mirror. They caught you looking and saw the humor dancing in your eyes.

"Come on, Dad, you know where we're going."

"Yes, of course, let's see, you asked if we were *there* yet. So we must be going...there. But when we get *there,* that will only be another here...AND..."

"Daaaaaaad," they interrupt with an elongated moan. But you continue, knowing that you only have about a minute more before they will want the real answer.

"...since we are always here, we are never really going. So that means, I suppose, that we have already arrived. And if we've already arrived, then *that* would mean that we *are* already there. So, yes, we are there."

Your oldest gives you a scowl with the hint of a smile. He leans over to the youngest to explain. "What he means is that we're really not there yet. Because, if we had been there yet, he would've just said, 'yes.' So we must be pretty far away from the hotel still."

At this semi-convoluted explanation that is intended to clarify, you burst with laughter. Like father, like son, you suppose.

As convoluted as Dad sounded, he does have a point, both about the question that was posed to him and the one that started this chapter. What he is attempting to say is that the journey, in this case, the car trip itself, is often overlooked as valuable. The car trip is only the method of getting *there*, to the destination. And the destination, end or goal is the object that is held up as the thing to desire. We extend the trophy of our "destination" high above our heads and gaze longingly toward it.

"Are we *there* yet?"

Here, meaning the present journey is tossed off as worthless and ordinary, a mere method of getting to *there*. The car trip is seen by the children as something to endure, to get through so that they can get to their destination, the hotel at the beach. Dad understands that the car trip is no more or less of an experience than the destination. He understands that the journey is just as valid as the end. In fact, he understands that the end is often mistaken for something other than just the continuation of the journey. In other words, it's *all* journey and he knows it. Now, even with this translation of what Dad was trying to say, it still might all sound like a bunch of philosophical mumbo-jumbo.

"Yeah, yeah, here, there, everywhere, journey, end, right. What does this *really* mean?"

In our lives, we hold up many "destinations" as trophies to be gathered along the way. If we're following the way of the flock, the destinations are the ends of the prescribed paths that we talked about earlier. The prescribed paths imply that we will have a sense of life satisfaction when we have arrived at our destinations of financial security, physical health, and emotional security perhaps. And we can back these up by pointing to the concrete things or people that underline them: the house, the wife, the car, the family get-togethers, the physical exercise. It all fits together to form the destinations that the followers of the flock will strive toward. Of course, in looking always toward the destination, we are missing the gold in the journey of getting there. The journey is tossed off casually as *only* the method. How we get to our destinations is pushed aside as the worthless work that must occur in order to arrive. That car ride is so much less fun than actually arriving at that beach hotel.

But, then, if we finally *do* get to the hotel, the excitement will certainly carry us for awhile. We'll scurry through the halls, check where the ice machine is located so that we'll have an excuse to go out of the room later, and bound onto the bed of our room with gleeful abandon. We *have* finally reached our destination and snag that trophy with hunger. Eventually, though, if we stay long enough, that gleeful abandon will fade and we'll soon be into a rhythm not unlike the rhythm we were in at home.

Same thing happens when we arrive at our emotional security, our financial security, etc. At first, we spin with excitement. Then, of course, the excitement wears off. That's when we look around and think, *Okay, now what?* This sort of befuddled looking around occurs because we're failing to see that the journey of getting to the destination *was* the point. So, when we arrive and the excitement has worn off, we are stunned to find more…well, more journeying to do. The journey continues even after we have "arrived." The arrival is no more than a continuation of the journey. The journey just assumes a different form. For some of us, particularly those who are wedded to the prescribed paths, this comes as a bit of a shock. The idea takes a little getting used to, particularly when you've spent several years of your life, living through other assumptions. Disillusion can taste bitter at first.

Now, you might think that mistaking the destination as the thing to desire, the thing to strive towards, is limited to the followers of the flock. But it's not. We can make this same mistake, even if we choose to embrace a method of living where the focus is on Aligning ourselves with the Sacred that is within us and around us, on our nourishment and evolution. That is, even if we choose to focus on flying, we are susceptible to thinking of a destination. And here it is: Soaring. Here is the destination that we might tend to hold up.

"Oh, so *this* is what we're working towards," we say to ourselves. "Let's see, if I can turn down that reactionary tendency over there… and practice a bit more with that little red guy and the box that is sitting right next to him…and take care of those ghastly themes darting around over there…well, then I could probably, finally, Soar."

So, when we have done all this work, trudged through the hours of meditation, painfully dug around in themes and transcended, we can finally ask that back seat question, "Are we Soaring yet?"

But if we do, we are just like those children in the car. We have missed the point. For, the minute that we turn our focus to the

Alignment of ourselves to the Sacred that is within us and around us, we are *already* Soaring. We are already engaging in the journey for the sake of the journeying. The very minute that the moments are viewed as precious, tiny Sacred tidbits of life that we can immerse ourselves in, that we can grow from, then we are focusing on the journey of living. And the journey of living, quite simply put, just continues. There is the journey in how we are and what we are struggling with now and the journey that is later, in how we will be and what we will be at that time. Sure, through our practice and efforts, we might be better flyers later. We hope so. But we'll still be focusing on flying, won't we? The journey is now and continues. So, there is really no place to go. We are already there. What this all means, then, is that we are Soaring when we simply focus on the journey of living. To Soar is simply to focus on flying. Dad would be right, then, to say, "yes, we are there."

YET, (notice just how big that "yet" is), the very idea of Soaring seems to imply a destination, something to strive towards, doesn't it? It seems to imply a gliding, gentle, effortless way of being where Soul is guiding us, where peace infiltrates the very pores of our skin. And this way of being is not something that we can do without practice and effort, no? With all those efforts we have progressed and evolved. We have learned and changed. We actually *are* better flyers, and fly with greater ease. We are not so reactionary nor are we so easily blown off course. And we have cleared away some of those dangling themes that were so dictatorial. We have managed to Align ourselves to the Sacred, at least some of the time. We have managed to live from Soul, at least some of the time. So, are we not striving after all? Are we not striving towards being better flyers, towards being able to Soar, at least some of the time? It would seem so. We seem to have stumbled on a contradiction, although I would rather call it a paradox. In one sense, we have the idea of Soaring as the simple act of focusing on flying and in another sense, there is the idea of Soaring as the enhanced flying that comes with extended effort. Hum… But it's not so difficult to clear up really. Because Soaring is both. Soaring is both the journey as it is now and the journey as it is later. Later, after some lengthy practicing, we might be able to better manage the winds, themes and reactions, and we may even be able to have some of that enhanced ability, but we will still be focusing on flying. The idea of Soaring incorporates where we are now in our simple focus on flying and where we will be in our enhanced flying and continued focus. So the answer to that back seat question, "Are we Soaring yet?" will always be "yes" and "no." For, if we choose this way of living, then we will always be focusing on flying. And, because of this focus we will be Soaring. That's the "yes" part of the answer. But there will always be more to learn and practice. That would be the "no" part.

Now, hopefully, you followed all of that, but if you didn't, don't worry. I just didn't want you to forget that Soaring is focusing on flying, the *process* of Aligning ourselves to the Sacred that is within us and around us. And you might easily forget it when we start to look at all of the results of this method of living. Which is what we're about to do. Aside from the initial chapters that honed in on the concepts, we have been spotlighting the *journey* aspect of this way of living. In other words, we have been focusing on Soaring as it means focusing on flying. And rightly so. The journey is and continues. But here, we are going to attempt a glimpse at what it might be like when we are flying better, when we can Soar with that enhanced flying ability from time to time. Please be wary about holding these results up as destinations, ends to aspire to, though. Remember that they are only pieces that we experience along the continuing journey. With all of this in mind, then, we can broaden the definition of Soaring to these results and allow it to quietly expand outward from there.

Soaring Is Clarity of Our Perceptions About Life

Something happens after we have been practicing our flying skills for awhile—life starts to look different, clearer somehow, like we're looking at it through a clean window instead of a smudgy one. We begin to have a clarity of our perceptions about life. Now I realize that what I consider to be a clearer view of life might be radically different than what you consider to be a clearer view. And, if we were interacting face to face, the above statement would likely spark a rather lively conversation. I am hoping that some of what is written here will indeed ignite some juicy philosophical debates. ("What do you mean, 'clarity?' Life may look different, but it doesn't mean that it's 'clearer.'") But, since I am limited by ink and paper, an interaction is impossible, at least for the moment. What this means, then, is that the conversation will be one-sided with only one opinion showing. I get to go first.

Now, we have already tiptoed up on this subject of perceptions about life in several places. You remember back in the chapter about the basic positions of flying when we were talking about those bumps in life, those inevitable foiling of plans. We made all those meticulously laid plans about love, careers, children. Our plans were as detailed and meticulous as an architect's. We relish being the architects of our lives. But then the bump happens, some unplanned event that life casually seems to toss at us. Astonishment and fury at these seemingly chaotic and random injustices were two of our preferred ways of reacting. And when these emotional reactions were not satisfying enough, we would turn to action. We would attempt to force our plans into fruition or bow our heads in defeat. This was the usual way of perceiving the bumps in our lives.

Another way was to view life's unplanned events with acceptance and meaning. "Whoa, that was a sharp turn…Looks like a new direction…Wonder what I can learn here." With some practice, this basic perceptual position begins to grow on us like a slow, gentle moss. After awhile, we begin to make our plans more tentatively and relinquish them more quickly when those unplanned events insert themselves into our lives. And our reactions. How different the reactions to these bumps become, once acceptance has infiltrated our perception in a more automatic way. Instead of that wild-eyed astonishment and fury, mild surprise is more likely going to come up first. It shows in a raising of the eyebrows in our best unperturbed Spock imitation.

Life Is Lighter and More Meaningful

What happens, after we've been adopting this basic flying position for awhile, is that it starts to expand. Most of these bumps just don't seem as heavy as before. Here is when we start to notice the lightness of life. Life doesn't seem so heavy and dark. The hues of life just don't seem so solid packed, dense or leaden. Life starts to take on the ephemeral colors of lightness. With this clearer view, the bumps seem less serious. Particularly with the smaller incidences, those mishaps, mistakes and faux pas, we might even be tempted to, well…giggle. Before, "giggling" probably wasn't even on our list of behaviors. But somehow, we seem to find ourselves tee-heeing at the oddest times. Okay, if you're not comfortable with "giggle," then you can just do a coy smile. Either way, we're finding that these bumps are not only innocuous, they are funny. Humor has now made its appearance among our reactions, causing the edges of life to curl a bit. So, when your wallet flies off of the roof of the car because you accidentally left it there and your wife says that all those colorful flying plastic cards look a bit like firecrackers, you laugh. And when your son leaps through the air in his underwear, half-yelling, half-singing "Tra-la-la" and claiming to be Captain Underpants during the dinner party with your boss, you laugh. It's funny. (Please notice just how closely humor is related to freedom here. Humor can be a weapon against our usual astonishment and fury, which leads us to this freeing perspective. Humor is also a sign of this freedom. Freedom often writes her signature with humor. Look for it—it's there.) After we've been viewing the bumps of life with acceptance and meaning for awhile, life appears to be lighter.

And what this means is that more of these bumps fit in the small stuff department. Here is another place where the basic flying position starts to expand. For this small stuff department is getting quite large. It seems to be gradually swelling. More and more of life's unplanned events are fitting so neatly here. Mud ground into the carpet was always small stuff, but now, so is the report that you can't seem to find. And your car being totaled does indeed fit into this growing department, especially considering that you weren't hurt when the wreck happened. Indeed, this small stuff department is getting so large that we might begin to wonder if *all* of it might not fit in there.

Well, okay, maybe not *all* of it. At least for now, there are those bumps in the ride that weigh more heavily on us, that just don't fit quite so easily in the small stuff department and that we can't quite laugh at yet. Perhaps we never will laugh at some of these heavier bumps. Still, even without the giggles or coy smiles, we don't react in the same way that we used to. Now we gaze at these sometimes painful unplanned events and scan with our deeper understanding.

We dig with our perceptions in search of the meaning that we are certain is there. The unplanned pregnancy makes us wince, but we don't wallow in the pain of the dashed future that we had so meticulously planned. Instead, we readjust our lives and our plans to incorporate this new addition. We begin that deep scan for meaning. And we know that meaning often blooms through our growth and evolution. Certainly, this inserted, unplanned event will teach us something. Maybe, like Susan, a child will help us develop that atrophied nurturing side. Or maybe we begin to realize that we were expending way too much energy on ourselves and that we needed to expand our limited perception. This last chunk of evolution is not something our egos could foresee or plan. Only this unique event so casually inserted by life, could point this out to us in this way. With the heavier bumps, those unplanned events that cause us to temporarily wince in pain, the ones that don't seem to fit in with the small stuff, we turn to growth and meaning.

Viewing the unplanned events of life with acceptance and meaning can expand into perceiving life as being lighter and less serious. Mild surprise and humor replace that astonishment and fury from before. Life seems to brighten considerably as we begin to think that more and more of these bumps slide right into the small stuff department. Life seems clearer. It's not all gummed up with the grime of our reactions and the onerous weight of our usual perceptions. We can see those bumps through a much cleaner window. But we've only been talking about the *bumps* in life. All of this perceptual positioning has been revolving around these. What about the rest of life? We might have a clearer view of the unplanned events, but life isn't limited to these.

Life Is a Ride

When I was pregnant with my first child, I was naturally anxious about the pain of labor, especially since I would be doing it naturally.

After several questions that obviously showed this anxiety like it was on display in a lighted bookcase, my midwife looked me dead in the eye and said something like, "Look, once labor starts, your body will take over and there will be absolutely nothing you can do about it. So just hang onto your hat and enjoy the ride."

At that moment, I hooked on to the word "enjoy." All I could think was, *enjoy it? She's telling me to enjoy the pain of labor?* Once I got over the shock of this idea, I was better able to absorb what she had said. She was trying to tell me that, for as long as the labor lasted, I would not be in control of my body. I needed to understand that it was a ride that I was on, a ride that I had no control over. There was nothing I could do except to go along with it. Anxiety, planning, and taking calm breaths would do absolutely nothing to change the course. The child would be born. (Of course, being anxious or calm during labor would definitely affect the *experience* and even the length of it. But whether I was anxious or calm, the child would be born anyway.) My midwife was attempting to get me to perceive the upcoming experience in a clearer, more realistic way. No illusions here please.

She had a good point about labor. And about life. For, when we step away from the immediate experience of our lives and look from the long view which includes the bumps and everything else, we come to have a penetrating understanding that life is a ride. We're born and the ride starts. The pace just keeps going, moving along as we grow older. Sure, we can orchestrate parts of it. We can say what we'll have for dinner, at least some of the time. (There are always those bumps to take into account.) We can say what careers we will choose, at least some of the time. But the ride keeps going despite our choices or attempts to choose.

We really don't have much say in the pace, either. We keep getting older. We reach the peak of adulthood, but before we have too long to marvel at our sinewy bodies and minds, we're already starting to wrinkle and broaden. The ride just keeps going. *Okay, okay, we understand what the deal is now*, we think, and so we try to slow the ride down a bit with exercise, diet and a nightly regime of Oil of Olay. We can't stop those wrinkles, though, can we? Not even with our desperate attempts like cosmetic surgery. And there's not much to do about the general deterioration, like the joints that ache and the eyes that suddenly seem to need glasses. It's the ride again. It just keeps going.

"Um, excuse me," we say to no one in particular, for we don't know exactly where to direct this next query, "Could we take a break from this ride for a while?"

Silence answers and we just keep going. That is, we keep going until the ride is over. We don't have much say about how it ends either, unless, of course, we consider ending it ourselves. Almost always a mistake. Further contemplation of the ride's end will send a brief, rippling shiver up the spine. We recognize the shiver of fear. Quickly, because of the burning discomfort of this contemplation, we'll want to shake these thoughts and those shivers right off. Um, can we do something else, now? Anything else at all will be just fine, thank you.

We don't much like thinking of the ride's end because it reminds us too directly about the whole damn thing being a ride to begin with. It all seems so chaotic. So beyond our control. That's what we don't like about it. But, once we start to approach the bumps of this ride with acceptance, once we begin to perceive life's unexpected events as sometimes humorous and always meaningful, once life takes on a lightness, then we don't squirm so much when we come to contemplate the nature of the entire ride itself. Even the end. There's not so much fidgeting and flinches and darts toward escape when we come to take that long view of life and realize that we're on a ride and there's no stopping until the ride is over. No, we might not snuggle up comfortably with this idea initially. It takes some getting used to. The rippling shivers tend to linger. Yet, the perceptions of acceptance, humor, meaning and lightness that we adopted for life's bumps, can begin to seep deeper into our psyches and leak onto the idea that life is a ride. And when this happens, we begin to warm up to the clarity of this idea. We feel more comfortable and at ease with it. *We* can choose our approach to living. *We* can choose our perceptions, our way of doing this ride of life. Certainly, our approach is going to affect our *experience* of the ride and the *type* of ride we have, but the ride happens anyway. No illusions here, please.

Life Is Mysterious

All that warmth and comfort might even increase when we stop to contemplate the mystery of the ride. Somewhere along the journey, we start to become suspicious. We start to consider that maybe, just maybe, the ride is not such a blur of chaos after all. Because, sometimes…the chaos seems to have a tinge of order to it. We squint our eyes and look a bit closer.

"Those coincidences," we say, pointing our finger accusingly, "they keep happening at an abnormal rate."

There do seem to be quite a few of these odd synchronicities around, don't there? Sometimes the circumstances of our lives dovetail so neatly with what we need at that moment. You're glad that the cleaners was still open because you almost didn't make it in time to get your shirt. You had to pop out of your car quickly to make it. Relieved, you walk back to your car and pull at the door handle, only to find that your hand flies up in front of you. It's locked. You can see the keys still swinging in the ignition. You're peering in, simply trying to absorb the fact that you are locked out when you see through the other window that a truck has pulled up. On the side is written, "Joe's Locksmith Service."

Small oddities, these can be, but even the small "coincidences" still make us cock our heads to one side, squint our eyes and murmur, "Wow, do you believe that?"

The synchronicities occur on the grander scale as well. I once heard of a woman who won a state lottery the day before she was scheduled to go into bankruptcy court. Our lives are sprinkled with these synchronicities. They occur with a frequency that is much too great to be accounted for by randomness.

Of course, we may not see the significance of the event, at first. The elegance is not often revealed or obvious. Sometimes, we have to wait until later to get a full view of understanding. You interview for two radically different jobs, one in the computer field, the other in public relations. When your spouse calls you to the phone with a gleam in her eye, you know that it's one of these potential employers. The public relation folks want to hire you. You tell them that you want to think about it. Two hours later you call them back to accept. The phone is not even fully nestled in the cradle before it is ringing again. This time it's the computer people. They want to offer you the job. Twenty years later, you glance around your office. You're the head of the public relations office for a major firm downtown. You reflect for a moment about your career path and you wonder, *What if I had gotten the other call first?* Indeed. A whole other life would have formed.

And there are those events that life inserts into our lives that teach us something about ourselves or about our living. Yes, we're back to those bumps again. Only now, we're looking at them in terms of their synchronous presence in our lives. Susan's crash over an argument between her two children lead her to discover an aspect of herself that was cramping her approach, stunting her evolution. And with the focus on her theme, events occurred that helped her to clarify it further. The car accident that she witnessed, the song on the radio, the conversation with her business partner; all were events that "coincidentally" appeared in her day. Now I know that Susan is all ink and paper, but these types of synchronicities do happen in three dimensions as well.

The synchronicities, the bumps that teach us something that we never could have planned for ourselves, and the events that seem to blow up with significance years later; all seem to point to an order that disguises itself as random and chaotic. It is a mysterious order that we become suspicious of, early in our lives. We do those double takes, feel the eerie sense of mystery, and continue to marvel with our, "Wow, can you believe that?" until one day, we contemplate the idea that perhaps this old ride can be trusted. We won't always know what's coming. We won't always see the significance of those events that life casually places in front of us, but we could consider that the event or bump might be exactly what we need to Align ourselves with our Souls and ultimately Soar.

Here is where someone in the back stands up, points that finger and says something like, "But what about all the pain and struggle in life? What about those events that devastate us?"

This is always a good point, isn't it? There is no denying the excruciating pain in this ride. At some point, the ride becomes treacherous, heated with pain that seems to soak down to the pit of our Souls. The catastrophes explode upon us with nothing less than a nuclear power, a searing rip of the core. The death of someone close to us, the earthquake that killed thousands, the acts of terrorism that slayed adults and children. One glance toward these events and we could easily slide into fury. A mild version of this fury comes over us when we even think of these devastating events in the most general terms. At the moments when they actually occur or we are actually a part of the devastation, we feel a blinding sense of chaos and betrayal.

292

It may take an extended period of time, years perhaps, before the initial burn of pain and betrayal stings less. And any trust in life that we had, gets catapulted right out of the widow. But somewhere along that journey, we can still choose how we will perceive these events. Catastrophes are always life altering. Perhaps we could be a part of choosing how. And in our choosing, couldn't we, eventually, move towards growth? Couldn't we, for example, allow the acts of violence to show us that hurting each other is not in Alignment with who we truly are? At this point, you may be cheering with agreement about the idea of trusting life, or you may be scowling with disagreement. The idea and arguments about it are ancient, so they're not likely to be resolved here. No matter what you tend to believe about this idea, though, we could probably agree that there is a mystery to life that eludes explanation, that defies logic. We shall leave this subject here, then. Take it where you will.

Life Is a Continuing Series of Present Moments

Our continued gaze from this long view points to the nature of this ride. And we get another piece of clarity. Life is a continuing series of present moments. What else could it be? Sure, we could consider the past and the future. These seem to be as alive as any concept of the present. But they're not. Past and future exist in our memories and our fantasies, but outside of our minds, they become the translucent phantoms that they are. The past seems to be a more solid sort of phantom. We can point to events past with a certainty of memory. We can say with a definitive nod of our heads that this happened, then this, and after that, another event loomed up. We can remember and record our personal and societal histories. The history books are full of various accounts of our past memories. Yet, once past, the luscious reality of the moment, that immediacy of the present that seems so full, loses some of its radiance. The present moment dies and takes on the pallor of the phantom of the past.

This is not to say that the past is not useful. The past is enormously useful if we dig at our memories in a constructive manner. Looking at the past we can see our trends, our patterns, our themes. We can analyze and see what worked for us in our continuing journey of growth and what didn't work. We can see where the brilliance of our Souls shone and where we blew it. We can accept, forgive, grow and evolve. The past does this for us. It is one of the most powerful tools of evolving towards an Alignment with our Souls.

And the past can be fun, too. We can pull up alongside an old pleasant memory and, if our imaginations are particularly vivid, we can almost relive the event. The whole thing can be almost re-experienced, complete with our thoughts and the feelings.

But the past is past. It exists in our minds, a phantom that fades to a negligee translucence when it steps out of our craniums. And the future is even less solid of a phantom than the past. This is obvious. The future stays continually in front of us. The phantom of the past at least had some shape. This future guy just keeps changing forms, depending on our moods. One minute, the future looks bright and hopeful and we look forward with a drooling anticipation. The next minute, the future takes on the bleak, drawn appearance of an apparition and we're already running in another direction. A veritable shape shifter, this guy is.

When we get right down to the nitty and the gritty, the hard core consideration of this ride, what we see is the gleam of the Sacred present. Because, after awhile, we start to recognize the past and the future for the phantoms that they are. So when the Sacred present takes its proper place on center stage, sashaying up to the middle in the warmth of that spotlight, we greet it with the respect and dignity that is called for. We recognize the radiant nourishing color of the present. The present is touchable, full, solid. The present is where we are and always will be. Then we realize that the ride is a continuous series of heres and nows, moving and infinite.

As we focus on flying, particularly after we have been practicing for awhile, we start to get a clarity of our perceptions about life. Meaning and purpose become obvious first, because the moment that we make that shift, they are there. But we also begin to perceive life as that mysterious ride that is sometimes so ordered and trustworthy and sometimes so apparently chaotic. Our acceptance of this perception frees us from illusions. We can see life for what it is. There is no need to run, manipulate or force. We see its lightness and the meaning behind its heaviness. We are free to immerse ourselves in the golden, full, radiant present. We can experience the peace and the beauty of the Sacred in this continuing series of present moments. And it is through these continuing series of present moments that we can evolve to a point where the Sacred within us, our Souls are directing our lives. This is how life looks after we've been practicing awhile. Refreshing, penetrating, meaningful and definitely clearer.

Life is a ride, so hang onto your hat and enjoy it.

Soaring Is Restoration

If we choose to do this ride with a focus on Aligning ourselves to the Sacred that is within us and around us, on our nourishment and evolution, we will be gradually moving toward restoration. You remember this idea from the earlier chapters? (It's easy to get bogged down in the details and forget the big picture sometimes.) Well, Soaring is restoration or a bringing back to an original state. Gradually, through all of our practice and attention, through the onslaught of reactions and the density of themes, we are Aligning ourselves more and more with our Souls. We are restoring ourselves to our original state of pure love and then attempting to live from this source, in all manner of being. And living from a state of pure love changes things, doesn't it? Even if we are able to come from the Soul for only a few moments, for those few moments, we can be sure to soak up the results. One of the first things we will notice is freedom.

Restoration Means Freedom

In a country where we can voice rancid opinions about the President and still not have to worry about persecution, the idea of freedom is certainly not new to us. We can even toss around nasty opinions at the same time that we wear blue hair, burn the flag and make up a new form of religion. At least in this country, we have a lot of freedom. But the freedom that I'm referring to here, is of a whole other variety. It has an entirely different flavor. And it is not limited by any country's borders. We had a little taste of this kind of freedom before, when we were talking about the winds and the themes. You remember, a sort of kick-up-your-feet-dance-in-the-sun freedom. This is the type of freedom that we discover along the journey of focusing on flying.

Before, thoughts and emotions seemed to be the ones that so often planted themselves in that director's chair behind that curtain. They seemed to perpetually overpower us, leaving us reeling with the shock of our own behaviors. We would peer around the corner of the future and gasp in fear when we saw the next wave of emotion and fueling thoughts spinning toward us with the speed of a tornado. We would plant our feet fully and lean into this wind ready for battle, only to be casually bandied about. Our reactions and crashes were the result. Oddly enough, we would still loudly proclaim that we *were* indeed the ones behind the curtain. Of course, we really didn't believe it. We knew it was that damn coo-coo again or some roaring bull or some wacky Kansas professor. But we would ready ourselves for the next round and weather the wind as best we could. Screaming energy would pore out of us through the sweating effort of attempting to force those lids on those boxes. Pushing and pulling, poking and prodding. But it never seemed to do much good. Somebody would get out of the box or somebody wouldn't stay out. And we would be overwhelmed with our thoughts and emotions.

We were overwhelmed, that is, until we began to realize that those thoughts and emotions didn't have to be the ones sitting in that director's chair, running the drama of our lives. We could do it. Or rather, we could allow our Souls to quietly take the helm. The Soul naturally conducts our lives if we're Aligning ourselves with it, instead of Aligning ourselves with those pushy, bullying whirlwinds of thoughts and blasts of emotion. And once we realized that the power lay solidly within our Souls, we started to take some of that same power back. Half of this power we took back when we understood that our emotions and thoughts are no more than just aspects of experience. They are not as domineering as we had once thought. Once we understood this, then we got that first jolt of one freedom, the freedom from victimization by our own thoughts and emotions. Because what this meant is that we would not have to be overwhelmed. We could practice training our thoughts to go where we wanted them. We could watch those boxes dance and blow without reacting. We may be amazed by the explosions from the box, but they don't affect us as much. We're just not as impressed. We no longer Align ourselves to them. We know *who we are*.

More pieces of freedom float our way when we realize that we no longer need to peek around the corner of the future with such dripping anxiety. We don't have to be constantly watching those boxes anymore, waiting for the pop. Never quite being sure when we would crash next had left little goosebumps of fear. Well, they're not so many of those goosebumps around anymore since we're less likely to be overwhelmed. This is the freedom from anxiety about our own emotions and thoughts. There is so much less to worry about when we are assured about who is behind that curtain.

And there is the freedom from struggle. For all this journey we are practicing: practicing a sinking into the Sacredness and peace of the present moment, practicing paying attention, practicing changing perceptions or reactions, transcending themes. It seems that we are always practicing, always struggling with some aspect of living that we're working on, always attempting to Align ourselves with our Souls. So much effort it seems to take, this focusing on flying. The effort that it takes is enormous and relentless. This is true. But then, one day, you notice something. You notice an absence. An absence of struggle. Suddenly, you realize that for a moment, you were just gliding, maybe Soaring. It can start small. Like when the orange juice spilled on the new carpet and that orangish splash really *didn't* bother you. *And*, you didn't even have to work at this perception. It was automatic. No struggle at all. In fact, once you start to consider it, you can think of several recent situations that would have ordinary jolted the little red guy's box. But they didn't. That anger box didn't even move. Maybe the little red guy was sleeping. He seems to be sleeping a lot lately, you notice. With the smaller instances, the absence of struggle may not be so loud. You might have to make an effort to notice it. Like when you've had a cold, then suddenly notice that you can breathe through your nose again. When exactly did that happen? The absence of struggle can be quiet like this.

It gets louder, though, when we transcend a theme. In fact, it can be so loud then, that we can get a blast of exhilaration from the experience of this freedom. We saw it with Susan. For years, she had been a victim of the dictations of a furtive ghost. It infiltrated the corners of her interactions, her perceptions, her life. Years. That's a long time to be chained to some ghastly Siamese twin. Then, after she got a full, intimate glimpse at this twin and understood that she was victim to its dictations, she struggled and battled against it. With transcendence, though, came a lovely void. The glorious absence of struggle. You bet she went ahead with that casual wink.

Restoration Means Delight and Spontaneity

Without the worry of being overwhelmed or out of control, without the anxiety, without the struggle, we are Free. After all, the Soul is firmly planted in that director's chair more often. And what this means is that *we can play*. We can delight in the experiences, the events, emotions and thoughts. We can truly relish the richness and texture of life. This includes not only those moments that are smothered with beauty, elegance and grace, but also those moments that twist our hearts, tug on us at our roots of being. So you can truly savor that angst when you look at some faded photos from twenty years ago, since you are less likely to let it expand into tearful regrets and sadness. At least, not without your permission. And you can relish the electric lust that tingles when your lover sweeps aside your hair to plant a tender kiss on the back of your neck. You can feel it and allow yourself to swoon and let go or just stay in place. It's your choice. Our freedom allows us to sink into life as deep as we choose. There's that click again.

And our freedom gives us something else that is as precious as it is delightful—spontaneity. For, the more that we are Aligned with our Souls, the more that the Soul is in-charge, the more spontaneous we can afford to be. In-charge *and* spontaneous? It seems like we've stumbled on another paradox. (I like paradoxes. They tend to be more weighty with truth.) Yep. Spontaneous and in-charge. And I'm not talking about that sort of herky-jerky motion that takes place when we self-consciously decide to be "spontaneous." You move out on the dance floor, thinking to yourself, *I need to let my hair down more, let myself go a little.* So you start to concentrate on the rhythm of the music that seems to pulse through the floor, and move your body. *There,* you think, as your body stays consistently off-beat, *I think I've finally got it.* If you could see yourself at this point, Steve Martin might come to mind. It might be good training to get you out of a rut, but it is not spontaneity. No, spontaneity has nothing to do with forcing. It's more like a trusting display of emotions and thoughts, an uninhibited genuine behavior. We can recognize spontaneity in ourselves or someone else. It's what makes us so uniquely charming. And spontaneity is a treat that we can certainly afford when we've been practicing at letting the Soul be in-charge for awhile.

Being in-charge and being spontaneous still sound odd in the same sentence, don't they? But think of the idea this way: the more that we practice with our thoughts and emotions, the less reactionary we will be which means then that we can *trust* ourselves. And, the clearer we are of the dictations of those old themes, the more we can *trust* ourselves. With practice and clearing, we can trust ourselves not to freak out, bolt, blow up or crash. With the Soul holding that seat more often, our behavior is reflective of its natural love, peace, wisdom and compassion. Certainly, we can trust these. And with this trust comes the freedom of spontaneity. Now the trip to the dance floor seems entirely different. You're chatting with a friend, when the DJ puts on a new song. You recognize it and instantly feel that pulsing rhythm leaking into your body.

"Ooo," you say, interrupting your friend with a light touch on her shoulder, "I just gotta dance to this one."

You're up before she can respond. And before you even make it to the dance floor, you're already pumping your head and your walk…well, it's not really a walk anymore. You have already started dancing. Without having to watch for those winds and with a quiet certainty that we truly *are* the ones behind the curtain, we can dance spontaneously almost anytime we feel like it. But that's redundant isn't it?

Delighting and playing with and through our emotions and thoughts, and being spontaneous are the results of freedom from victimization, freedom from anxiety and freedom from struggle. That wacky professor from Kansas who we thought might be hovering behind the curtain, left on some balloon ride. So he's just gone. As for the coo-coo, well, he makes an appearance once in a while, but not so often anymore. And we're not so haunted anymore by the swirling ghosts of themes because we've done some clearing. There are just less of them around. Maybe they went on that balloon ride with the professor. Wherever they've gone, they have left more room, more room for the Soulful qualities of love, peace, wisdom and compassion, and thus more room for delight and spontaneity in life.

Restoration Means Transformation

That transformation is involved with this way of approaching life should not be at all surprising. That is, after all, what this book is about—a transformation of perceptions and positions, a transformation of thoughts and emotions, a transformation of patterns. Even the word restoration literally means a transformation to our original state of love. So why the redundancy?

Well, one reason for such redundancy is simply to underscore the lovely effects that such a transformation can bring forth. We have already talked about a few of these: clarity of the perceptions about life, freedom, humor, delight and spontaneity. These effects will most certainly begin to seep into the air of your life when you take on that new focus. And they *are* truly lovely. But notice here that the transformation has been *internal*. In fact, our external lives may appear to be pretty much the same from the outside. We may still have that same job with the same rhythm of activities. And it may not be the glamorous, "respected" job that would be envied by others. We may still have the same life partner. The same house. Maybe even the same car. But somehow, our lives have been transformed. And it is *because* these externals remain the same that the transformation seems so magical. Harry Potter couldn't have done better. Everything appears the same on the outside, but quiet seismic shifts have saturated the inside. Our ordinary lives, our ordinary circumstances are twinkling with meaning, sparkling with opportunities. And this is true, no matter what job we have, no matter what partner we have, no matter what house or country we live in.

However, as we continue in our focus on Aligning ourselves to the Sacred that is within us and around us, on our nourishment, evolution and gradual restoration, the transformation may expand, stretch its wings a bit and move into the *external*. Now I'm not referring to that frantic ripping apart of our relationships or dashing from one job to another in a desperate, rocking search for meaning. No. The meaning that we so desperately searched for, has been found through our new, conscious focus. What I am referring to is a gradual movement towards people with whom we can form healthy relationships, careers that tend to be more in tune with our natural gifts and talents, and activities that are more Aligned with who we are.

Let me explain. When we Align ourselves with our Souls, we are in sync with the pulsing rhythm of love. And love is a higher frequency energy that is quite powerful. There is absolutely nothing wimpy about it. So the more we Align ourselves with love, the higher the energy we'll be putting out. And what *this* means is that we will be attracting a similar type of energy back to us. Are you getting this? It's important. The type of energy we put out is what we will get back. Think about it this way. Let's say that the universe has millions of tuning forks in it, all tuned to different frequencies. (You may be giggling now, but stay with me.) There's the tuning fork of indifference, the tuning fork of criticism, the tuning fork of sadness, the tuning fork of joy and millions of others as well. Each time we harmonize ourselves to the tone of one of these frequencies, the sound goes out and vibrates the corresponding tuning fork, causing that tuning fork to sound and bounce back toward us. We may not always get back the same exact *form* of the tone, but it will come back to us in one form or another.

You are the head of your own business and as the CEO, you are constantly inundated with major decisions about purchases, marketing, profit spending, personnel. On top of all of that, you are on committees at the church and at the local hospital. *And* you have young children who are into ballet lessons and baseball. You try to go to all of their rehearsals, practices and games. With this version of life, you are stressed, stressed, stressed.

To be sure, this guy is sending out the frequency and sound of stress, which vibrates that particular tuning fork loud and clear. Right next to that tuning fork are the ones for irritation and meaninglessness. They start vibrating too, along with several others near that frequency. Soon, he has a whole host of tuning forks vibrating some massive negative sounds. And they're not likely to sound anything like the melodies of a symphony. With the long-term, unbroken chain of vibrations of this sort, the same noise is going to start coming back at him. Physical illness might rebound back. It tends to be attracted to the tuning fork of stress. And there's depression, which might set in. That could come from a sense of meaninglessness. Not to mention some potential nasty turns in the business, which will, of course, put this guy under more stress. Well, that is, after all, what he is putting out.

The type of energy that we put out, we get back. Like attracts like. When we choose a way of living that moves us toward an Alignment with the Soul, that puts us in sync with love, we are putting out a *potent* form of energy. The tuning fork of love is the largest of all of those positive tuning forks and tends to make them vibrate as well. Imagine what will be coming back when we send out the vibration of love.

Transformation. Transformation comes as a direct result of increasing the level and type of energy we are putting out. We become more drawn to activities that are more nourishing and the other, previous activities tend to fall away. We become drawn to people who are similar in their level of vibrational energy while the old acquaintances, friends, and lovers tend to move out of our lives. We become drawn to jobs and careers that are more reflective of our natural abilities and talents, careers that can become our gifts to the world. Gradually or perhaps suddenly, we realize that some of the external forms of existence we have surrounded ourselves with, just don't seem to fit so well any more.

A massive internal transformation has occurred. And it is because of this internal transformation that the *external* circumstances of our lives may begin to rearrange themselves. Now, instead of plopping ourselves down in front of that TV, we tend to prefer a hot bath with candles and quiet music. It's not a New Year's resolution that prompts such a change. The bath is simply what we have come to prefer. It just feels more nourishing. Now, instead of scrambling to be on a prestigious board or committee, we prefer to spend that time simply hanging out with our families, being in the Sacred present. The Soul moves us toward such a choice. Now, instead of thinking mostly about how we're going to put food on the table, we might even contemplate a career change. With so much love and optimism floating around, we dig up our old career dreams and think that maybe, just maybe we could start living a dream. Heck, we might even write a book. *External* transformation does occur when we take up this focus on flying. It is a direct result of the type of energy and vibration that we're putting out. With our new focus, we now have a symphony. And it sounds like the music of the Angels.

Soaring Leads to a Perception of Oneness

Somewhere along our journey, with all of our practice on Aligning ourselves to the Sacredness that surrounds us, we have probably stumbled upon an experience of complete immersion into the present. We have talked about this a bit before. Some gorgeous detail of living will capture us totally. Time seems to slow down, maybe almost stop. You soak in the vision of your daughter's sleeping face — those eyelashes stenciled so gently by the rising glow of the sun. There is absolutely nothing else that exists at the moment. That face is the universe. Or so it seems. During moments like these, there is a feeling of merging, a loosening of physical and mental boundaries. We *become* the beauty that we witness. The beauty is us. Somehow we have merged with the experience. Later, when we reflect back on the experience, we marvel at what happened. The boundaries between us and the beauty, between us and that gorgeous face, melted. And we become suspicious about our ordinary perception of separation. For now, though, we shrug and go on about our focus, simply enjoying this nourishment with our attention.

Then another process begins to unfold that causes even more suspicions about the perception of separation. We start to pivot slowly around to check out the other people who are on this ride with us. For so long, certainly for the length of this book and probably for much of our lives, *we* have been the center of our attention. *My* emotions, *my* thoughts, *my* themes, the messages that *I* need, *my* point of view, *my* growth, *my* evolution. Even *my* Soul. This is as it should be. We *are* the ones to do the work of clearing and of gradual restoration. It is a healthy, temporary narcissism. But, after awhile, we shift our gaze to others. It's an odd thing, this turning outward. It seems that once we have practiced a bit, cleared a bit, transcended a bit, the ego shrinks a bit. And we find that there is more space. We're not squeezed into our lives so much. Our attention turns outward.

Without so much clutter around our own Souls, too, our turn outward is more direct and more penetrating. We give up our old position of self-importance and gaze deeply into the nature of someone else. Without the filters and grime of our own themes, reactions and other stuff, we can perceive the entirety of another person. What we will see initially, of course, is that person's unique version of stuff. They have those limiting perceptions, domineering thoughts and emotions, crashes and themes too. But if we look deeper, we can see glimpses of something that we might recognize. There is a quiet, steady radiance buried beneath all those layers of grime. It's the Soul. Look deep enough and we might realize that this person's Soul is of the *same essence* as our own—love. *Hmm,* we think, *why would it be so very much the same?* Then we recall those other experiences when we sank into the present and seemed to merge with the experience. Faces and minds contorted with consternation, we hesitate. *I become the beauty; I become the experience; the essence from one person to another is the same...* We start to consider that maybe, just maybe, separateness is the grand illusion that we always suspected. And we're caught with our spiritual pants down, pointing to the idea of oneness, despite our egos' screaming attempts to keep us from this contemplation.

Our egos detest it when we even consider the idea of oneness, because it would mean instant ego death and the ego won't stand for it. Any consideration at all of the perception of oneness and the ego begins to employ logic as a weapon.

"Look," it says, pointing to those other people, "it is obvious that they are separate from us. I mean, come *on*. They don't share the same body, have the same thoughts or feelings...well, okay, not *exactly* the same thoughts or feelings. And they have different lives, perceptions, and opinions. Oneness? Please, get real."

Not bad. Not bad at all. The ego would come up with an even better argument, give more time, but this one might be enough to make us throw the whole idea right out the window. Of course, I'm not going to do that. (But you knew that already.)

If we can fend off the ego long enough to fully contemplate the idea of oneness, we can expand and eventually embrace it. We start with *energy*. Think about it for a minute. Everything, absolutely *everything* is energy. Everything has molecules and atoms, electrons and protons and neutrons floating around in it. Everything includes the trees, the leaves, the birds, the bees, the air, the door mat, the interactions between people, the fax machine, the petals of a flower, the thoughts in your mind, you and me. It's all in there. Everything is energy. This energy is the basis of our essence. And this same energy is the basis for the essence of everything that we experience with our senses, (all six of them.) This is the energy of the Sacred, the foundation. Some call this energy God, some call it the Tao, some say that it is nameless. But however we think about it, the energy permeates all. However, the energy takes different *forms*. There is the form of a tree, the form of an interaction, the form of soft petals. Same energy. Different forms. Do not be fooled into believing in separateness because of the illusion of form. It *is* an illusion. We could think of the essence of creation as a mirror. Hold up the mirror and it reflects all of the various forms that creation can take. The essence of the mirror never changed. Only the reflections. The *essence* is the same.

When the boundaries between us and our experience loosen and we merge with the beauty, we are removing the illusion of separation and allowing ourselves to realize what we already are. The essence of that beauty and us *is* the same. When we make that slow pivot outward to gaze at the other people that surround us, we recognize the Soul of love. The essence of us and others is the same. Our spiritual pants down, we begin to consider the grand illusion of separation.

What this means then, is that all of creation is intimately connected through our commonality of the energy, the spiritual essence of who we are. All of creation is intimately connected through God, the Tao, the nameless. In other words, we are all One. And what *this* means is that any subtle or massive change in part of that essence is going to affect the larger whole of energy. The effect is much like the rippling that occurs when you toss a rock into a pond. Energy waves emanate outward from the center, gradually lessening in intensity with distance. From a less abstract point of view then, everything about one person affects all others, especially those who are closest to that person. Thus, what I do, how I think, how I feel, how I interact with others ripples into the larger whole, greatly affecting those closest in proximity.

The effect is easy enough to observe. Simply walk into a room where someone has just had an argument. Heavy and thick in there, isn't it? Stay there long enough and you might catch some of that irritation yourself. Or, on the other end of the spectrum, you can interact with someone who seems filled with love and lightness. Within a few minutes, you're filled with it as well. It's the rippling effect. Because we are all connected through this energy, this essence, we are affected. (Of course, if you are focusing on Aligning yourself to the Sacred, then *you* will be the one who is rippling love and light toward everyone else.)

Oneness Means Compassion

When we embark on our journey with a focus on flying, *already* we are attempting to live from the Soul of love. We are practicing on deleting any blocks of the Soul, so that it will Soar into our lives. We want to allow love to direct us. At first, we may take on this focus for our own selfish reasons, namely to find meaning and purpose, to find peace and contentment and abundance, to just feel plain less stressed.

But when we allow the idea of oneness to infiltrate, when we perceive others as being reflections of our own essence, then we naturally begin to hold a deep affinity for others, indeed for creation in its entirety. And compassion blooms. Here is this other person, a reflection of ourselves dealing with all of the grime that surrounds the

Soul. The grime — those reactions, crashes, blowing thoughts, emotions and themes will bring up a strong compassion for that person, who is a reflection of us. After all, we have been intimate with the struggle ourselves. Compassion swells easily and naturally with a perception of oneness.

With all that compassion reverberating around in our hearts and craniums, we might be tempted to start going around telling other people how to think, how to behave, how to live their lives. Especially when we consider that this part of us, (the other people who might not be doing so well), are affecting *us* with their rippling energy.

We might be tempted to say, "Listen, you've got to do your part because you're affecting all of us. Okay? So here's what you need to do." And we proceed with a litany of requirements to move that person toward some form of enlightenment. Of course, it won't work.

When we step back and slip into the perspective of oneness, what we see are individuals who make up the different forms of a whole Sacred essence. Each of these forms or individuals is on a unique journey, designed by their own Souls. They are exactly where they need to be. If we use the analogy of school, then we could say that some are in first grade, others are in college and others are scattered in-between. You are in college and I'm in first grade. Because you see the difference so clearly, you decide to try to teach me calculus. I might listen curiously at first but, by the end of the conversation, I'm likely to think that you're speaking some other language, that maybe you're even from some other planet. Despite your smiles, gentleness and loving manner, at the end I'll roll my eyes and wander away. It's not going to work.

If we go back and consider only our own individual journeys for a moment, we can probably think back to a time when we came across an issue or theme that we were just not ready to even contemplate, much less deal with. We were not ready to face it. That part of us is in first grade. Now, within our own individual evolution, what do we do when we're not ready to deal with something? We don't deal with it. We simply go along dealing with those themes or patterns that we *are* ready to address, moving at a pace that we can handle. The part of us that holds on to that theme may be in first grade, but it's not ready for calculus yet, so we wait patiently and compassionately until it is ready.

And this is exactly what we do when we look around at all the other parts of ourselves, those other people that make up the different forms of the same Sacred essence. We may glance around and spot a few first graders. Gently, lovingly (after all, we're coming more often from our Souls), we hold their hands and accept where they are in their individual journeys, allowing them to move at the pace that they set for themselves. We let the compassion fill us without allowing it to turn into preaching or parading our own advances. We won't try to teach them calculus.

Of course, in our glancing around at the other folks on this ride, we're likely to find some advanced college students milling around. If we're wise enough, we will observe them closely and ask for a calculus lesson or two. We might just be able to understand a little of it after all. (Well *you* might be able to understand it. Calculus is way over my head.)

Oneness Means Harmlessness and...Love

Oneness—the idea that all of creation is of the same Sacred essence, that the forms of this creation are only illusions. If we come to truly embrace this idea, the implications are rather, well, enormous. How we act and interact with every part of creation would come under scrutiny, for all of it, all of creation is...us. You would come to think about: how you treat your cat, how you interact with your boss, how you interact at church, how you drive, how you treat your house, how you treat your food, how you treat your plants, yard, neighbor, neighborhood, community, local park, local grocery clerk, local politician, rivers, streams, trees, roads. All of it is a part of the Sacred essence that we share. All of it is us. So, we would not want to damage, destroy, belittle, mistreat any of it, would we? Because that would be mistreating a part of ourselves. Indeed, we would be mistreating a part of the energy and Sacred essence that makes up who we are. Why would we intentionally do something so absurd?

Why indeed.

When we embrace the idea of oneness wholeheartedly, then we are also embracing a value of harmlessness, since we perceive all of creation as another aspect of ourselves. Quickly and suddenly sometimes, we come to realize that it doesn't make sense to harm any aspect of this creation. And, almost as quickly, we might realize that it makes complete sense to show love towards all of creation. Now, we are no longer thinking only of not harming the Sacred essence of ourselves, we are moving toward loving all the forms that the Sacred essence takes. With oneness firmly planted in our hearts, we plunge toward subtracting harm and adding love in our treatment of creation. And the addition of love propels us towards service and giving. (Not to mention that we are continuing to Align ourselves with our Souls at the same time.)

Wonder with me what would happen to the world if most of its inhabitants embraced the idea of oneness, including the resulting values of harmlessness and love. There would be no more wars, would there? For we would be fighting ourselves. There would be fewer deceptions between people and nations of peoples. For the deception would be against ourselves. Pollution would be intolerable. For we would want to love the earth and treat this part of ourselves well. Starvation would be unacceptable. For we would not allow a part of ourselves to die from neglect, especially when there is enough. All of creation would garner the respect it deserves from the smallest insect to the entire universe. We would think about what we do, how we are evolving, what effect we are creating by all of our actions. Big stuff, isn't it?

But what we are coming back to, really, is the idea of living from love. It goes around full circle, doesn't it? We begin with our own journey, consciously undertaken with our new focus. Through our living, through our Alignment to the Sacred essence that is within us and around us, through our nourishment and evolution, we move back to our original state of love. We restore ourselves to our original states. And as the restoration gradually dawns, our perceptions of life become clearer, we experience levels of freedom, delight, spontaneity. We are transformed, restored to our original state. Coming from love, we begin to embrace the idea that all of creation is of the same Sacred essence. Coming from love we would do no harm.

Instead we seek to treat all aspects of creation with love. In other words, we would be coming from love. Period. And isn't that what we have been trying to do all along with our new focus? It does appear rather circular, doesn't it? But circles are like that you know. Infinite and continuous.

We have arrived at the end. We have arrived at the beginning. I heard in a rock song that "every new beginning comes from some other beginning's end." (Who says rock doesn't have wisdom?) At any rate, here we are. The vacation dad would agree. We are there, meaning of course that we are here. We are born into this ride that moves along at its own pace in its endless series of present moments. We can't do much about that. But for each one of those moments, we can choose our approach to life. We can consciously choose to Align ourselves with the Sacred essence that is within us and around us. And each time we choose this focus, this way of being, we are moving in a direction. We are gradually restoring the shining brilliance of love in our Souls. We are freeing ourselves. We are transforming a part of the essence of the whole, moving that part toward love. We are Soaring in Life. And the effect ripples throughout the whole of creation.

May you and your children revel in the light of being, the joy of growing, and the peace of restoration.

Genuinely, Gently and Lovingly sent,

Mary Whittle

THE BEGINNING

The Practice Begins...

Would you Soar with me?

"Would You Soar With Me?"

This is the beginning, the time for choosing. You have read about what it means to Align yourself to the Sacred that is within you and around you. You have read about methods and you have read about results. In every moment that you live, you are moving toward your restoration. This is guaranteed. But you may choose to consciously and deliberately pursue your Alignment. You may choose to consciously and deliberately practice immersing yourself into the Sacred that is around you. You may choose to consciously and deliberately live from Soul. In fact, every moment of your life, you are choosing. You are choosing what you will Align yourself with in every "now" there is. So you see, every "now" is just another beginning, another moment of choice. With the realization of the meaning and purpose of living, with a few methods and understandings under your belt, then, you can consciously begin again and again and again.

But you might need some help, more than just words on a page. Certainly, you can use this book as a guideline. That is why it was written. Yet the warmth of a living teacher, a guide through the initial stages of your conscious beginning may prove to be just the jumpstart you need. And the warmth of other people, all journeying together offers a synergy that is beyond the written word. I have designed a workshop for people who wish to pursue their conscious beginning through a teacher and the synergy of a group. The workshop is called Soaring 101. It is a balance between teaching, discussions and experiential exercises. The teachings underscore the concepts and methods of this book. The discussions tap into the wealth of wisdom from other participants. The experiential exercises...well, they amplify both the beauty of your Soul and the forms of the barriers that prevent that beauty from coming into your life. In other words, you will see yourself in a clearer way and you will have time to practice some of the methods here, applying them to your life.

For more information on content and scheduling for Soaring 101, please check the website at www.SoaringInLife.com. If no workshop is scheduled in your area, we may be able to make arrangements to schedule a workshop especially for your group. Or you may contact the author at:

Mary Whittle
SoaringInLife@aol.com

Printed in the United States
29232LVS00003B/59